Building Societies : Structure, Performance and Change

Building Societies : Structure, Performance and Change

Donal McKillop
School of Finance and Information
Queen's University Belfast

and

Charles Ferguson
Ulster Business School
University of Ulster at Jordanstown

Graham & Trotman
A member of Wolters Kluwer Academic Publishers
LONDON/DORDRECHT/BOSTON

Graham & Trotman Limited
Sterling House
66 Wilton Road
London SW1V 1DE
UK

Kluwer Academic Publishers Group
101 Philip Drive
Assinippi Park
Norwell, MA 02061
USA

ISBN 1 85333 880 X

First published 1993

British Library and Library of Congress Cataloguing-in-Publication Data is available upon request.

Printed and bound in Great Britain by Hartnolls Ltd, Bodmin, Cornwall

Preface

As a sector undergoing a period of major transition, the building society sector provides an interesting area of study. Building societies occupy an important role within the UK financial services arena, and broadly the purpose of this text is to provide an in-depth examination of their structure and performance. Given the context of a deregulated business environment, and the increasing competitiveness within financial services, an analysis at this time of the adaptations that have been made by building societies to the challenges associated with these factors is particularly appropriate. There is also a concern in this text to address, in a non-prescriptive way, the broad future directions that the sector might take.

The themes of structure, performance and change determine the scope of our text. To explore these themes in a meaningful way has necessitated not only having recourse to existing published material but also placing a heavy emphasis on our own empirical investigation of key aspects of building societies. The survey work undertaken on organisational change, relocation policy, product diversification, information technology and marketing is worth mentioning here, as is the Data Appendix provided in the text, as both provide original information on the UK building society sector. Our intention has been to provide a comprehensive audit of developments within the sector over the past few years, not purely of internal operational features, but also in terms of the evolving legal and regulatory framework. Moreover, we felt that a text of this nature would be deficient without consideration of the European legal dimension.

Our text aims to be of value to managers within the building society sector, to students within this sector, and to others within the financial services sector interested in tracking recent developments. Much of the data contained in this text will also be of direct relevance to researchers in the field of financial services. As far as possible, we have attempted to make this text user-friendly and suitable for a wide readership.

Needless to say, the opinions herein expressed and any errors are entirely our own.

Donal McKillop
Charles Ferguson

Acknowledgements

Our first debt of gratitude is to those building societies that participated in a series of surveys carried out by the authors between the middle of 1991 and the end of 1992. Without their excellent co-operation, reflected in an average response rate across the respective surveys in excess of 70 percent, this text simply could not have been completed.

As part of the background work for this text personal interviews were conducted with a selection of individuals from within the building society sector. Particularly helpful and informative were representatives from the Alliance and Leicester, the Beverley, the Bradford and Bingley, the Catholic, the Chesham, the Britannia, the Greenwich, the Halifax, the Lambeth, the Leeds and Holbeck, the Nationwide, the Yorkshire and the Woolwich. As an integral component of the personal interview programme we are in addition grateful for insight and advice obtained from representatives of the Bank of England, the Building Societies Association and the Building Societies Commission.

The final version of this text benefited greatly from helpful criticism of an earlier draft. On this count we would like to thank Ivor Oswald (the Alliance and Leicester), Daniel Corr (the Nationwide) and Joseph Nellis (Cranfield Institute of Technology).

For their invaluable research assistance we owe much thanks to Liam Barton, Suzanne Bradley and Mary Tohill. We would like to thank Freda Neil for typing a number of the initial chapters in this text and we extend special thanks to Margaret Sturgeon for her patience and perseverance in typing the bulk of this manuscript.

Contents

To our wives and children

Janice, Ciara and Barry

and

Joan, Michael, Kate and Conall

1. Introductory Comments

Rationale

Within the financial services sector a gradual erosion has taken place, since the mid-1980s, in the traditional barriers between markets for different financial services. Instrumental in this process of change have been the twin forces of information technology and financial market deregulation. This breakdown in demarcation lines has also extended outside national boundaries. Implementation of the single banking licence, at the start of 1993, coupled with technological advance, has enabled financial institutions to more effectively diversify outside their domestic market and into the markets of other European Community countries. As a consequence of these changes the financial services sector has become much more competitive in the provision of financial services; increasingly customer orientated in its business approach; and global as opposed to insular in terms of market horizons.

Therefore, it is within this framework of a new and evolving financial services environment that the analysis of UK building societies is conducted. Indeed building societies can, in many ways, be viewed as the financial grouping most profoundly affected by the changed market environment. Prior to the mid-1980s, building societies were essentially single product firms with a virtual regional monopoly on mortgages and savings. Today the major societies in particular, are multi-product institutions heavily involved with other high street rivals in competition for market share. Some societies have even stepped outside national boundaries in the provision of financial services.

Societies have in general responded positively to these new challenges. This market effective response has not, however, come easy. It has necessitated that societies revise their internal operational procedures, re-evaluate and re-define their objectives and monitor performance not only relative to other societies but also *vis a vis* those institutions with which they now compete. One drawback faced by societies is that they have not had total freedom in the moulding of this new focus, rather it has been achieved within the domestic and European legislative constraints under which societies are obliged to operate.

The scope of this text is obviously related to an examination of change within the UK building society sector. In order to undertake this, a distinct focus is applied to a variety of important issues. First, an audit is provided of the internal aspects involved in adaptation by building societies to this new market environment. Included in the audit is, for instance, consideration of the adoption of information technology, the changing relationship between head-office, front-offices and back-offices; the prevalence of a customer focused approach to business development; and the shift towards a more performance based ethos in terms of revenue generation. Secondly, both the market structure and the legislative framework are examined since they dictate the extent and the degree of adaptation open to societies. Thirdly, a comparative focus is provided in the evaluation of building societies particularly in terms of their rivalry with the retail banks in order to gain a more accurate appreciation of their corporate performance. Fourthly, societies are not viewed as a homogeneous group. Differences in the level of available resources and differential treatment under the legislation, has necessarily implied that there has been marked variation in terms of the extent to which societies have been able to embrace change. In an attempt to make provision for these differences, the sector has been divided into three mutually exclusive subcategories - national societies, regional societies and local societies. Thus the issues in this text are not only viewed from the perspective of the building society sector as a whole, but are also delineated in terms of the national, regional and local society segments.

A text on UK building societies at this juncture is both timely and relevant. Six years have elapsed since the advent of a more deregulated environment for building societies. Building societies are involved in a learning curve, critically in respect of issues such as product diversification, organisational restructuring, information technology adoption and new marketing techniques. Sufficient time has now elapsed to undertake an appraisal of their performance in respect of these and other issues. In addition, the experience of societies to date allows them to also critically evaluate the impact of existing legislation on their operation, and societies are now at the stage where they are in the process of formulating their views on necessary future legislative reforms.

Content

The structure of the text mirrors the points so far identified. The historical and legislative framework relevant to UK building societies is documented in chapter 2. Key developments affecting the emergence of a more competitive environment are also outlined in this chapter. Aspects of building society structure are examined in chapter 3. Attention focuses upon amalgamations and transfer of engagements between societies, trends in employment, branch rationalisation, the asset and liability structure and the regional orientation of societies. At strategic points, a wider comparative perspective *vis a vis* other financial institutions is provided. In addition, it is in this chapter that the typology of national, regional and local building societies is developed. In chapter 4 attention shifts to an analysis of building society performance. Capital strength, income generation capabilities, cost management and profit performance are discussed for the respective society groupings and also in comparison to a selection of retail banks. The theme of cost management is further explored in chapter 5 where a cost function model is utilised to provide measures of economies of scale and economies of scope for the various society groupings.

The changing role of information technology applications within the building society sector is pursued in chapter 6. Given the huge investment differential between banks and building societies particular attention is paid to the strategic use of information technology in these two institutional groupings. In chapter 7, an effort is made to provide insight into the factors which influence the nature of product diversification. Emphasis is also placed on the identification of differences in the degree of product diversification between societies, and the extent of retrenchment from the product lines which initially formed part of their diversification programmes. The marketing strategies of societies are examined in chapter 8 and an appraisal is made of the extent to which they have adopted a more rigorous marketing approach in a deregulated business environment. Chapter 9 provides an overview of organisational change, and examines both changes in organisational structure and culture within the sector. In chapter 10 the factors of influence in the relocation decision are considered. In terms of this discussion, relocation is viewed to be the situation where a society relocates its business operations in part or in full from one geographic area to another.

Chapters 11 and 12 broaden the focus to include the wider European dimension. The legislative framework is considered in chapter 11, whilst the potential that exists for expansion into European markets is scrutinised in chapter 12. In the final chapter, a commentary is provided on the key issues that arise from discussion in earlier chapters. The potential for evolutionary or radical change is examined in terms of the broad strategic options that exist in relation to the conversion option, further legal and constitutional reforms and possible future regulatory convergence.

Methodology

Much of the empirical evidence for changes within the sector is original and based on surveys carried out between June 1991 and December 1992. A total of 5 surveys were completed in respect of information technology, product diversification, marketing, organisational change and relocation. Data was also extensively drawn from the published accounts of societies for the period 1989 to 1991. While information from this source appears in the body of the text to amplify the analysis provided, it has also been utilised in the construction of a detailed Data Appendix. Comprising a total of 24 separate information categories, the Data Appendix is a comprehensive source of comparative information on each of the 89 societies in existence at the time of the completion of this text, December 1992.

2. Historical and Legal Development

Introduction

Any consideration of building societies requires, as a starting point, an examination of the key features that have influenced their historical development. In this chapter the origins of building societies are traced to their 18th century roots with the legal regulation which shaped such a distinctive role for them also examined. The legal framework established during the 19th century proved to be enduring and it is only with the enactment of the Building Societies Act of 1986 that any significant revision of the traditional functions of building societies can be seen to occur. Undoubtedly, the building society sector has enjoyed a prolonged period of stability and growth throughout its history. The context within which building societies currently operate though is far more dynamic and unpredictable than at any other time in their history, and this is largely attributable to the consequences of competition and deregulation.

Since the early 1980s, due initially to changes in the regulatory framework of the banks, building societies can be seen to be competing more directly with the banks. During the 1980s the mortgage market proved attractive not only for banks, but also new entrants such as centralised mortgage lenders, and the effect of this new competition at times undermined the traditional dominance of the building societies in the mortgage market. The traditional practice of rationing mortgages by building societies through the operation of an interest rate cartel proved unsustainable in the new competitive environment. Equally, competition has been intense on the investment side with the banks and building societies battling to attract savings. The themes of competition and deregulation are of course inter-related, and a major purpose of this chapter is to examine the impact of these in changing the nature of building societies. Here, particular attention is paid to the diversification by building societies into new services permissible under the 1986 Act.

It is obvious that the concept of a level playing field provided the impetus for deregulation of the building society sector in 1986, since building societies desired to compete on equal terms with other financial institutions. The effect of the 1986 Act and the regulatory framework governing building societies is the subject of current debate and this chapter also examines the question of future reforms within the sector.

Historical Distinctiveness of Building Societies

As one commentator put it,

> "the early societies were true building societies in that they built homes and were mutual." (Boleat, 1982).

Originating in the second half of the 18th century, these early mutual societies were founded on self-help principles and were dedicated to addressing the housing needs of the newly urbanised population created by the industrial revolution. The logic of these early societies was a simple one where 20 to 30 members banded together to regularly contribute funds in order to finance house building. Once all the members had been housed, the society was terminated since its purpose had been achieved.

If structure is a purpose of function, then the development of permanent societies can be viewed as a consequence of the need to speed up the provision of housing. First appearing in the middle of the 19th century, permanent societies paid interest to investors and charged interest to borrowers who required funds for house purchase. As the title implies, permanent societies expected to be enduring corporate entities into the future, unlike the earlier terminating societies which had a limited life span. By 1873 there were 540 permanent societies compared with 959 terminating societies (Cleary, 1965). By 1912 the number of terminating societies had fallen to half the total of all societies and by 1936 constituted only 16 percent of all societies (Drake, 1989). In 1980, the last remaining terminating society was dissolved.

Clearly establishing themselves as the dominant form of building society throughout this century, permanent societies have become substantial financial institutions, aided by a relentless process of concentration within the building society sector. At the start of this century there were 2,286 building societies with 585,000 share investors and total assets of some £60m. By the time the

Mid-Sussex building society transferred its engagements to the Cheltenham and Gloucester in August 1992, the number of societies had fallen to 89. The number of investors by 1992 had grown to 45m and total assets were in excess of £246bn.

The nature and scope of building society activity was largely established in the late 19th century by legally defining their corporate status as building societies owned by members. Thus, the ownership basis of building societies was totally different from that of commercial banks and companies established on the basis of share capital. It was the Building Societies Act of 1874 that first offered a clear definition of the distinctiveness of building societies as legal entities. Basically, this was achieved by closely circumscribing the activities of building societies through restrictions on their functions to those of accepting savings from the public and making loans on the security of land. This Act also established that societies were not permitted to build or own land except for the purpose of conducting their business. Furthermore, societies were required to invest surplus funds in mortgages or government securities. Restrictions were placed on mergers between societies and the Act protected societies from being controlled by another institution and prevented societies gaining control of other organisations.

The period following this landmark Act was one of economic depression which proved traumatic for building societies. Failure in 1892 of the Portsea Island and the then largest society, the Liberator, seriously affected investor confidence in the building society movement as a whole. Practices in these societies revealed important weaknesses in the 1874 Act. Resulting from speculative lending backed by inadequate security, these society failures,

> "tested the boundaries of building society business and demonstrated the dangers of over-stepping them." (Boddy, 1980).

A new Building Societies Act of 1894 further defined the boundary of building society activity by prohibiting suspect financial operations such as second mortgages. Also, the powers of the Chief Registrar were strengthened and similarly the reporting requirements on societies were tightened.

Further refinements in building society legislation occurred in 1960 and 1962. The 1960 Building Societies Act brought in measures to remedy the dubious practices of some rogue societies during the 1950s. Consequently, restrictions were placed on the types of property which societies could take as security for loans and placed limits on special advances to ensure that building society lending was channelled into traditional mortgage business. The 1962 Building Societies Act consolidated the existing legislation. It should be appreciated that the major legislation governing the activities of building societies still largely rested in the provisions first defined in the 1874 Act. Substantive change occurred to the boundaries defined by the 1874 Act only with the advent of greater competition in the 1980s and these are encompassed in the deregulation measures contained in the Building Societies Act of 1986.

The historic purpose of building societies can be categorised as the specialist provision of housing finance directed towards extending home ownership, although it should be added that until the 1950s many societies also provided mortgages to landlords to buy housing to offer for rent. As stated earlier the mutual status of building societies makes them fundamentally different from commercial organisations in that they have no equity shareholders but are owned by their investing and borrowing members. As a distinctive form of business organisation, mutual building societies have been successful financial institutions playing a significant role in the UK financial sector. The defining features of their historic role was neatly summarised by the Governor of the Bank of England in 1987,

> "At present they are, I would judge, held in particularly high esteem by the general public in this country. In part this reflects their mutual status - although this has its disadvantages in limiting their access to the capital market - but also the fact that societies have had a well defined function which has been carried out effectively." (Bank of England Quarterly Bulletin, 1987).

For most of their history, building societies have indeed operated within a well defined segment of the UK financial services market. This has been a reflection of the structure of the financial services sector in the UK which has traditionally been highly segmented and where, historically,

> " order and stability rather than competition and innovation were the values aspired to." (Hutchinson and McKillop, 1991).

In recent years, increased competition and innovation has dramatically affected the contours of the financial services sector and has made it increasingly difficult to view it as comprising of distinctive segments. Deregulation has led to a blurring of the boundaries between segments of the financial services sector and this is particularly the case with UK building societies and banks. Order and stability are no longer the dominant values, instead the financial services sector is typified more by competition and innovation. Before proceeding to describe in detail the provisions of the Building Societies Act of 1986 it is perhaps useful to outline the distortions to competition that existed in the period prior to deregulation. As stated in the introduction, a major intention of deregulation was to create a level playing field particularly between banks and building societies.

Distortions to Competition

The period 1950 to 1980 was one of unprecedented growth by building societies. Not only did they prosper in a huge and growing mortgage market to achieve virtual dominance, building societies were also successful in making significant gains, largely at the expense of the banks, in the retail deposit market. Effectively, building societies were able to exploit both these markets with only minimal competition from the banks. The segregation between the banks and building societies during this period can be explained by their differing histories, structure and corporate philosophies, but most importantly by differences in their regulatory regimes. Banks were subject to a variety of controls on their lending and deposit taking activities as part of monetary control policy which prevented them from being active in the personal sector financial market. Also, the preference of the banks to fund primarily in the wholesale market, further helps to explain the lack of bank competition to the building societies during this period.

The nature of the business environment prior to 1980 has been described as artificially created (Pawley et al, 1991) being the product of unique bank and building society regulatory regimes. That there existed a lack of competitive neutrality in the regulatory regime of building societies was certainly claimed by the banks. The Wilson Committee established in 1977 provided a forum whereby the banking sector highlighted a number of special advantages it believed that the building society sector enjoyed. For instance, the ability of the building societies to provide lower mortgage rates than banks was attributed to the existence of the composite rate tax system and it was alleged that building societies gained a competitive advantage in attracting money from taxpayers. Similarly, it was alleged that a lower corporation tax rate for building societies also conferred advantage.

A more important aspect of the artificiality of the business environment prior to 1980 was the operation by the building societies of an interest rate setting cartel through the Recommended Rate System. The effects of this cartel by the end of the 1970s were such as to be described in the following way,

> "Prices were not responsive to supply and demand; the lenders, the building societies, were not responsive to what the consumer wanted, and the process of borrowing could be a long drawn out affair." (Boleat, 1987).

From another perspective, the same writer makes the point that the existence of the Recommended Rate System ensured orderly market conditions and a low mortgage rate which suited both government and home owners.

Since a major effect of the cartel was to stifle price competition between societies, non-price competition became the norm and this took the form of growth of building society branches. In other words, a major corporate objective of building societies during this period was growth of assets. The cartel was also held to be important in protecting the inefficient societies from interest rate competition and this was consistent with a philosophy that saw all constituent mutual societies as sharing in the common social purpose of a building society movement. Self-imposed, the cartel was generally adhered to within the sector with the exception of some of the smaller societies which used their low management expenses ratios to offer premiums above the Recommended Rate. A key feature of the Recommended Rate System was that it was very sticky, in that adjustments in building society interest rates tended to lag behind movements in market rates and mortgage lending rates were kept, for the most part, below market clearing levels. Serious excess demand for mortgages existed as a consequence of the Recommended Rate System with building societies having recourse to non-price rationing of mortgages. The impact of technology, which served to radically reduce the entry barriers to financial services markets, combined with the deregulation of the financial services sector, were the main contributory factors leading to the demise of the Recommended Rate System. If the analysis now returns to the business environment prior to 1980 the evolving nature of competition in both the retail and mortgage markets can be considered.

Although competition between the banks and building societies had been increasing in the 1970s, this was largely restricted to the retail deposit market. Building societies had successfully built up their market share by offering term deposits and premium interest accounts for deposits above stipulated amounts. An obvious consequence of offering new retail deposit products which provided rates of interest above the ordinary share account was to increase the average funding costs for building societies. Similarly, to compete successfully in the retail deposit market posed the same kind of difficulty for banks in that the internal migration of funds from interest free accounts would increase their cost of funds. Competition from the banks heightened dramatically with the abolition of exchange controls in 1979 and the corset in 1980, and impacted on both the retail deposit and mortgage markets.

This relaxation of regulatory controls on the banks was a powerful influence, allowing them to engage in balance sheet expansion. Not only were banks freed from artificial lending constraints, Llewellyn (1988) also highlighted the impact of change in Bank of England regulations governing the capital base of banks which created a capital injection of £8.4bn between 1980 and 1986. This capital injection was used to fuel an expansion in bank lending. Given the reduced profitability of their corporate business in the 1970s and the excess demand that existed in the mortgage market, the banks deliberately targeted expansion in the mortgage market as a matter of strategic policy. The view was taken that the mortgage market offered multiple attractions in that it was perceived as being profitable, low risk and held the potential of providing a forum for the cross-selling of financial products. This entry by the banks into the mortgage market signalled the beginning of the end for the Recommended Rate System where traditionally the mortgage rate had been kept below market clearing levels. As a consequence of the entry by the banks to the mortgage market, the mortgage interest rate structure became much more market related. Banks were initially successful in penetrating the mortgage market and by 1982 had achieved a 36 percent market share of new lending.

Banks were not the only competitive threat to building societies in the mortgage market. A further impact of the structural change in mortgage interest rates - where the mortgage rate was rising relative to interest rates generally and relative to money markets in particular - was to further intensify competition by making the mortgage market attractive to new financial institutions, including foreign banks and quasi-secondary market institutions funded via the wholesale markets. These new institutions, such as National Home Loans, Mortgage Corporation and Mortgage Express, having access to cheaper funds and utilising new technology to obviate the need for an expensive branch structure, deliberately aimed to undercut building societies on price. By 1986, the combined market share of both the new centralised lenders and the banks was approaching 50 percent. These new lenders in particular, proved to be innovative in the creation of new mortgage products and offered consumers a variety of fixed rate, low start or deferred interest mortgage products in place of a single standard mortgage. In 1986, when the banks abolished the differential charged on endowment mortgages, building societies were obliged to follow suit even though 50 percent of their mortgage balances were linked to endowment policies. That there was, therefore, an increase in the rate of product innovation in the mortgage market and a reduction in profit margins is clear. And as perhaps has become apparent since, the level of risk increased with restrictions on income multipliers being competed away and 100 percent mortgages being made more available as a consequence of increased competition.

Competition in the retail savings market intensified during the 1980s. Building societies faced heightened competition from the banks as a consequence of a strategic shift in bank funding policy aimed to reduce their dependence on wholesale funds. Increased competition also emerged from National Savings. As a result of this new competitive environment, the personal sector witnessed a wave of new product development. In the case of building societies, this led to a propensity to launch new accounts offering interest premiums well above those on the traditional share account. It is interesting to note that over the decade, the composition of building society retail accounts was to radically change. Prior to the 1980s, funds held in ordinary accounts comprised nearly 90 percent of all building society retail deposits. By 1989, this proportion was to decline to less than 8 percent. Similarly, the banks were forced through competitive pressure to introduce new products in the retail market and by the mid-1980s they were offering interest paying current accounts. As stated before, these kinds of retail product developments served to increase the cost of retail funding relative to wholesale funding. Non-price competition also escalated during the 1980s. In 1980 the banks and building societies spent £8.6m. and £8.8m respectively on TV advertising. By 1987 this had risen to £50.3m and £41.1m respectively, (Speed,1990).

Clearly, the competitive environment of the 1980s was a force for change within building societies. It was nevertheless clear that a level playing field did not exist in relation to banks and building societies given the legal constraints described earlier which confined societies to their traditional role of collecting savings and making mortgage loans. In other words,

> "the building societies faced key disadvantages in that banks were better able to compete in the traditional business of the building society than were the building societies in the business of the banks." (Bank of England Quarterly Bulletin, 1990).

Besides offering money transmission facilities, savings accounts and mortgage loans, additional products such as estate agency services, unsecured loans and insurance services could be offered by the banks. If the banks were able to offer a full and flexible range of products, building societies could not. In the few cases where building societies did offer cheque book accounts for instance, this in the main was undertaken in conjunction with a bank[1] since legal restrictions prevented societies from providing cheque guarantee cards and overdraft facilities on these accounts. The enactment of the Building Societies Act of 1986 created a deregulated framework whereby building societies could better respond to the competitive pressure that had built up in the financial services sector.

The 1986 Building Societies Act

If both the Government and building societies recognised the need for new legislation to put societies on a more equal footing with other financial institutions, this was not to be done at the expense of a radical departure from the existing primary functions of building societies. Thus, shifting the boundaries of building society activity would be

> "incidental to these [primary functions] and should enhance their achievement." (Boleat, 1988).

The Building Societies Act of 1986 currently governs both the powers and constitution of building societies and is exclusive to them. As mutual institutions owned by investing and borrowing members, societies are not subject to either banking or commercial legislation. As a restrictive piece of legislation, building societies are able to do only those things laid down in the 1986 Act and subsequent statutory instruments made under the Act. Any society with aspirations to undertake activities outside the legal parameters of the Act, and not wishing to be frustrated by *ultra vires*, must convert to public limited company status.

Effectively, a building society converting to plc status would become a bank and require approval from the Bank of England to operate as such. Besides side-stepping any restrictions on their activities imposed by the Building Societies Act, perhaps the major attraction of conversion is the access it gives to additional capital. The procedure involved in the conversion process requires the recognition of a number of safeguards. Firstly, there must be adequate membership support for such a move. Here, there is a requirement that 75 percent of shareholders who vote and 50 percent of borrowers who vote support conversion. The minimum percentage of shareholders that must vote in the case of a conversion proposal is set at 20 percent. Secondly, the conversion procedure must be fair between members. Since the members of the society collectively own the reserves of the society, it follows that some distribution of reserves should occur in recognition of this. Finally, conversion should not provide the opportunity for gain through speculation. The device used to help prevent this is when a society announces proposals for conversion it must also announce a qualifying date where entitlement to benefits arising from conversion will depend on shares held at that date and for two years previously.

The 1986 Act also established the Building Societies Commission, (BSC) as the regulatory body for the sector. Broadly the functions of the BSC are to ensure the protection of building society investors, foster the financial stability of the industry and make recommendations to the Government on its future. Specifically, the BSC is charged with administering the system of regulation provided for by the Act, especially the criteria for prudent management (Section 45 (3)). Guidance on achieving compliance with prudential requirements occurs through the issue of prudential notes. The prudential notes relating to the capital adequacy of building societies are the most important and therefore worthy of closer examination. Essentially, determining the capital adequacy of building societies involves the BSC in grading the different categories of assets held by a building society according to their degree of risk. Depending on the degree of risk involved, a specified minimum percentage of the value of the asset is required by the BSC to be held as capital, with the higher risk assets requiring more capital backing. Taking each building society on an individual basis, the BSC makes judgements about the proficiency of the management, particularly their capability to engage in new business activities. Therefore, the prescribed minimum capital level determined for each building society reflects not only the composition of its assets, but also an assessment of the proficiency of its management. By convention, each building society is expected to keep its capital adequacy at least 0.5 percent above the BSC's prescribed minimum level. Capital adequacy requirements for building societies have been increasing since 1987 as a reflection of the diversification process permissible under the

Act.

It is also worth noting that since 1987 when the Act first took effect, the BSC has been running, in parallel to the requirements outlined above, the capital adequacy standards laid down in the European Community directives on Own Funds of Credit Institutions and the Solvency Ratio for Credit Institutions, both of which are due to come into effect from January 1, 1993. Currently, every building society is reporting its solvency ratio to the BSC on a quarterly basis. The European regime for capital adequacy employs a different methodology. The solvency ratio approach involves the calculation of risk-weighted assets. According to the Solvency Ratio Directive, the ratio of eligible capital or own funds to the value of the sum of the risk weighted assets, must be at least 8 percent. A building society which reported an actual or expected solvency ratio below 8 percent would be required by the BSC to take immediate steps to rectify its position. In chapter 4, the capital strength of building societies is discussed in more detail.

Returning to the BSC's overall supervisory role, it can be stated that its supervisory approach relies on monitoring the key aspects of building society activity to ensure that the management, systems and capital of a building society are all adequate for prudent management. Persuasion and a pro-active stance in identifying any prudential problems well before they become a risk is the hallmark of the BSC's approach. As a last resort, the BSC has an impressive armoury of statutory powers, including ultimately the power to present a petition for the winding up of a society.

The 1986 Act sets out quantitative limits on categories of building society commercial assets which, in conjunction with the services specified in Schedule 8 of the Act, define the extent to which societies can develop new services. Under the Act, three classes of commercial asset were introduced - class 1 assets are primarily first mortgages to owner occupiers; class 2 assets are other advances secured on land; and class 3 assets are essentially unsecured advances, investment in land and investment in subsidiaries. The importance of the introduction of class 3 lending lay in the fact that it provided building societies with the opportunity to issue credit cards, provide money transaction accounts with overdraft facilities and also unsecured loans for non-housing purposes. In other words, the Act basically permitted building societies to diversify into traditional banking activities but only within carefully defined quantitative limits. Thus the proportion of total assets available in each class were at least 90 percent of assets in class 1, and of the remaining 10 per cent not more than 5 percent could be in the form of class 3 assets.

With minor exceptions, within class 3 assets, the range of individually specified assets included in each of the classes has altered very little since the 1986 Act. The two main changes have been with regard to the Building Societies (Commercial Assets and Services) Order which came into force in August 1988 and the Building Societies (Money Transmission Services) Order which came into force in July 1989. Both Orders permit societies to hold additional forms of class 3 assets. The Commercial Assets and Services Order entitles societies to hold four additional forms of class 3 assets: residual mortgage debts, rights under instruments relating to mortgages, personal property for leasing, and rights arising from bridging loans. This order emanated from the review of Schedule 8 in 1988 which in extending the range of powers available to societies also recognised that this required additional powers to hold new forms of assets. The Money Transmission Services Order empowered societies with qualifying assets to operate accounts on which a person other than an individual can temporarily overdraw in the course of receiving money transmission services with the requisite debt counting as a class 3 asset.

There are two quantitative restrictions placed on societies with regard to their holdings of commercial assets. The first is that unsecured lending and acquisition and development of land cannot be offered by societies with commercial assets of less than £100m. The second is that there is an upper limit placed upon unsecured lending. Initially, under the 1986 Act, the upper limit was £5,000. This was raised to £10,000 in the 1988 review of Schedule 8, and currently, November 1992, proposals are before Parliament to raise the limit to £25,000. Finally, the limits upon the proportion of commercial assets which societies can hold in each of the classes have been revised. Currently, a minimum of 80 percent of a society's commercial assets have to be in the form of class 1 lending. Up to 10 percent of commercial assets can be in the form of class 3 lending with an upper limit of 20 percent placed on the sum of class 2 and 3 assets. A further revision of the percentage weights takes place at the start of 1993 when the limits on class 2 and 3 lending are to be further raised so that in total they can account for 25 percent of commercial assets, with a limit on class 3 assets of 15 percent. The exact range of land services and financial services which a building society is entitled to provide under the Act is detailed in Schedule 8. Amended in 1988, Schedule 8 covers services in the categories of banking, insurance and investment, and also in respect of trusteeship, executorship and land services. In respect of banking services, building societies have the power to provide every banking service to individuals, although they can only provide limited services to corporate customers. Under the power to provide investment services, building societies are able to manage collective investment trusts, manage pension schemes, operate a stockbroking service, operate personal equity plans and give investment advice. Societies have the power to arrange the provision of insurance of any description. The services of trusteeship which they can offer is restricted to express trusts where the majority of the beneficiaries are individuals or charitable trusts. Building societies can administrate the estates of deceased persons and can assist in the making of wills under their power to provide executorship services. Finally, the definition of land services under Schedule 8 includes the provision of estate agency services, although building societies are required to undertake this through a subsidiary.

Under Schedule 8 of the 1986 Act societies were initially prevented from underwriting insurance business. This restriction was eased somewhat in the 1988 Review of Schedule 8. Building societies were given the power to underwrite life assurance business with societies permitted to wholly own a life assurance company. In addition societies were permitted to take an equity stake up to 15 percent in a general insurance company.

One other feature of the 1986 Act deserves to be highlighted, namely the establishment of a Building Societies Investor Protection Board. The main purpose of this body is to protect investors' funds in the unlikely event of the insolvency of one of the societies. The Board is funded via a levy on societies and, should compensation be required, investors receive up to 90 percent of their deposits subject to a maximum of £20,000[2].

Restrictions Imposed by the 1986 Act

The restrictive nature of the Building Societies Act should now be examined to appreciate the perceived need, particularly by the larger societies, for a more permissive stance to be taken towards building societies if they are to operate effectively in the ever intensifying competitive environment of the 1990s. Responding to developments in the financial services market in the future may well be constrained under the legislation as it stands.

The principal purpose of a building society is defined by section 5(1) of the 1986 Act where it states that a building society must be established,

> "for the purpose of raising, primarily through the subscriptions of members, a stock or fund for making to them advances secured on land for their residential use."

There are a series of restrictions, or nature limits, which further prescribe the extent of building society activity by defining specific requirements in key areas. Amongst these are the provisions relating to the lending constraints within determined asset categories which were discussed earlier. Similarly, important restrictions are placed on the funding activities of building societies.

Restrictions on funding, and the impact of this on the core activity of building societies, could be regarded as potentially limiting the future market responsiveness of building societies. Initially, the wholesale funding limit was set by the Act at 20 percent, although this has been raised by statutory instrument to 40 percent in recognition of the increasingly important role played by this funding source in the prevalent market conditions of the late 1980s. Although only in the case of a limited number of societies has the level of wholesale funding even reached 25 percent, (see both chapter 3 and the Data Appendix), and therefore is well short of the permitted ceiling, there is still a desire to see restrictions on funding removed. This reflects an awareness that should, as in the past, retail funds become less plentiful or more expensive, it is in the strategic interests of building societies to have the funding flexibility to respond to any anticipated problems relating to an over-reliance on retail funding. The same perspective can be applied to asset limits. Whilst building societies are also short of the permitted maximum in terms of commercial asset limits, their ability to foresee market problems and opportunities should, arguably, be accompanied by the ability to adjust their strategy in terms of class 2 and 3 lending to suit judgements about best business policy. The balance between retaining the principal purpose and mutuality elements of building society distinctiveness and a loosening of the boundaries defined for funding and lending in the current legislation is an issue to be addressed in the 1990s. A recent study undertaken by Price Waterhouse (1991), and commissioned by the BSA, articulates this issue concerning the further reform of building society powers,

> "Our findings suggest that, especially in the short term and in the light of the uncertainty surrounding the financial services market place worldwide, there is no great desire to significantly change the nature and scope of the activities of individual building societies. However, it is recognised that such a change is likely to be necessary in the medium term and that preparing for such a change must start now. The key desire lay in the ability to undertake new activities in response to changes in the financial markets. This flexibility was not only seen as essential from a competitive standpoint, but would also eliminate the significant amount of time currently being spent by managers and lawyers on the question of what a building society can and cannot do."

If flexibility is essential from a competitive standpoint, building societies may feel that they suffer poorly in comparison with banks. Under the banking regulatory framework, banks can, in principle, offer any financial service they choose. Building societies cannot. The restrictive nature of the Building Societies Act can be further documented by reference to several illustrations of the sector's ability to develop new financial services being legally thwarted *ab initio.*

Restriction on the lines of business a building society can enter can be seen for example when the Alliance and Leicester bought Girobank in 1990 and had to sell off the bank's leasing and commercial lending operations since the society would fall foul of *ultra vires* if it undertook these forms of business. Similarly, a building society is prohibited from owning more than 15 percent of a general insurance company. Although building societies can at present undertake class 2 lending secured on land, they are prohibited from undertaking other forms of corporate lending whether secured on corporate assets or unsecured. Initially, building societies were restricted from taking part in syndicated loans, although recently the BSC has issued guidance notes on this and they can now engage in such loans provided they do so through a subsidiary. A building society can lend £10,000 in aggregate by way of a mix of unsecured loan, overdraft or credit card to an individual under permissible class 3 lending, but despite further liberalisation which allowed an additional £10,000 lending from each of a society's subsidiaries, the class 3 limits are still felt to be restrictive, especially in terms of lending to customers with a high net worth. As was stated above, the limit of £10,000 is about to change to £25,000. Building societies face restrictions on the use of hedging and swap arrangements. Finally, building societies face considerable restrictions on their ability to undertake international operations and it is worth considering this more fully.

Diversification through international operations is still in its early stages within the building society sector. Until recently, building societies faced considerable restrictions on operating in the European Community. The 1986 Act did not allow them to operate directly in other European Community countries. Although section 14 of the Act permitted societies to lend direct on the security of land outside the UK, the power to do so had to be conferred by Treasury Order and until recently these had only been issued in respect of the Isle of Man, the Channel Islands and Gibraltar. Whilst societies were allowed to lend outside the UK under the mechanism just described, the only means open to building societies of doing business in the European Community was through subsidiaries, provided that the society in question had commercial assets of at least £100m. The Act did not permit these subsidiaries to offer a full range of services since the business conducted in the European Community had to be in mainly secured lending. Subsidiaries established to operate in the European Community could not raise deposits in the UK nor lend in the UK. Furthermore, such investment in a European subsidiary had to be counted as a class 3 asset contributing towards a society's holdings in this asset category.

When set against the impending enactment of the European Community's Second Banking Co-ordination Directive, due to come into effect in January, 1993, the above measures governing the operation of UK building societies in the European Community placed societies at a serious disadvantage to other financial institutions. Under the Second Banking Directive, a credit institution can obtain a single banking licence which allows them to trade in other Community countries without further authorisation. Central to the operation of this Directive is the concept of home country authorisation and supervision, but crucially the single banking licence is only valid in respect of activities that can be carried out in the home country. Mindful that societies should be allowed to take full advantage of the potential afforded by the Second Banking Directive, a Treasury Order came into effect in July 1992 which permits societies to lend directly in Europe and to provide all the services they currently provide in the UK. The European theme is further explored in chapters 11 and 12.

The Financial Services Act, 1986

The Financial Services Act is an important aspect of the current legal framework as it contains a requirement that building societies obtain authorisation to undertake investment business. Under the original provisions of this Act, the mechanisms for authorisation included direct authorisation from the Securities and Investments Board or through membership of one of five self-regulatory bodies then recognised by the Securities and Investments Board. Most societies obtained authorisation directly from the Securities and Investments Board. Investment business excludes traditional building society share and deposit and mortgage business, but encompasses a wide range of activities such as endowment insurance and mortgage protection policies, personal pensions, personal equity plans, unit trusts and staff pension schemes.

Controversially, the Act introduced the concept of polarisation whereby intermediaries had to choose to be either wholly independent acting on behalf of the customer, or tie themselves as the appointed representative of a particular company selling only their products. It should be noted at this point that polarisation applies only to life assurance and unit trusts and not to other investment products. The intention behind the legislation was to better ensure investor protection. Societies are bound by guidance given by the Securities and Investments Board on the conduct of investment business which includes, *inter alia*, the obligation to provide best advice, to ascertain the suitability of potential investors, to disclose fees and charges and to disclose material particulars involved in a transaction. The Clucas Report (1992) recommended a rationalisation of the five original self-regulatory bodies set up under the Act, and suggested that independent financial advisers and tied agents be regulated by the same body rather than separately.

Currently, the only two societies in the top fifteen which are independent under the polarisation rules are the Bradford and Bingley and the Yorkshire. Most societies have opted for appointed representative agreements and have either formed a joint venture with a life assurance company or acquired a mutual insurance company. Investment business is of growing importance to building societies. An assessment of investment business is provided in chapter 7.

Future Issues

The major legal changes that have occurred as part of the deregulation process have now been considered. Whilst this has permitted diversification and, to an extent, the breakdown of the traditional demarcations between the building society and banking sectors, there currently exists a state of unstable equilibrium in the building society industry. For a sector that has enjoyed long periods of stability and continuity, the dynamic flux of the 1980s and early

1990s has undoubtedly created an agenda of change. A momentum, led by the BSA, for new legislation to modify the prescriptive regime of the 1986 Act already exists. This is perhaps motivated by a recognition that failure to remove the limits on building society activities might result in the larger societies being attracted down the route of conversion to plc status, thereby putting at jeopardy the existence of a distinctive building society sector. It is apparent that the BSA favours the continued development of the building societies sector on the basis of mutuality, and would prefer to see the larger societies remain mutuals. Although we have already postulated a convergence thesis in respect of building societies increasingly undertaking banking activities, it is likely that building society distinctiveness and the identity of mutuality, may strongly inform the debate about the future evolution of building societies, particularly in respect of greater involvement in the banking arena. The emergence of mutual banks from the ranks of current building societies is therefore entirely conceivable,

> "Time was, if a British building society wanted to behave like a bank, it had to become one. That is why Abbey National, the second-biggest building society, spent £80 million in promotions and fees to become a publicly quoted bank in 1989. A few years from now Abbey may wonder why it bothered. Britain's mortgage specialists are pressing for new laws that would allow them to do everything that banks can do and still work as mutual societies, owned by their customers, free of the obligation to pay dividends, and immune from takeovers." (The Economist,1990).

The development and growth of mutual building societies in this country has been a success story and mutuality as an organisational form has proved to be enduring and effective. At this point it is perhaps helpful to more clearly define the distinguishing characteristics of mutuality. This can be done by comparing the key differences between the mutual form of a business organisation and that of a limited company. Clearly, the basis of member ownership of a mutual differs significantly from that of a plc. In return for the risks involved in investing share capital in a plc, the owners of this capital are entitled to receive the payment of dividends and to accrue the benefits of increases in share prices. Although the members own a mutual building society, their claim to the residual value of the institution cannot be exercised directly on the same individual basis in the same way as a shareholder. Also, building societies are not required to service their reserves in the way that a plc does through the payment of dividends. A further major difference between the two organisational forms relates to the ability of a plc to increase its capital through the issue of new equity. Mutuals, in contrast, do not have access to an external capital market but rather have to generate capital internally from surpluses. This latter point does however, require to be qualified in the light of the introduction of Permanent Interest Bearing Shares, (PIBS) within the building society sector in 1991.

PIBS can be compared in many respects with equity shares in a limited company. For instance, they are not covered by the building society compensation scheme described earlier, and PIBS holders would be last in line for payment in the unlikely event of a building society failing. Thus, they are comparable to ordinary shares in a limited company. PIBS are real risk capital and are not available from the building society that issues them, rather they have to be obtained through a stockbroker or investment adviser. They pay a fixed rate of interest and can be compared to gilts. Currently, building societies can issue PIBS as additions to their capital base, subject to BSC guidance that not more than 50 percent of free reserves[3] be used in this way. So far, twelve building societies have issued PIBS and it is likely that the use of PIBS will quickly spread throughout the sector. PIBS are again examined in chapter 4 in the section which considers the capital strength of building societies.

Continuing the comparison of the two business organisation forms it is the case that ownership and control is seen to be more directly linked in plc's than in mutuals. Since ownership of mutuals is widely dispersed, the implication is often drawn that management accountability is therefore weaker than in plc's. Similarly, the fact that there is an absence of adverse takeover threat in the building society sector is often counterposed with the situation governing plc's where the threat of takeover is omnipresent and acts as a discipline on managers to run the company as efficiently as possible. This implied lack of accountability within mutuals can be used as justification of special restrictions being placed on them. Without restrictions, mutuals might otherwise be less cost efficient and more risk taking than plc's. In other words, there are features inherent in the nature of mutuals that give rise to the need for special provisions to regulate their activities in order to guarantee competitive neutrality with other forms of business organisation, particularly plc's.

A recent consultancy report commissioned by the BSA (Price Waterhouse, 1991) counters the perspective outlined above, and argues that the reasons advocated for

> "special restrictions on the activities of building societies are weak, implausible or inconsistent."

Plc's are seen to be no more accountable than mutual building societies where members have a very effective mechanism for ensuring management accountability via their right to remove their funds. Higher costs could be taken as an indicator of lack of management accountability, yet evidence to be reported in chapter 4 would tend to suggest that building societies have lower cost to income ratios than banks and in addition are more profitable than their plc rivals. The efficacy of takeover threat to ensuring greater efficiency in plc's is also severely questioned, since empirical evidence here suggests that a major defence mechanism against takeover threat is the adoption of a growth, rather than an efficiency strategy. Similarly, arguments concerning the competitive advantage that might accrue to building societies through free reserves are refuted; seeing free reserves as a funding advantage fails to take account of the gains to members of the lower insolvency risks created by reserves. That investors should choose to accept the opportunity cost of lower insolvency risk by foregoing larger interest margins negates the notion that reserves are in fact "free".

The concept of a building society as a staid institution which simply takes deposits and makes mortgage loans is an outdated one. Stimulated by competition in their core business, building societies have become more commercially sophisticated and more recognisably profit-orientated. The extent to which building societies engage in higher risk business is an important factor since the control of risk may provide a powerful justification for the retention of controls on building society activities beyond the less defensible reasons already outlined.

One key feature which suggests that in fact building societies are likely to be risk averse relates to the difficulty of re-building capital once it has been lost since new capital has to be generated internally. Thus, unlike plc banks, building societies cannot issue new equity (with the exception of PIBS) to rebuild their capital base. It would also appear that if building societies do desire to engage in more risky activities, then it is as an extension to their core business. Building societies do not appear to be attracted to the more high risk forms of bank lending. To the extent that they are engaged in banking activities, it seems equitable to suggest that, rather than have to meet special requirements as building societies, they could be governed by similar prudential regulations to the banks. Some commentators see regulatory convergence between banks and building societies as a natural consequence of the current developments in the financial services industry. Discussion of the issue of a single regulator is considered in chapter 13.

Summary

In providing an overview of the context of UK building societies, this chapter has attempted to provide a framework for understanding the development of societies from their origins to the present day. Building societies have a unique history which has had a powerful effect in making them quite distinctive institutions in the financial services sector. This distinctiveness was traced to the legal definition formulated in the 19th century, which stressed a restricted purpose and function for building societies. The building society sector has displayed the dual characteristics of growth and concentration, mostly within the context of a stable, external business environment, throughout most of its history.

The context within which building societies now operate is in stark contrast to the days when societies enjoyed a dominance within a segmented financial services sector. The features that resulted in competitive distortions within the personal financial sector prior to 1980 were examined with this linked to changes in the banking regulatory framework which escalated competitive pressures in the markets where building societies are active. Based on the logic of the creation of a level playing field, the Building Societies Act aimed to liberate societies from the strictures of 19th century legislation, but not in a radical way. The net result appears to be a dissatisfaction with this legislation as still being too restrictive, and a concern that building societies cannot in fact compete with their rivals, the banks, on an equal footing.

The restrictive nature of the 1986 Act was examined in detail. Both funding and lending policy are carefully regulated by this legislation and an attempt was made to explain the mechanics of this. The role of the BSC was also briefly explained, particularly in respect of the monitoring of capital adequacy requirements for prudent management. Obviously, as the legislation is constantly evolving, some of the initial restrictions contained in it have been modified, the case of international operations being a good example of this. There are, nevertheless, still sufficient irritants within the legislation to fuel calls for its replacement by new legislation. Strategic flexibility in the long term perhaps requires greater freedom of action on the part of building societies. How far they wish to stray from the core identity of a building society is the key question. Transformation to the status of mutual bank is not inconceivable, conversion to plc remains an option, and legislative reform is certainly intended for the future. In the final chapter, the future options confronting building societies are considered as are the implications of these options.

It was also viewed as important to pay some attention in this chapter to examining the characteristics of mutual organisations in comparison to plc's. Drawing on a recent consultancy report commissioned by the BSA, arguments regarding the sustainability or otherwise of special provisions for building societies were explored. It would be entirely wrong to be prescriptive in any way at this stage about major issues. Rather, the preference is, in the initial chapters that follow, to conduct an audit of key operational features before returning to a more strategic focus in the final chapters of the book. From the discussion in this chapter, it should be clear that building societies are in a period of transition or, as was put earlier, unstable equilibrium, and that the sector is destined to undergo major changes in the 1990s.

Notes

[1]One exception was the Abbey National which offered a cheque book account from 1983 without overdraft and cheque guarantee card using a bank only for clearing.

[2]Under the 1986 Act the maximum level of compensation was initially set at £10,000, this was subsequently raised in 1987 to £20,000.

[3]Free capital is defined as gross capital minus fixed assets. Gross capital includes general reserves plus qualifying subordinated debt plus PIBS.

3. Structure and Market Position

Introduction

The purpose of this chapter is to present a structured overview of the building society industry. This overview focuses upon a number of dimensions where building societies are examined in isolation of other financial institutions. In addition, the overview also endeavours to broaden the discussion at strategic points in order to identify the importance of building societies as a general group within the UK financial services industry.

Aspects of building society structure which are examined within the confines of the industry include: amalgamations and transfer of engagements between societies; distribution of building societies' head-offices; trends in employment; branch rationalisation; and, the asset and liability structure of building societies. In terms of the wider focus, an attempt is made to identify the position occupied by societies in both the savings and the mortgage markets *vis a vis* other financial institutions.

As a start point, the discussion in this chapter commences with the construction of a framework within which subsequent analysis in this chapter, as well as in later chapters, is based. This framework is essentially built upon the recognition that building societies are not necessarily a homogeneous group of financial institutions. Differences in the geographical distribution of their branch networks, and more importantly, differences in asset size, are likely to result in the emergence of, for example, significant differences in their product portfolios. On the basis of the joint criteria of network distribution and asset size, societies are consequently defined as being national, regional or local in form. Statistical material is then, where possible, presented for not only societies as a whole, but in addition, for each of the subgroupings.

Society Classifications

As of August 1992, there were a total of 89 building societies authorised by the Building Societies Commission, (BSC) to accept investments from the public. It is these 89 societies on which the analysis in this and future chapters is based.

Much of the statistical material published elsewhere on building societies is presented either in aggregate terms or on the basis of asset size groups. The classification of societies by asset size, as set out by the BSC, is based on each society's assets expressed as a percentage of the total assets of all societies. The classification itself has been revised on a number of occasions with the most recent of these revisions having occurred in 1990. The effect of these changes was to increase the number of societies within the first group which is made up of the larger societies; to generally reduce the asset size range within each group; and to reduce the number of groups from 6 to 4. These four groups are now labelled A, B, C and D.

In terms of the format of this text, it was felt that an alternative typology of society groupings was warranted. Specifically, it was decided to regroup societies in terms of a national, regional and local classification system. Asset size coupled with the number and geographical distribution of a society's branch outlets were the criteria utilised to allocate societies into the respective groupings.

One slight problem when it comes to an analysis and classification of societies, based on information primarily obtained from their annual reports and statement of accounts, is that all societies do not report on an end calendar year basis. A total of 26 societies have end reporting periods which do not coincide with the end of the calendar year. The manner in which this problem was dealt with was that information obtained from accounts which had an end reporting year in the first six months of the year was classified under previous year data, while information from accounts which had an end reporting year in the second half of a year was classified under the specific year in question. For example, the last annual report and statement of accounts obtained in 1992 and included in the database on which the statistical analysis in this text is built, was that of the Clay Cross Benefit building society. The accounts of the Clay Cross were published in September 1992 with the end reporting period, May 31, 1992. The data in these accounts were consequently classified as 1991 information.

National societies are defined as having a network of branches throughout the UK and a consolidated asset base which exceeds £5bn, (end 1991). A total of 10 societies were defined as national societies. Coincidentally, those societies classed as national societies are exactly the same as those categorised as group A by the BSC.

Regional societies are societies which have an extensive branch network presence in a particular region and an asset level in excess of £200m, (end 1991). In total, 33 societies were categorised as being regional societies. Local societies, in contrast, have a few branches in a town or county, a strong local identity, and an asset base of below £200m, (end 1991). The remaining 46 societies were all viewed to fall into the local category.

As would be expected with the use of a joint criteria classification system, there are one or two societies which potentially transcend more than one of the categories. A case in point is that of the National Counties. It is allocated to the regional classification primarily because its asset base of £340m, (end 1991), places it as a middle of the range society within this group. National Counties has, however, no branch outlets and operates only through a head office, consequently on the branch criteria it could be viewed as a local society. To further compound the problem, National Counties as a postal based society, covers most of the UK and so in consequence it may be judged by some to have many similarities, particularly in terms of the geographical spread of its customer base, to that of a national society.

While accepting that the classification is not perfect, there are two main reasons for the organisation of societies into national, regional and local groupings. The first relates to the fact that many of the issues which are explored in the text lend themselves to an analysis from the joint perspective of branch numbers and asset size. The study of economies of scale and economies of scope in chapter 5, and product diversification in chapter 7, are the more immediately obvious examples. The second reason for the new classification is that it is both more cosmetically pleasing and indeed more meaningful for the reader to be informed about national, regional and local societies as opposed to group A, B C and D societies.

Mortgage Market

Although under the 1986 Act societies have been permitted to expand and diversify the range of activities that they can undertake, the majority of their business still centres upon the provision of mortgage finance. A statistical overview is presented in Table 3:I of loans for house purchase both in terms of residential mortgage balances outstanding and also in terms of annual net advances for house purchase. The information is documented for the years 1986 through to 1991 and is presented for banks and other loan institutions as well as building societies. In any time series analysis of aggregate bank and building society statistics, it should be remembered that from Q3, 1989 the Abbey National is included as a bank rather than a building society.

Table 3:I
Loans for House Purchase 1986-1991

Year	Net Advances During Period, £m			Balances Outstanding End Period, £m		
	Building Societies	Banks	Other*	Building Societies	Banks	Other*
1986	19,541	5,196	2,279	116,938	26,307	11,698
1987	14,588	9,644	4,259	131,518	35,951	15,965
1988	23,677	10,909	5,423	155,195	45,337	21,389
1989	24,041	7,186	2,518	152,432	79,196	25,570
1990	24,090	6,419	1,616	176,572	85,688	30,814
1991	20,585	4,909	1,145	197,107	90,490	31,959

*other relates to local authorities, other public sector, insurance companies and pension funds, and miscellaneous financial institutions.

At the end of 1991 residential mortgage balances outstanding stood in total at £320bn. The building societies' share of the market was £197bn, (62 percent). Of more importance to mortgage lenders is the volume of new business attracted. On this count the 1991 figures were somewhat of a disappointment. Net advances for all mortgage lenders in 1991 totalled £26.6bn, with 1991 the third successive year of falling mortgage advances. The underlying reasons for the fall were the combination of high interest rates and static or falling house prices which reduced the turnover in owner-occupied housing. Building societies, however, took an increasing share of this declining market. Their share in 1991 was marginally in excess of 77 percent. This marked the fourth year in succession, from a low point of 51 percent in 1987, that societies' share of net advances has risen. The increase in market share by societies has largely been at the expense of the new specialised mortgage lenders. Many, although not all, of the centralised lenders which came into the mortgage market during the 1980s have, since the end of 1989, been attempting to quietly withdraw. In the main, these centralised lenders consist of foreign banks and life assurance groups.

The *modus operandi* of these new mortgage market participants is relatively straight-forward. Funds are obtained from wholesale money markets and mortgages are sold through panels of insurance companies rather than through branch outlets. Through operating in this manner, centralised mortgage lenders avoid the overheads which building societies face in both the generation of funds and in the sale of mortgages. Coupled with lower costs of production, centralised mortgage lenders were very much in the vanguard in the design of tailor-made mortgages. Indeed, they are viewed as being the catalyst for the plethora of new mortgage products now to be found in the market place. In addition, centralised operations also come into their own during periods of low interest rates. During such periods, there is a tendency for the cost of retail funding to rise significantly in relation to that of wholesale funding.

The peak market share for centralised lenders was obtained towards the end of 1986. At that stage, they had managed to capture 20 percent of total new lending. Between 1986 and the third quarter of 1989 the market share of centralised lenders tended to trend around 15 percent. Thereafter, there was a sharp decline in their market share and by the end of 1991, they accounted for a mere 5 percent of net new lending.

The key players among the centralised mortgage companies were, and in most cases still are, National Home Loans, Household Mortgage Company, Mortgage Corporation, Mortgage Funding Corporation, First Mortgage Securities and Mortgage Express. Mortgage Express, the centralised mortgage lending arm of the TSB Group, was the first major centralised lender to withdraw from the market. It withdrew at the start of 1991. The relative importance of Mortgage Express to the mortgage market may be viewed from the fact that at its height, towards the end of 1988, its mortgage book was comparable in size to that of a top regional building society. National Home Loans, at the time of writing, had also all but collapsed. It is estimated that in the market there are currently some two dozen mortgage books for sale, (Barchard, 1991a).

There is not one cause but several for the difficulties faced by centralised lenders since the end of 1989. First, from a price perspective, the reversal of the downward drift in interest rates at the end of 1988 shifted the cost advantage back towards building societies with their ability to fund their lending more cheaply from retail deposits. Indeed a number of the national societies deliberately held retail deposit rates as low as possible in a deliberate effort to put a squeeze on centralised lenders.

A further cause of the difficulties faced by centralised lenders relates to the fact that they tended to attract more high risk borrowers, particularly first time buyers who required a relatively high percentage of the value of the property.

> "With many advances at or near 100 percent of property valuations and with mortgage interest rates then rising rapidly, it was inevitable that when property prices collapsed, the financial exposure of the centralised lenders would make them particularly vulnerable." (Fleming and Nellis, 1992).

In addition, the problems faced by centralised lenders have been further exacerbated by the fact that a large percentage of the loan book of centralised lenders has been concentrated in the south of England. The property market collapse has, therefore, disproportionately impacted upon centralised lenders.

For the future, the expectation must be for a further decline in the number of centralised lenders operating in the UK mortgage market. Indeed, given that the Household Mortgage Corporation, very much against market trends, has pursued a policy of acquiring other centralised lenders, an exit route has opened up for centralised lenders wishing to vacate the mortgage market.

Recovery in the house market is also unlikely to lead to a reversal in this reduced participation by centralised lenders in the mortgage market. The reasons invariably cited for such a conclusion are

> ".... many of the mortgage arrears problems are still in the pipeline; and .... some companies have come to realise that the UK mortgage market is no longer the friendly environment that it once was, and the future of centralised lenders in the UK is therefore uncertain." (Fleming and Nellis, 1992).

A more sustained level of competition for mortgage business has emerged from the retail banking sector. After the abolition of controls on their lending, retail banks aggressively entered the mortgage market in 1981, and by the end of 1982, had a market share of 36 percent. Price competitiveness was the primary reason for the rapid inroads made by banks into the mortgage market. At that stage, rates in the wholesale market were profitably below the mortgage rate and banks, unlike societies, were freely able to access the wholesale markets. As with the centralised lenders, the banks' share of the mortgage market has, over the years, been subject to wide fluctuations. Furthermore, and in line with the experience of the centralised lenders, the banks' share of the mortgage market has since 1989, been considerably squeezed by the building societies. Particularly important in this turn-around in fortunes has been the price competitiveness of building societies' mortgages. Two factors have been important in the attainment of a price advantage by societies. First, the opportunity to access wholesale markets has enabled societies to reduce their retail savings rate which has, in turn, permitted societies to cut the costs of mortgages at the margin. Secondly, banks have been hit by historically high levels of bad debt, not only on their mortgage book but in other aspects of their business, such as corporate loans. To counter the adverse effect of bad debt on profitability and hence upon capital ratios, (see chapter 4), banks have engaged in a policy of widening their domestic lending spreads. This widening of spread has eroded their competitive position in the mortgage market. During 1991, the banks' share of net mortgage lending stood at approximately 18 percent.

Retail banks, unlike many centralised lenders, are not going to withdraw from the mortgage market, and when societies revise upwards their highly competitive mortgage pricing strategy, the banks' mortgage share will again increase. Competition for retail savings, particularly from national savings, is likely to result in the occurrence of such a revision sooner rather than later.

UBS Phillips and Drew (1992a) cited a selection of reasons why retail banks may, however, be unable to recoup market share levels similar to that of

1982. Particularly pertinent from among these reasons are that banks no longer hold an advantage in mortgage product innovation; societies over the last 5 years have built up estate agency chains which can be utilised to channel business to the society; and the strategic alliances now being formed with life companies with their own distribution networks and sales forces, can also be employed to generate mortgage business.

Other Commercial Assets

Mortgages are, of course, only one component of the commercial assets of building societies. As indicated in chapter 2, the commercial assets of building societies have, under the 1986 Act, been subdivided into three classes: class 1 assets, which are first mortgages to owner-occupiers of residential property; class 2 assets which are other advances secured on land; and class 3 assets, defined as unsecured advances to individuals, investment in land and investment in subsidiaries and associates. In Table 3:II the opportunity is taken to detail, for societies as a whole, the respective share of each asset class as a proportion of total commercial assets.[1]

Table 3:II
Asset Class as a Proportion of Commercial Assets, %

Asset Class	1989	1990	1991
Class 1	96.42	95.60	95.72
Class 2	2.86	3.45	3.28
Class 3	0.72	0.95	1.00

From Table 3:II, it is clear that first advances to owner-occupiers play a dominant and pivotal position in the commercial asset portfolio of societies. Although societies as a whole are well below their prescribed limits for class 2 and class 3 assets the general trend in Table 3:II is one of an upward movement in both class 2 and class 3 assets as a proportion of commercial assets. The exception to this general trend is the slight dip between 1990 and 1991 in class 2 assets as a proportion of commercial assets. In chapter 7 which examines the product diversification strategies of building societies, a much more extensive and disaggregate analysis of the commercial asset holdings of building societies is provided.

Liquid Assets

In addition to commercial assets, the asset portfolio of societies also encompasses a liquid asset component. Liquid assets are held by societies primarily to finance short term cash outflows arising from a society's normal business activities. The regulation on liquid assets which came into force in 1987 was revised in December 1991. The rationale behind the revision was that for large societies particularly, the regulations were proving over-restrictive in that they permitted the holding of only a very narrow range of assets. The effect of the new regulation was

> "to permit building societies to hold a wider range of high quality investments and to replace detailed statutory restrictions with prudential requirements." (BSC Annual Report, 1991-92).

Earlier in 1991, the BSC also widened societies' powers to hold each others certificates of deposit and floating rate notes as well as enabling societies, for the first time, to hold deposits with other societies. In essence, 1991 saw the introduction of an inter-building society deposit market.

The composition of the liquid asset holdings of societies has itself altered over time. In 1987, bank deposits (including certificate of deposits and bills) accounted for 57 percent, UK government securities 30 percent and building society certificates of deposit 7 percent.[2] Comparable figures for 1991 were 76, 7 and 6 percent respectively. This shift in the liquid asset structure of societies has primarily been due to three factors. The first relates to the abolition in 1984 of tax relief on capital gains made by societies on the disposal of government gilts. Not surprisingly the abolition of tax relief reduced the attraction of holding government stock for societies. The second factor is the increased volatility of retail funds in recent years which has encouraged societies to move out of long dated assets and move into assets with shortened maturities. The third factor relates to the reduction in the supply of government securities over the period as a consequence of the decline in the public sector borrowing requirement.

Liquid assets as a percentage of total assets are detailed in Table 3:III.[3] The information is provided for societies as a whole as well as for the national, regional and local subgroupings. Note that the average ratios reported for each of the groupings are calculated on a weighted basis. The weights in this instance are determined by the relative proportion of a society's total assets to the total assets of the particular group under consideration.

Table 3:III
Liquid Assets as a Proportion of Total Assets, 1989-1991

Building Society Groupings	1989	1990	1991
National Societies	15.98	16.80	16.75
Regional Societies	17.62	17.66	17.75
Local Societies	19.92	19.45	19.26
All Societies	16.29	16.98	16.95

From Table 3:III it is clear that regional societies have a greater proportion of total assets tied up in liquid assets than national societies and local societies have in turn, an even more pronounced holding of liquid assets than regional societies. Part of the explanation for the differential relates to the maturity mismatch that societies face. In simple terms, the maturity mismatch refers to the fact that societies borrow short and lend long. Drake (1989) suggested that this mismatch has been exacerbated in recent years by factors such as the reduced average maturity of retail deposits and the increasing interest rate sensitivity of retail deposits. Societies, through their access to the wholesale money markets, can, to some extent, limit the magnitude of the problem. The scope and diversity of wholesale funds open to smaller societies is, however, much more limited. In consequence the BSC to combat the increased risks faced by smaller societies due to maturity mismatch, encourages higher percentage holdings of liquid assets.

Retail Savings

The important position occupied by societies in the savings market can be seen through examination of Table 3:IV. In this table, annual net increases for a select group of personal sector liquid assets are reported for the period 1986 to 1991. These liquid assets are savings with building societies, deposits with banks, and National Savings. All three are essentially alternatives for risk free personal saving.

Table 3:IV
Increase in Liquid Assets held by the Personal Sector, 1986-91

Year	Building Societies		Banks		National Savings		Total
	£m	%	£m	%	£m	%	£m
1986	11,847	50.3	8,442	35.8	2,523	10.7	23,574
1987	13,590	57.8	7,312	31.1	2,439	10.4	23,499
1988	20,237	50.8	17,049	42.8	1,408	3.5	39,805
1989	16,421	41.9	23,440	59.8	-1,519	-3.9	39,178
1990	17,959	49.5	17,198	47.4	783	2.2	36,248
1991	17,347	67.3	6,117	23.7	2,181	8.5	25,773

Source: Financial Statistics.

The overall increase in the holdings of liquid assets by the personal sector was much lower in 1991, falling back to around the level of 1987. This fall back was a result of increased competition from long-term contractual savings, (pension funds and life assurance) and further recovery in equity-based investment, (BSC Annual Report,1991-92). The pivotal position of societies in the savings market is underscored by the fact that they secured some 67 percent of the increase in liquid asset holdings. Banks in contrast have seen their share of the increase in liquid assets fall for the second consecutive year. In part, this is due to their adoption of a less aggressive approach in the generation of retail savings. As UBS Phillips and Drew (1992a) stated

> "The key reason for this pull back from the retail savings market is that banks have been forced to widen both lending and savings spreads in order to compensate for the effect of record domestic bad debt .... . Banks' balance sheets have hardly grown since 1990. This is the price they have had to pay to preserve their capital adequacy ratios."

Set against this fall in the retail share of the banks over the last two years is that in the five years prior, banks actually managed to recoup market share from societies. While part of this increase in market share by the banks was due to the switch in 1989 of the Abbey National from the building society sector to the bank sector, also of importance was the relative fall in the retail saving rates on offer from societies and the renewed focus by banks on retail savings. The retail banks were becoming increasingly aware that a healthy personal sector customer base offered added opportunities for the cross-selling of financial products. In consequence, banks copied the building societies and offered a range of new savings products including interest bearing current accounts and various forms of term and instant access accounts. Product innovation in the savings market is a theme returned to in chapter 7.

Building societies in 1991 also faced somewhat increased competitive pressure in the retail savings market from National Savings. The government has increasingly utilised National Savings to help them meet their expenditure commitments on welfare and unemployment which have risen as a consequence of the prolonged recession.

Non-Retail Funds

In recent years non-retail funds have become an increasingly important funding source for building societies. Access for societies to the wholesale markets dates back to 1980 when the Nationwide issued the first negotiable bond. At that juncture, societies were offered the opportunity to pay interest gross and in consequence became a much more attractive investment vehicle for institutions. Under the 1986 Act a 20 percent upper limit on wholesale funding was imposed on societies. This limit was subsequently raised in 1988 to 40 percent. At present the BSA are lobbying to obtain a further increase in the wholesale funding limit. They feel that with, for example, 7 of the national societies having at present in excess of 20 percent of their funding from the wholesale markets that

> "by the mid 1990s, a number of societies will feel constrained by the current limit and this will prevent them from offering the most competitive mortgage products to their members." (Coles, 1992).

The popularity of wholesale funding for societies centres around a number of factors. The first relates to cost. For large periods of time since 1983 the gross retail deposit rate has been in excess of, for example, the three month LIBOR. In addition, if the generation of additional funds requires an increase in the rate of interest on offer, this need only be paid on new wholesale funds, but is likely to apply to both new and old depositors in the retail market. A second advantage of the wholesale market is that the society can more closely tailor the structure of liabilities with that of its assets. In particular, wholesale funding can be utilised to lengthen the maturity of a society's liabilities. A final advantage alluded to earlier is that due to a reduction in maturity mismatch, liquid asset holdings can be reduced.

Time deposits and commercial paper are the most important source of wholesale funds for societies. In 1991 they accounted for 43 percent of societies' non-retail funding. The importance in part relates to restrictions placed on smaller societies in terms of their ability to issue certificates of deposits and become involved in the bond markets. Bond financing is a further important source of non-retail funding for societies, accounting in 1991 for some 32 percent of wholesale funds. With respect to the issue of bonds, it was observed in the Bank of England Quarterly Bulletin (1990) that

> "The Euro-sterling floating-rate market has been a particularly attractive one for the building societies, as they have been able to use it to obtain long-term funds more cheaply than in any other form. The ability to undertake swap transactions has meant that funds can be raised in the fixed-rate bond and the non-sterling Eurobond markets and swapped into floating-rate sterling liabilities .... ."

Certificates of deposit at 20 percent of total wholesale funds in 1991 and bank borrowing at 5 percent are the remaining sources of non-retail funds utilised by societies.

Information on wholesale funds as a proportion of total share, deposit and loan liabilities is presented in Table 3:V.[4] The material is again provided for all societies in addition to each of the society subgroups. The average ratios are reported on a weighted basis. In this case the weights are calculated as the relative proportion of a society's share, deposit and loan liabilities to the total value of the share deposit and loan liabilities of the group under consideration.

Table 3:V
Wholesale Funds as a Percentage of Share Deposit and Loan Liabilities, 1989-91

Building Society Groupings	1989	1990	1991
National Societies	17.39	19.47	20.16
Regional Societies	14.13	16.71	19.36
Local Societies	3.45	4.15	5.11
All Societies	16.69	18.82	19.83

Two points emerge from Table 3:V. The first is that over time, wholesale funding has become of increased importance to each of the society groups. This is particularly true in the case of national societies and indeed adds weight to the call by the BSA for the wholesale funding limit to be raised.

The second point to emerge from Table 3:V is that smaller societies utilise the wholesale market to a much lesser degree than the larger players. In part this is due to the fact that asset volume coupled with healthy credit ratings confer on national societies both cheaper funding sources and access to a wider range of markets. Indeed, access to many of the bond markets is dependent on first securing a credit rating and, given that ratings have to date been only awarded within the national society category, the non-involvement of regional and local societies in this market is to be expected, (out of the 10 national societies, all but 2 - the Britannia and the Bristol & West - have obtained credit ratings for long-term debt while all but the Bristol & West are rated for short-term debt).

Restrictions under the 1986 Act are of course an important reason for the more limited involvement of regional and local societies in the wholesale funding markets. For example societies with commercial assets less than £100m are not permitted to undertake interest and currency swaps. In addition, societies can only hold certificate of deposits if they have been issued by societies with assets in excess of £1000m. While technically this does not bar societies with assets of less than £1000m from issuing certificates of deposit, it effectively limits their involvement as there would be no secondary market within the industry for their issues.

Transfer of Engagements

With the transfer of engagements of the Mid-Sussex to the Cheltenham and Gloucester, which took effect from 1 August 1992, only 89 societies remain with current authorisation to accept investments from the public.[5] There are a further 16 building societies which, while registered, are no longer authorised to accept investments from the public. These latter societies are not included in the analysis. The number of societies operating in the UK has been subject to almost unabated decline since the peak figure of 3,642 societies in 1895. As explained in chapter 2, the decline in the pre-1950 period was primarily a consequence of the dissolution of terminating societies. Thereafter, the fall in numbers can be more accurately ascribed to mergers between societies. Mergers can take one of two forms. Societies can either merge through the amalgamation of two or more societies or through transfer of engagements from one society to another.

Amalgamations have tended to be much less common than transfer of engagements. For the most part, amalgamations have occurred between societies in the local and regional groups. The primary reason given for such amalgamations is that the society is then better placed to exploit its regional/local identity. A secondary reason is that the new society can produce services more cost effectively through availing of scale economies.

Towards the middle to late 1980s, a series of amalgamations also occurred between national societies. Notable examples are the mergers between the Alliance and the Leicester and the Nationwide and the Anglia. The rationale underlying these mergers was to create sufficient critical mass to both allow the society to offer an enhanced range of financial services and to enable it to compete on a more equal footing with the retail banks.

Transfer of engagements in the main have been from the local and smaller regional societies to the national players. Gough (1982) argued that the directors, employees and members of the local society all benefit from the transfer of engagements. For directors, there is the opportunity to serve in a larger organisation with enhanced conditions. Whether this argument is now valid is somewhat questionable in that with more recent transfer of engagements directors have usually lost their position totally. Employees can avail of better work conditions in terms of training, salary, pension rights and promotion possibilities. The benefit to members is usually in the form of a cash bonus paid immediately following the effective date of the transfer. In recent years the cash payment has been equivalent to around 2 percent of their investments. For the national society, the advantage of the transfer centres upon the capture of asset size and perhaps a network of branches in a geographical location where the society considers itself to be under-represented. The Bradford and Bingley and the Cheltenham and Gloucester are the two national societies which have been most actively involved with the transfer of engagement process in recent years. From the beginning of 1991 up to the transfer of the Mid-Sussex to the Cheltenham and Gloucester there have been a total of 16 transfers of engagements. The Bradford and Bingley has been involved in 3 and the Cheltenham and Gloucester in a further 6. Increased geographical coverage particularly in the south of England is the rationale underlying the involvement of the Bradford and Bingley. In contrast, the objective of the Cheltenham and Gloucester is aimed more at generally building up its branch network. While accepting the strong postal emphasis of the Cheltenham and Gloucester, a network of 210 branches is still extremely small for a society which, in asset terms, is the sixth largest in the UK.

One noteworthy feature of a transfer of engagements or amalgamation is that only the board of a society can put an offer to its members for approval. This is done in the form of a transfer statement. The statement describes the terms of the offer and explains the consequences of the transfer for members. The board of the society can, nevertheless, reject the transfer offer simply by not putting it to their members. A case in point occurred with the takeover of the Frome Selwood. The Frome Selwood received an offer from the Stroud and Swindon in which members were offered a cash payment equivalent to 2 percent of their investments. Subsequently the Cheltenham and Gloucester made a competing offer worth 3 percent. The board of the Frome Selwood refused to put the improved offer to a vote on the grounds that a transfer of engagements to the Cheltenham and Gloucester would result in redundancies and the elimination of the society's local identity. The transfer of engagements to the Stroud and Swindon was eventually approved and became effective from July 1, 1990.

In recent times transfer of engagements have not solely been passive affairs just between the two negotiating societies. The violation or near violation by a limited number of societies of minimum capital requirements has resulted in the BSC stepping in and, depending upon the seriousness of the problem, either ordering or actively encouraging the offending society to seek a rescue through a transfer of engagements to another society.

Capital requirement problems have occurred due to the housing slump in the UK which has pushed arrears on mortgages and repossession of property to record levels. In certain cases, societies have also exacerbated their already weak position through ill-advised high risk secured lending strategies. Mid to upper range regional societies based in the south of England are the ones which have experienced the most acute difficulties. Given the asset size of these offending societies the onus of rescue has fallen upon the larger national societies as only they have sufficient scale to absorb poorly performing societies without adversely impacting upon their own financial position. A recent example is the transfer of the Town and Country - then, in terms of asset volume, the 19th largest society in the UK - to the Woolwich. The transfer took place on May 2, 1992. For the reporting year end 1991, the Town and Country had actually recorded a loss of £43m on ordinary activities before tax.

With regard to the rescuing society, it should be recognised that there is no question of a poison chalice. Indeed, among national societies there has even been some competition as to which society performs the rescue function.

> "The attraction of merging for the rescuing society, is that it will take full control of the ailing society at an extremely low cost (less than 15% of the acquired society's net assets in most cases)." (UBS Phillips and Drew, 1992a).

Company Status

An additional, although minor, reason for shrinkage in the number of societies is that of conversion to company status. Under the 1986 Act a building society has the option to become a plc. Only one society has to date availed of this option. The Abbey National obtained a full quotation on the stock exchange in July 1989. In the intervening period, while a number of other societies have been considered strong contenders for company status, none as yet have followed suit. Flotation plans by the National and Provincial were said to have reached a very advanced stage when they were dropped in October 1990. It is still unclear what halted the flotation plans of the National and Provincial. At the time, the reason most commonly given for the U-turn was the depressed nature of the housing market coupled with recognition by the board that the National and Provincial simply was not ready for flotation.

Rumours abound that other top national societies are actively considering flotation as an option. Names which are frequently mentioned are the Alliance and Leicester and the Cheltenham and Gloucester. The housing slump plus commercial loan book problems has, however, led to the flotation plans of these societies and others with such intentions being placed on hold at least in the short to medium term.

For the future, an additional means through which industry concentration may occur is through the takeover of a society by an existing company, perhaps a bank or an insurance company.

> "It could be more attractive to some medium-sized societies to retain their identity either inside a larger financial services group as its mortgage lending arm, than surrender it totally in a merger with another society." (Frazer, 1990).

No such financial conglomerate has, as yet, been formed through the takeover of a building society, although there are frequent press rumours of foreign banks and insurance companies both approaching and being approached by building societies. At the start of 1990 such was the level of interest in acquiring building societies that the BSC felt it necessary to issue guidance about the law and procedures involved. Much of this guidance simply involved the highlight of the requisite part in the 1986 Act. The guidance, in summary, made the following points:

1. The BSC must first be of the opinion that the takeover is lawful. The Bank of England must be prepared to give authorisation under the 1987 Banking Act in the case of bank acquirors and the Department of Trade for insurance companies.
2. Given that a building society can only be acquired by a non-building society after it has dropped its mutual status and transformed itself into a bank, the Bank of England must also agree to licence the transformed society as a bank.
3. Members of a society which is taken over can be compensated in two ways, by receiving shares in the successor company, or by a distribution of cash, but only to members of two years standing.
4. Only the board of a society can put an offer to its members.
5. A takeover must be approved by two transfer resolutions, one by investing members and one by borrowing members.

Interestingly and at odds with speculation, where industry restructuring through takeover has to date occurred, building societies have been the acquiring agents. Examples which stand out are the acquisition of Girobank by the Alliance and Leicester, and FS Assurance and Crusader Insurance by the Britannia.

One result of the fall in society number has been an increase in asset concentration. At the end of 1991, the ten national societies' share of the sector's total assets was slightly in excess of 83 percent. Comparable figures for 1982, 1986 and 1989 were respectively 73.1, 76.6 and 79.1 percent.

Employment Trends

Perhaps surprisingly, given the fall in society numbers, there has been a general upward trend in employee numbers over the past ten years. The one break in this trend was in 1989 when figures for the Abbey National were removed from the aggregate statistics. This steady rise in employment within the industry has been due in large part to the product diversification programmes undertaken by societies. Diversification has necessitated the employment of new staff in both back-office and front-office functions. As in the case of asset share, national building societies have a disproportionate share of total employees. At the end of 1991 national societies accounted for 81 percent of full-time employees and 77 percent of part-time employees.[6]

Branch Networks

Branch outlets have also not tended to fall to the degree which might have been expected. Indeed, from 1980 through to 1988, there was a steady rise in branch numbers. Only since 1988 has the number of branches started to fall with the most marked decline between 1990 and 1991. In 1991 there were some 5,756 building society branches in the UK. This represented a fall in branch numbers of some 1,200 placing the number of society outlets barely above their 1980 position. Although this must be set against the fact that conversion by the Abbey National in 1989 removed approximately 600 branches from the aggregate statistics. Again the recession plus the high levels of bad debt provision were the main factors behind branch rationalisation. It should also be added that both building societies and banks are viewed to have an over-supply of branches per head of population, therefore, rationalisation would have probably occurred irrespective of the recession. National societies again have a disproportionate share of branch numbers although their share is not as pronounced as in the case of asset volume and employee numbers. At the end of 1991 national societies accounted for 71 percent of total branch numbers.[7]

Regional Structure

Presented in Table 3:VI for the years 1989 and 1991 is a regional breakdown of both building society numbers and the assets under the control of these societies. The various societies are allocated to the respective regions on the basis of the location of their head office.

Table 3:VI
Regional Breakdown of Building Societies, 1989 and 1991

Region	1989		1991	
	Number of Societies	Total Assets, £m	Number of Societies	Total Assets, £m
London	13	59,839.8	8	75,619.6
South East (excluding GL)	21	4,292.9	11	1,359.6
South West	9	15,732.5	7	27,452.9
East Anglia	3	1,352.7	3	1,694.6
West Midlands	12	15,040.8	11	18,224.3
East Midlands	13	2,205.2	13	2,910.2
Yorkshire and Humberside	11	83,069.0	11	104,380.4
North West	7	1,277.2	6	1,552.6
North	12	5,392.0	11	8,014.3
Scotland	3	558.8	3	745.2
Wales	3	878.4	3	1,180.2
N Ireland	2	169.5	2	261.3
TOTAL	109	189,808.8	89	243,395.2

It is of course recognised that while all societies have a region of origin and in consequence are more closely identified with that region than others, the breakdown does not control for the fact that the top 10 societies now have a national as opposed to a regional identity.

If initially the analysis concentrates upon the information provided in Table 3:VI for 1991 it is clear that, in terms of assets attributed to the respective regions, two regions are dominant - Greater London and Yorkshire & Humberside. Although other regions, notably East and West Midlands and the North, are home to either similar or greater numbers of societies, Greater London and Yorkshire & Humberside are almost exclusively the region of origin of the national societies.

In terms of their geographical distribution, building societies are almost unique among financial institutions. Unlike building societies, most other financial groupings are headquartered in London and operate in the rest of the UK on the basis of a branch network system which reports to the London head-office. The attraction of London relates to the fact that it is the location of the national money markets. In addition, there are mutual benefits arising from the concentration of financial firms in one location. These benefits relate directly to improved market liquidity, efficiency and information flows plus an enhanced opportunity for intermediaries to feed off each other in the conduct of their business. Concentration also encourages the establishment of extensive back-up services such as legal, computing and consultancy services of various forms, (see McKillop and Hutchinson, 1990).

Such an analysis does not, however, explain the strength of building societies in the Midlands and particularly in Yorkshire and Humberside. Essentially, the location of building societies in these areas is historical in nature. Building societies emanated from the plethora of co-operative and friendly societies, established in the eighteenth and nineteenth centuries to support the influx of migrants to the new industrial urban areas. Boddy (1980) indicated that in the first 30 years of the nineteenth century cities like Birmingham, Leeds and Manchester more than doubled in size.

For the future, the expectation might well be that as societies increasingly shift from being focused and limited financial product institutions, there will be a stronger incentive to locate within or in close proximity to the central capital markets of London. Although set against this argument is the fact that new technology now makes geographical location less relevant.

What also emerges from Table 3:VI are the regions over the period 1989 to 1991 which experienced a significant decline in building society numbers. It is clear that regions in southern England have experienced much more dramatic falls in society numbers than elsewhere. While most of the decline has been in the smaller asset volume local societies, a number of middle to upper range regional societies have also disappeared. The Town and Country and the Guardian in London, and the Regency and the Portsmouth in the South East are all examples of the latter.

The regional nature of the decline in society numbers has to a large extent been dictated by the impact of the recession on the housing market which has resulted in a more pronounced level of mortgage arrears and repossessions in the south of England. Coles (1992) documented a range of arguments for the fact that the housing slump is more acute in southern England compared to elsewhere. The more pertinent of the arguments put forward are that house prices were bid to higher levels, both in absolute terms and in relation to income; unemployment has grown much more rapidly; and house prices have fallen much further since 1988 leaving many borrowers with negative equity.

Whether the full effect of the recession on society numbers has now been played to its final conclusion is a matter of conjecture. Although the profit performance of the vast majority of local and regional societies is at present healthy, (see chapter 4), the expectation must be that a prolonged housing slump is likely to force more societies to enter into transfer of engagements not only in the south of England, but also increasingly in other regions of the UK.

Summary

The structure of building societies and their position in the market place has come under scrutiny in this chapter. The analysis revealed that as a financial grouping, societies occupy a dominant position in a number of domestic financial markets. In the retail savings and mortgage markets, after significant falls in market share in the mid-1980s, building societies have fought back strongly and now have approximately a 70 percent share of each market.

Within the building society industry itself, it was also amply clear that a process of change is currently on-going. Particularly apparent was the rising pace in the decline of society numbers. In most instances the decline was a consequence of transfer of engagements from either local or regional societies to national societies. One worrying feature of the transfers was the high proportion "encouraged" by the BSC as a consequence of societies finding themselves in financial difficulties, with this a particular problem for societies based in the south of England. Furthermore, the expectation was that a continuation of the housing slump was likely to result in additional transfer of engagements with the process no longer confined merely to the south of England.

The analysis also revealed the extensive branch rationalisation programmes currently being carried out by societies. This was as expected, given the economic downturn and the fall in society numbers. Somewhat surprising, however, was that the numbers employed by societies has continued to rise. Although some societies have shed labour and others have adopted an "informal hiring freeze", there has been a significant increase overall in both full-time and part-time employees within the building society industry. One possible explanation put forward was that the diversification programmes undertaken by societies have necessitated the hiring of labour with new skills.

The commercial asset structure of societies was also examined in this chapter. While it was obvious that societies have pursued substantial diversification, it was also evident that societies were still very much within their nature limits for class 2 and class 3 lending and that first mortgages to owner occupiers were still the dominant component on the asset side of the balance sheet.

Diversification in contrast was much more pronounced on the liability side of the balance sheet with societies increasingly turning to the wholesale markets as a source of finance. Differences did emerge between societies with the use of wholesale markets most pronounced for societies with high volume asset bases and good credit ratings. Indeed, it was argued that for some societies an upward revision in the 40 percent wholesale funding limit was starting, even at this stage, to take on an increased importance.

A final feature of this chapter was the creation of a framework within which the building society industry could be analysed. The framework was designed on the assumption that building societies were not a homogeneous group of financial institutions and could be subdivided into a number of mutually exclusive groupings. The society categorisations chosen were those of national societies, regional societies and local societies.

Notes

[1]Information on class 1, class 2 and class 3 assets, each as a proportion of total commercial assets, is detailed for individual societies in the Data Appendix.

[2]Other liquid assets held by building societies include cash, sterling treasury bills and local authority debt.

[3]Information on liquid asset holdings as a percentage of total assets is documented for each society in the Data Appendix.

[4]Information on wholesale funds as a proportion of total share, deposit and loan liabilities is presented for each society in the Data Appendix.

[5]On 31st December 1992, with the transfer of engagements of the Haywards Heath to the Yorkshire, the number of societies with current authorisation to take money from the public reduces further to 88.

[6]Information on the total number of employees of each building society is presented in the Data Appendix. Part-time employees are included and are allocated a weight of 0.5 in the computation of the total number employed by each building society.

[7]Information on the number of branch outlets of each society is detailed in the Data Appendix.

4. Performance

Introduction

In the previous chapter an effort was made to identify the position occupied by building societies in what they would consider to be their key markets. In this current chapter attention shifts to an analysis of building society performance. The importance of such an analysis, particularly when it is conducted relative to the performance of competitors, is that it enables an objective assessment to be made of the likely future position of building societies in their respective markets.

A number of aspects are involved in the judgement of building society performance. The most obvious is that of capital strength. The necessity for capital strength rests with the fact that not only is capital required to support current and future developments but perhaps more importantly a strong capital base is needed to protect investors and to generally ensure the financial stability of the building society industry. In this chapter the capital requirements laid down by the BSC and the European Community are both examined. In addition capital ratios are computed for building societies and a selection of retail banks in an attempt to judge the relative capital strength of both banks and building societies.

Income generation is another aspect of organisational performance which must be considered in any relative assessment. For financial institutions income generation has two components, net interest income and fee-based income. Net interest income is scrutinised on the basis of differences in interest rate margins between building societies and banks while the fee-based analysis simply considers the relative importance of commission to banks and building societies.

The cost side of the equation is also examined with the cost to income ratio utilised as the statistic for comparative purposes. An additional factor which has impinged on the cost and performance of both societies and banks is that of bad debt. A separate part of the analysis is devoted to an examination of relative bad debt problems. The analysis, however, suffers from the fact that institutions do not employ a standardised procedure to account for bad debt.

To complete the discussion the cost and income analysis is tied together with institutions scrutinised on the basis of their profit levels. To ensure a complete and rounded picture two measures of profit performance are computed. They are pre-tax profits as a percentage of mean reserves, (pre-tax profits as a proportion of average shareholders' funds in the case of banks), and pre-tax profits as a percentage of mean total assets.

Capital Strength

Societies require a strong capital base to support new developments; to expand existing services; to ensure the protection of investors; and to generally promote the financial stability of the building society sector. Capital requirements are prescribed for building societies by the BSC. These requirements are imposed on a society by society basis and are dependent upon the risk composition of the society's assets coupled with the BSC's perception of the society's management ability.

In assessing the desired level of capital to support a society's business the BSC applies a ratio to each type of asset held and aggregates the resulting amounts. Mortgage assets are divided into four groups based on the nature of the borrower, level of security and length of time that the loan has been outstanding. The amount of capital required against a particular type of asset held therefore derives both from the amount of such assets outstanding and the relevant capital ratios, (the BSC Annual Report, 1988-1989 sets out in Table H the relevant figures for each type of asset).

For societies as a whole the capital requirement, as desired by the BSC, has steadily risen each year with the exception of a small fall between 1990 and 1991. Desired capital as a proportion of share, deposit and loan liabilities stood at 4.13 percent in 1989, rose to 4.72 percent in 1990 before it fell to 4.63 percent in 1991. Product innovations coupled with the increase in arrears have been the main reasons for the increase in capital required. The sharp rise in the requirement between 1989 and 1990 is, for example, explained by the implementation of the Commission's Prudential Note 1990/1. This note raised the capital ratios applicable to certain higher risk categories of mortgage lending (low start mortgages and mortgages on shared ownership properties) and introduced a contribution to the capital requirements based on the level of arrears.

The capital position of building societies under the BSC criteria is relatively healthy. For 1991 the BSC in its Annual Report, 1991-1992 estimated that the average society exhibited a gross capital ratio of 6.16 percent. This represented a margin of 1.53 percent in excess of the desired capital ratio of 4.63 percent for 1991. Comparable estimates for 1989 and 1990 of the margin of gross capital in excess of desired capital were respectively 1.65 percent and 1.22 percent.

Computation of a desired capital ratio on a society by society basis is somewhat unwieldy in that it involves the application of a ratio, determined by the Commission, to each type of asset held by the society. The availability of capital to a society can, however, be adequately assessed through the consideration of gross capital and free capital measures. Gross capital comprises reserves plus qualifying subordinated liabilities plus subscribed capital, (PIBS), plus minority interests. Free capital is simply gross capital less investment in fixed assets. Gross capital and free capital measured as a percentage of share, deposit and loan liabilities are documented for the respective society groupings for the years 1989 through to 1991 in Table 4:I.[1] Note that the average ratios reported for each of the groupings are calculated on a weighted basis. The weights are determined in this instance by the relative proportion of a society's share, deposit and loan liabilities to the total value of share, deposit and loan liabilities of the particular grouping under consideration.

Table 4:I
Capital Ratios

Building Society Groupings	Gross Capital as a % of SDL			Free Capital as a % of SDL		
	1989	1990	1991	1989	1990	1991
National Societies	5.48	5.56	5.83	4.12	4.19	4.5
Regional Societies	6.47	6.48	6.45	4.94	4.87	4.93
Local Societies	7.01	7.09	7.08	5.81	5.84	5.71
All Societies	5.64	5.75	5.95	4.26	4.32	4.5

The availability of capital, expressed in terms of both gross and free capital ratios, shows an inverse correlation between capital strength and society size. This inverse relationship can be explained on two counts. First the smaller the society the higher the capital ratio since the smaller society is likely to have proportionately more capital for the type of business it is undertaking. Secondly the disparity is in part historical in that previous regulatory treatment permitted larger societies to maintain proportionately lower reserve ratios. Over time it is also evident that the difference between the capital ratios for national societies and those for local societies has tended to narrow. While the capital ratios for all groups of societies have generally increased the pace of growth has been more marked for the larger national societies.

In Table 4:II the opportunity is taken to document the proportion of gross capital which is made up of issued capital, (that is issued capital as a percentage of share, deposit and loan liabilities). The average ratios are reported on a weighted basis. In this case the weights are again calculated as the relative proportion of a society's share, deposit and loan liabilities to the total value of share, deposit and loan liabilities of the group under consideration. Issued capital includes qualifying subordinated debt and subscribed capital, (PIBS).

Table 4:II
Issued Capital

Building Society Groupings	Proportion of Gross Capital which Encompasses Issued Capital		
	1989	1990	1991
National Societies	0.85	0.91	1.12
Regional Societies	0.57	0.70	0.79
Local Societies	0.0	0.03	0.03
All Societies	0.8	0.87	1.05

The opportunity for societies to issue supplementary capital instruments existed for the first time in 1988. The total issue of supplementary capital in 1988 by societies was £1,105m. This comprised only term subordinated debt of approved types, and for any individual society the amount of such debt that may qualify as capital is limited. Furthermore such capital is treated as supplementary as opposed to core capital, (see chapter 2 for additional details).

In 1989 the total issue of supplementary capital at £383m was much lower than the 1988 level, in 1990 the level of issue reduced further to £200m, while in 1991 there was somewhat of an upsurge with societies raising £800m of issued capital. The growth in capital resources during 1991 was primarily to enable societies to absorb the impact of higher arrears on their capital requirement. Furthermore as argued in the BSC Annual Report, 1991-92

> "This strengthening of societies' capital base leaves them well placed for a prudent expansion of their mortgage lending when demand recovers."

In 1991, for the first time, issued capital also included subscribed capital, (PIBS). The breakdown of the £800m of issued capital raised in 1991 was £300m PIBS and £500m subordinated debt. PIBS are unique to building societies although they do have many of the characteristics of non-cumulative preference shares which are currently being utilised by the retail banks in the generation of core capital. As indicated in chapter 2, PIBS are subscribed risk bearing capital which can be aggregated with reserves. Unlike subordinated debt PIBS, in consequence, rank as core capital. On the winding up of the issuing society's business PIBS must, however, rank after all types of ordinary investments and other liabilities including subordinated debt.

From Table 4:II it is clear that for each of the society classes there has been a steady increase over time in issued capital as a proportion of gross capital. The relatively sharp increase in issued capital for national societies between 1990 and 1991 can be explained by the fact that it is primarily national societies which have been involved in the issue of PIBS. It is also apparent that there is a significant difference between the requirement for issued capital by national and regional societies on the one hand and local societies on the other. The fact that smaller societies have tended not to tap the subordinated debt and subscribed capital markets and rely almost entirely on reserves for capital resources necessarily implies that £ for £ their capital is of higher quality than that of the national and regional societies.

To date no mention has been made of the European Community's capital adequacy framework. Of particular relevance to building societies within this framework are the "Own Funds of Credit Institutions" and "A Solvency Ratio for Credit Institutions" Directives. Together they require building societies, (as they do banks), to maintain sufficient capital resources in relation to their business to ensure a minimum solvency ratio of 8 percent.

More specifically the Own Funds Directive defines the categories of capital permissible for credit institutions. It follows in substance, but not terminology, the definitions adopted by the Basle Committee on Banking Regulation and Supervision:

> Tier 1, primary capital, includes reserves (excluding revaluation reserves) plus subscribed capital and minority interests.
>
> Tier 2, secondary capital, includes interim profits internally audited plus subordinated debt, (up to 50 percent of Tier 1 capital minus intangible assets) plus general provisions for bad debt and revaluation reserves both of which are shortly to be designated.

Gross own funds are then calculated as the sum of Tier 1 plus Tier 2 capital minus intangible fixed assets. The solvency ratio is in turn computed as the own funds of the society divided by the sum of risk weighted assets and off balance sheet items, expressed as a percentage. The risk weights attributed range from 0 to 1. Residential mortgages, (class 1 assets), are allocated a weight of 0.5. Most class 2 assets, class 3 assets and fixed assets are assigned a risk weight of 1. The risk weights for liquid assets range between 0 and 0.2 with the higher weights kept for assets with longer maturities.

This new capital adequacy regime takes effect from January, 1993. During 1993 the solvency ratio framework will actually run in tandem with the current BSC capital adequacy calculus. The BSC, however, propose to move to the solvency ratio calculation, as the single measure of capital cover, in the first few months of 1994. In the 1991-92 Annual Report the BSC stated that their capital adequacy calculus is addressed essentially to mortgage asset risk and the present more diverse product portfolios of societies now stretch beyond a precise implementation of the 1987 capital adequacy framework. Not only will the BSC monitor compliance with the minimum 8 percent solvency ratio but it will in addition establish on a society by society basis a higher threshold ratio which they consider to more accurately reflect the risk interest in the business of the particular society under question.

> "Among the factors which will go into establishing the threshold ratio as opposed to the minimum, will be boards, management systems, asset quality ...., treasury management ...., planning .... and operating performance (including consistency in financial results and vulnerability to external shocks, for example, through geographic concentration." (BSC Annual Report, 1991-92).

At the end of 1991 the BSC obtained detailed solvency ratio returns for all societies. All societies are reputed to have comfortably met the 8 percent minimum solvency ratio, 90 percent of societies had a solvency ratio in the range 10 percent to 22 percent with the weighted average for all societies 11.8 percent.

Solvency ratios are not as yet published by societies in their annual reports. Following the methodology of UBS Phillips and Drew (1992a) an attempt has been made to calculate not solvency ratios *per se* but rather a measure of capital strength which utilises the risk adjusted procedure employed in the computation of the solvency measure, (the UBS Phillips and Drew analysis covers only the top 20 societies). This alternative measure of capital strength is defined as Tier 1 capital as a proportion of risk weighted assets. In line with UBS Phillips and Drew, op.cit., Tier 1 capital is taken as reserves (excluding revaluation reserves), subscribed capital plus minority interests. The risk weights employed in the generation of the denominator are 0.2 for liquid assets, 0.5 for residential mortgages; and 1 for all other assets. Average Tier 1 risk asset ratios are reported on a weighted basis for the various society subgroupings for the years 1989 to 1991 in Table 4:III.[2]

Table 4:III
Tier 1 Capital Ratios

Building Society Groupings	Tier 1 Capital/Risk Weighted Assets, %		
	1989	1990	1991
National Societies	8.66	8.81	9.39
Regional Societies	10.86	10.49	10.36
Local Societies	13.53	13.35	13.29
All Societies	9.07	9.15	9.6

As with the capital ratios reported earlier in Table 4:I there again exists an inverse relationship between capital strength and society size. In addition there is also evidence of a narrowing over time in the differential between the larger players (national societies) and their smaller counterparts (local societies). While the ratios for national societies have been gradually trending upwards the ratios for both regional and local societies have shown a downward drift.

Although not designed to provide information on whether societies are able to meet their capital adequacy requirements under the new solvency ratio regime, it does appear from Table 4:III that societies generally are able to meet their commitments from Tier 1 capital alone. Indeed if the 1991 Tier 1 capital ratios reported in the Data Appendix are scrutinised it transpires that only 6 societies fail to meet their capital adequacy requirements out of core capital alone. It must be emphasised that this judgement is made in terms of the 8 percent minimum capital ratio requirement and not relative to the higher threshold ratios which the BSC is in the process of establishing on a society by society basis.

At this juncture if the opportunity is taken to introduce comparable Tier 1 capital ratios for a selection of retail banks, Table 4:IV, the capital strength of building societies relative to other financial institutions becomes much more apparent. The information provided on retail banks in this and other tables in this chapter is calculated from the individual banks' annual reports and statements of accounts.

Table 4:IV
Tier 1 Capital Ratios (Retail Banks)

Retail Banks	Tier 1 Capital Ratios		
	1989	1990	1991
Abbey National	13.8	12.6	11.4
Barclays	5.7	5.8	5.9
Lloyds	4.4	5.2	6.2
Midland	5.4	5.4	5.5
National Westminster	5.3	5.2	5.1
Bank of Scotland	6.8	5.8	5.6
Royal Bank of Scotland	7.2	7.0	6.6

It is evident that, with the exception of the Abbey National, the Tier 1 capital ratios for individual banks are generally much lower than the comparable ratios for building societies. The Abbey National's higher ratios relative to other banks relates to the funds raised at flotation and the fact that its asset portfolio is still very much in the mould of a traditional building society in that first mortgages to owner-occupiers dominate, (66 percent of total assets, end 1991). Mortgages as a secured loan are assigned a weight of 0.5 in the computation of risk adjusted capital ratios and in consequence require less capital backing relative to advances. Nevertheless what transpires from this comparison of the capital position between banks and building societies is that societies have the greater opportunity to pursue a policy of balance sheet growth without adversely impacting upon core capital strength.

Income

A crucial aspect of performance is that of the income generation capabilities of building societies. Income generation has itself two components. The first is that of interest income. In this instance the performance measure by which institutions are usually compared with each other is that of net interest income as a proportion of total assets, (net interest margin). The second component of society income and one which has taken on enhanced importance post 1986 is that of non-interest income. Fee income, particularly from tied arrangements with insurance companies has greatly boosted the earning power of building societies.

Net Interest Income

Reported in Table 4:VA are net interest margins for the various building society subgroups. The average values are reported on a weighted basis with the denominator, total assets, employed to compute the weights. While in Table 4:VB interest margins are documented for a selection of retail clearing banks.

Table 4:VA
Net Interest Margin (Building Societies)

Building Society Groupings	Net Interest Margin, % 1989	1990	1991
National Societies	2.01	1.94	2.03
Regional Societies	2.19	2.05	2.04
Local Societies	2.51	2.37	2.31
All Societies	2.04	1.96	2.03

Table 4:VB
Net Interest Margin (Retail Banks)

Retail Banks	Net Interest Margin, % 1989	1990	1991
Abbey National	2.06	2.05	1.99
Barclays	2.68	2.59	2.65
Lloyds	3.83	4.13	4.59
Midland	2.96	2.76	2.96
National Westminster	3.01	2.98	3.01
Bank of Scotland	3.05	2.88	2.62
Royal Bank of Scotland	2.49	2.77	2.65

Although not immediately apparent from the time period under scrutiny in Table 4:VA, building societies' net interest margins have been gradually creeping upwards over recent years. This upward trend is in part explained by the fact that post 1986 an increasing proportion of building society advances are being made on an unsecured basis. Given that these advances are in consequence subject to higher risk levels they must in turn be accompanied by higher risk premiums. On this count it then becomes somewhat of a paradox that the net interest margins of local societies, which have either limited or no unsecured lending on their books, are higher than that of both national and regional societies. Part of the reason for the differential relates to the fact that local societies, as will be seen later in this chapter, have higher cost to income ratios than national societies. In consequence they must compensate for this cost disadvantage through operating a relatively higher interest spread. Furthermore as local societies are only targeting a localised, in many ways, *niche* market for their financial products, and are not after blanket market coverage they can afford, at the margin, to be less competitive in the pricing of their products.

Although the net interest margins of local societies have been drifting downwards and are converging towards those of national and regional societies it should also be noted that the differential between national and local societies would have been more pronounced in 1990 and 1991 had it not been for the take-over of Girobank by the Alliance and Leicester. Historically banks have much higher net interest margins than building societies. This is very much apparent from Table 4:VB. Differences in the net interest margins between banks and building societies is not indicative of market exploitation by the banks but rather it reflects two factors. The first is that a higher percentage of bank lending is on an unsecured basis and thus must be compensated for by higher risk premiums. The second is that banks offer a much more diverse range of financial products which push up their cost to income ratios. These higher cost ratios are covered through wider interest rate spreads.

From Table 4:VB it does nevertheless emerge that the net interest margins of banks are gradually moving in a downward direction. Indeed in most years since 1985 banks' net interest margins have shown a fall. Factors which account for the decline include the new more competitive environment now faced by retail banks; the replacement of non interest current accounts with interest bearing accounts; and the bad debt problems of recent years which have resulted in loan, and in consequence interest income, write-offs.

Non-Interest Income

Non-interest income has taken on enhanced importance for building societies post 1986.[3] Prior to the 1986 Act, societies were constrained in the product areas in which they could generate fee income. Insurance products, investment products, money transmission, estate agency and share dealing are all product areas in which societies now have the opportunity to accumulate fee based revenue. The steady improvement for societies over time in the contribution of fee based income to total income can be seen from Table 4:VIA. Equally apparent is the fact that relative to national societies, regional and even more so local societies generate a smaller proportion of their revenue on a fee income basis. This relates to their more limited product diversification strategies. The fee earning capacity of local societies, for example, is constrained primarily to what they are able to generate from investment and insurance products. Again it must be emphasised that the 1990 and 1991 aggregate contributions documented for national societies received an upward boost with the acquisition of Girobank by the Alliance and Leicester. Fee income as a proportion of total income for the Alliance and Leicester rose from 19.54 percent in 1989 to 35.73 percent in 1990 to 41.71 percent in 1991.

Table 4:VIA
Fee Income (Building Societies)

Building Society Groupings	Fee Income/Total Income, % 1989	1990	1991
National Societies	20.1	24.6	26.2
Regional Societies	17.7	18.7	21.4
Local Societies	10.3	11.0	11.6
All Societies	19.6	23.4	25.6

Table 4:VIB
Fee Income (Retail Banks)

Retail Banks	Fee Income/Total Income, % 1989	1990	1991
Abbey National	18.51	16.51	18.82
Barclays	38.35	39.06	42.71
Lloyds	39.64	40.4	40.88
Midland	41.86	47.64	47.27
National Westminster	34.62	35.97	40.87
Bank of Scotland	28.99	32.17	39.95
Royal Bank of Scotland	37.4	33.7	35.3

Retail banks commonly generate much more of their income on a fee earning basis, (Table 4:VIB). As with building societies the contribution of fee income to total income for banks has also risen in recent years. Unlike building societies the main area of fee growth for banks has been from their corporate sector business. UBS Phillips and Drew (1992a) estimate that

> "Typically less than a third of the banks' fee income derives from the personal sector, this being mainly from personal current account charges and insurance commission."

Phillips and Drew add that banks are now adopting a much more proactive approach to the generation of fee income from their personal sector customer base. In particular they are upwardly revising the fees levied on overdrafts and have recently started to impose administrative fees on credit cards.

Cost

Turning to the question of production costs an effort is now made to gauge the cost efficiency of building societies. The analysis is conducted through a comparison of the relative cost efficiencies of national, regional and local societies and in addition through a comparison of building societies *vis a vis* selected retail banks. The measure employed to assess relative cost efficiency was that of cost as a percentage of total income. This statistic was viewed as more appropriate than the more traditional measure of cost as a percentage of mean assets in that the latter fails to accommodate the off-balance sheet activity of societies.

> "Traditionally building societies have measured their profitability and efficiency primarily in terms of surplus or management expenses expressed as a percentage of mean assets. As societies have begun to offer a wider range of services .... which do not necessarily involve the creation of earning assets, it seems appropriate to widen the performance indicators considered .... . An important measure of efficiency which is widely used in the financial services industry is the cost/income ratio," (BSC Annual Report, 1990-91).

Cost was measured as management expenses which encompasses staff costs (wages and salaries, social security costs, other pension costs and other staff costs) plus depreciation plus rents payable under property leases plus auditors' remuneration plus other miscellaneous items. Income was calculated as net interest income plus other income. Cost/income ratios are reported in Table 4:VIIA for the various society classifications under examination as well as in Table 4:VIIB for a selection of banks.[4] Average ratios for societies are again reported on a weighted basis with the denominator employed to assign the weights.

Table 4:VIIA
Cost/Income Ratios (Building Societies)

Building Society Groupings	Cost/Income, % 1989	1990	1991
National Societies	51.5	50.8	51.0
Regional Societies	47.0	50.1	49.6
Local Societies	48.0	52.2	55.5
All Societies	50.7	50.7	50.9

Table 4:VIIB
Cost/Income Ratios (Retail Banks)

Retail Banks	Cost/Income, %		
	1989	1990	1991
Abbey National	45.2	44.4	45.1
Barclays	64.0	65.7	67.8
Lloyds	63.8	64.3	61.8
Midland	72.4	76.3	71.5
National Westminster	66.6	70.0	67.5
Bank of Scotland	56.2	52.8	54.6
Royal Bank of Scotland	60.7	60.7	64.1

In the face of the economic downturn and the increasingly competitive nature of the UK financial services industry both banks and building societies have been forced to keep a tight check on cost levels. A comparison of Tables 4:VIIA and 4:VIIB suggests that building societies have been much more successful in the attainment of this objective than the banks.

Within the building society sector it is difficult to arrive at a consistent picture in that the trends across the respective classifications over the period 1989 to 1991 have tended to be somewhat divergent. Nevertheless it can be said that generally cost/income ratios have gradually increased over time. Diversification programmes, particularly for national societies, but also for many regional societies, have necessitated the employment of additional staff which has placed upward pressure on cost. Another factor instrumental in the rising cost levels of building societies is that of investment in information technology. On average building societies have spent 15 percent of non-interest cost on information technology investment, (see chapter 6).

Building societies have, however, endeavoured to place a break on spiralling costs through branch rationalisation programmes and in the case of some national societies through product disinvestment. Stockbroking, estate agency and property management are areas which have failed to generate the levels of income initially expected. A number of national societies in consequence have cut their losses and have withdrawn from these markets, (product diversification and product disinvestment are examined in chapter 7).

Given that local societies have not diversified to anything like the same extent as the national or larger regional societies the fact that their cost/income ratios have both risen more sharply and in absolute terms are much higher than the other two classifications is somewhat of a surprise. One explanation is that local societies have been involved in office refurbishment and information technology upgrade programmes which in relative terms have taken up a much greater proportion of their annualised income. Societies such as the Ipswich, the Haywards Heath and the Century all reported cost/income ratios in excess of

75 percent for 1991.

Banks generally have much higher cost/income ratios than building societies with the exception of the Abbey National which has a ratio very much in line with the top cost performers within the building society sector. The higher cost structure of banks relates to the more diversified nature of their business. Banks during the last two years have attempted to force downwards their cost/income ratios through a selection of cost-control programmes. The Bank of England in its Banking Act Report 1991/92 provides evidence of the overall success of these programmes.

> "1991 saw the reversal of the upward trend seen since 1985 in the larger banks cost-income ratios .... with income growth outstripping the rise in costs, this ratio stood at 66.7% at the end of 1991, compared with 68% a year earlier."

The cost control measures pursued during 1990 and 1991 by the banks included sharp reductions in employee numbers. Approximately 40 percent of bank income each year is taken up by expenditure on staff, present and past. Branch rationalisation was also targeted by many banks as a means of achieving cost reductions. Much of the savings in these areas were nevertheless eroded by continued heavy investment in information technology. Jenkins (1992) estimated that during 1991 banks, on average, faced a 14 percent increase in equipment expenses taken up by information technology investment and associated higher depreciation charges.

Bad Debt Provisions

Building society performance in recent years has been increasingly hindered through rising levels of bad debt. Unfortunately comparisons among building societies themselves not to mention comparisons between banks and building societies are less than meaningful in that institutions utilise different approaches in provisioning for bad debt.

Nevertheless what can be said with certainty is that almost all building societies have experienced, over the last two years, huge increases in their bad debt provision. The Halifax reported a jump in bad debt provisions from £107m in 1990 to £229m in 1991. The Cheltenham and Gloucester one of the industry top performers had a bad debt provision in 1991 of £71.7m compared to £17.2m in 1990. Among the bottom line performers the Alliance and Leicester made provisions of £215m for bad debt in 1991. Much of this provision was made against its large portfolio of commercial lending, a market segment from which the Alliance and Leicester has now significantly retreated. Commercial lending also caused major problems for the Skipton. Its bad debt provision for 1991 was £23m of which £15m was for commercial lending.

Given the diversity in bad debt reporting procedures and the bias which this is likely to introduce into aggregate statistics, as an alternative, Table 4:VIII documents 1991 provisions for losses on commercial assets for each national building society[5]. Information is also provided on the money value of loss provision set against the various commercial asset constituents: residential property, class 1 assets; advances secured on land, class 2 assets; and other commercial assets, class 3 assets.

Table 4:VIII
Provisions for losses on Commercial Assets, 1991

National Societies	Loss Provision /Commercial Assets, %	Class 1 Assets £m	Class 2 Assets £m	Class 3 Assets £m	Total £m
Halifax	(0.47)	191.0	15.8	22.4	229.2
Nationwide	(0.85)	205.3	26.2	4.4	235.9
Alliance & Leicester	(1.42)	69.7	117.4	28.0	215.1
Woolwich	(0.44)	54.6	10.7	7.0	72.3
Leeds Permanent	(0.32)	37.9	1.6	4.8	44.3
Cheltenham & Gloucester	(0.58)	64.7	2.9	4.1	71.7
Bradford & Bingley	(0.31)	26.2	1.2	3.1	30.5
National & Provincial	(0.56)	24.7	24.6	2.8	52.1
Britannia	(0.48)	8.8	24.9	-	33.7
Bristol & West	(0.27)	14.5	1.1	-	15.6

The percentage weights in brackets after total loss provisions give an indication of the volume of bad debts relative to the commercial asset base of the society. Those societies with above average ratios have tended to either run mortgage books with a heavy emphasis upon property in the south of England or they have become over exposed in commercial lending with the problem again more acute if the advance is secured on land in the south of England.

Relative to the volume of loans tied up in class 2 assets the commercial lending books of the Nationwide, the Bradford, the National and Provincial, the Leek, the Staffordshire, the Britannia and the Alliance and Leicester have suffered most during this current recession. The domestic property market has also taken its toll on building societies. The period since 1989 has seen an almost unabated increase in both house repossessions and mortgage arrears. House repossessions stood at 15,800 in 1989 before climbing to 43,900 in 1990 and to 75,500 in 1991. While loans in excess of 12 months in arrears rose from 13,800 in 1989 to 36,100 in 1990 and then to 91,700 in 1991. It is of course the case, that the money value of loss provisions set against residential property, overstates the mortgage book problem relative to the loss provision levels of the other two categories, in that first mortgages to owner-occupiers account for over 90 percent of the commercial asset base of most national societies.

Relative to building societies the bad debt problems suffered by banks have been much more severe. Among the four London clearing banks bad debt provisions in 1991 ranged from £903m (excluding exceptional provisions of £1.5bn for problem country debt) in the case of the Midland to £1,875m for the National Westminster. Accepting the difficulties posed by the different computational procedures utilised by financial institutions in the calculation of bad debt provisions UBS Phillips and Drew (1992a) estimate that in 1991 domestic bad debt as a percentage of advances was on average 2.78 percent for the four London clearing banks. This compares with an average value across the top 20 building societies of 0.71 percent. The problem for banks generally, with the exception of the Abbey National which had a provision level of £155m in 1991, is that their business is skewed towards the currently loss making corporate end. The small firms sector has been a particular problem area for banks. This is reflected in the fact that the majority of loan losses have been less than £100,000 although by early 1992 there was increasing evidence of loan collapse in the mid-corporate sector. The difficulties which banks now face dates back to the extended boom period of the mid-1980s. The euphoria surrounding the boom led to an almost underlying expectation that the UK economy would remain in a state of prosperity. This resulted in banks adopting more relaxed lending criteria. In addition, banks during the Thatcher years, were actively encouraged to lend to small firms. The chief executive of the National Westminster succinctly summarised the cause of the bad debt problems now faced by banks in an interview for the Financial Times, March 1, 1992.

> "We got the economy wrong. We thought in 1986-88 that we were in a German-type economy. There was low inflation and low interest rates; so a lot of businesses which had not hitherto got going in this country, or would not have survived, did get going. I don't think anybody would have foreseen interest rates higher than 12%."

Misjudgment by banks appears therefore to have compounded their bad debt problems. The corollary of this is not that societies with a relatively lower level of bad debt have in place management with superior expertise but rather through legislation building societies have been excluded from the high risk corporate loan market.

Overall Profit Performance

While an overview of the various components of income and cost is important in that it sheds light on the efficiency and operational performance of different parts of an institution, the bottom line in the judgement of the success or otherwise of an institution is that of its relative profitability. In this part of the discussion two measures of relative profitability are reported. They are pre-tax profits as a percentage of mean reserves, essentially this is a return on capital measure and pre-tax profits as a percentage of mean total assets.

In Table 4:IXA pre-tax profits as a percentage of mean reserves are reported for the various society classifications.[6] The average ratios are reported on a weighted basis with mean reserves employed to assign weights. Following the methodology of UBS Phillips and Drew (1992b) reserves include minority interests since the profit values also include the profit (or loss) originating from these minority interests. Furthermore neither subscribed capital nor subordinated debt are included, as profits are reported after subtracting the interest costs of subscribed capital and subordinated debt. In Table 4:IXB a comparable capital return value is detailed for retail banks. The measure computed is that of pre-tax profits as a percentage of average shareholders' funds.

Table 4:IXA
Pre-tax Profits/Mean Reserves (Building Societies)

Building Society	Pre-tax Profits/Mean Reserves, %		
Groupings	1989	1990	1991
National Societies	30.04	27.22	21.95
Regional Societies	29.96	24.3	18.69
Local Societies	25.23	18.21	13.71
All Societies	29.92	26.49	21.19

Table 4:IXB
Pre-tax Profits/Average Shareholders' funds (Retail Banks)

Retail Banks	Pre-tax Profits/Average Shareholder's Funds, %		
	1989	1990	1991
Abbey National	26.63	22.6	21.8
Barclays	11.6	12.32	9.0
Lloyds	-27.29	25.5	27.18
Midland	-9.22	0.41	1.51
National Westminster	6.79	8.5	1.92
Bank of Scotland	24.12	22.53	13.78
Royal Bank of Scotland	17.02	16.54	3.71

The impact that the recession has had on the profitability of societies is at once obvious from Table 4:IXA. For each of the classifications the return on capital has declined between 1989 and 1991 although it does appear that the national players have not been subject to as large a percentage fall as have regional and local societies. In addition it also transpires that the return on capital for local societies is generally much lower than that for both national and regional societies. A number of factors come into play in this instance. They include the proportionately larger capital ratios of local societies and of course their higher cost to income ratios.

When building society profit performance is compared with that of the retail banks, Table 4:IXB, two points of note emerge. The first is that building societies have tended to out-perform their high-street competitors with the exception again that of the Abbey National. The second is that relative to banks the return on capital for building societies has been much more stable. The key element in the differential performance between these two groups of financial institutions is the very much cyclical nature of the contribution of corporate lending to the loan books of the retail banks. In addition the highly adverse performance of a number of banks in 1989 stems from high levels of provision on account of country specific bad debt.

It is also the case that building societies have proportionately less capital than banks. In consequence it could then be argued that this portrays societies in a more favourable light in terms of a return on capital measure. Phillips and Drew (1992a), however, argue that it is the risk adjusted capital base which is important in that the risk weighted position makes allowances for the relative riskiness of institutions' loan portfolios. Measures of Tier 1 capital as a proportion of risk weighted assets were detailed in Table 4:III for building societies and in Table 4:IV for banks. A comparative analysis of these tables indicated that building societies operated higher risk adjusted capital bases than banks. This places in an even more favourable light the superior profit performance of societies relative to banks, (Table 4:IXA and Table 4:IXB).

Where ambiguity does arise is in the comparative performance of national, regional and local societies. As indicated local societies have a higher unweighted capital base than either national or regional societies with the differential even more pronounced on a risk adjusted basis. An alternative measure of profit performance was therefore computed, pre-tax profits as a proportion of mean total assets.[7] This alternative measure also suffers from problems not least that total assets are not risk adjusted, nevertheless it does provide additional evidence which permits a more rounded assessment of profit performance to be made. Pre-tax profits as a percentage of mean total assets are reported in Table 4:XA for societies, (ratios are reported on a weighted basis), and in Table 4:XB for banks.

Table 4:XA
Pre-tax Profits/Mean Total Assets (Building Societies)

Building Society Groupings	Pre-tax Profits/ Mean Total Assets, %		
	1989	1990	1991
National Societies	1.21	1.13	0.91
Regional Societies	1.5	1.22	0.90
Local Societies	1.55	1.15	0.89
All Societies	1.26	1.14	0.90

Table 4:XB
Pre-tax Profits/Mean Total Assets (Retail Banks)

Retail Banks	Pre-tax Profits/ Mean Total Assets, %		
	1989	1990	1991
Abbey National	1.46	1.39	1.19
Barclays	0.6	0.58	0.39
Lloyds	-1.31	1.05	1.21
Midland	-0.44	0.02	0.06
National Westminster	0.38	0.42	0.09
Bank of Scotland	1.42	1.2	0.66
Royal Bank of Scotland	0.93	0.91	0.19

The general picture to emerge is that of a superior and more consistent profit performance for building societies *vis a vis* banks. Although on the basis of this profit measure the differential between the two groups of financial institutions is much narrower than it was with the previous measure.

A more fundamental shift in profit performance occurs when the relative position of national, regional and local societies is considered. In 1989 and 1990 both local societies and regional societies generate higher profit returns than national societies. In 1991 the ranking is reversed with national societies, as in the case of the previous profit measure, Table 4:IXA, the lead performers.

The introduction of this additional profit statistic therefore tends to indicate that the higher capital base of local societies is the key determinant in their relatively lacklustre performance when pre-tax profits as a proportion of mean reserves are employed as the profit performance indicator.

Summary

This chapter has focused upon the performance of building societies. Judgement with regard to performance was scrutinised on a number of counts. Capital strength was the initial area under consideration. From the analysis it emerged that in terms of both the BSC capital adequacy guidelines and the EC solvency ratio requirements that building societies are well capitalised. Significant differences did arise in terms of the relative capital strength of the various society subgroups, with the capital ratios of local building societies particularly high. In addition given that the capital base of local societies consisted essentially of reserves it was found to be £ for £ of higher quality than that of national and regional societies. The analysis did also suggest that recently the capital ratios of the larger and smaller societies have begun to converge. National societies, in part through the issue of PIBS, have started to build up their capital bases. When the capital strength of building societies was then compared to that of the retail banks it became clear that societies were in a somewhat healthier position. From the analysis of capital strength it was therefore clear that when the economic upturn does materialise that building societies are in a healthy position to expand existing product ranges and diversify into others.

The income generation capabilities of building societies were next considered. Income generation has two facets, that of net interest income and fee based income. In terms of net interest income societies were compared on the basis of net interest margins. It turned out that local societies operated somewhat higher margins than either national or regional societies. This was somewhat of a paradox. The expectation, *a priori*, was that as national societies have diversified into higher risk activities their net interest margins would have been higher. This assessment was based on the fact that retail banks traditionally operate much higher margins than building societies. Two reasons were put forward for local societies' higher margins. First they could get away with higher margins as their customer base essentially stemmed from a *niche* market. Second they required higher margins to cover their higher cost levels.

The analysis of the other component of income, that of fee-based income, was relatively straightforward. The computed statistics indicated a rapid rise in the contribution of fee-based income to total income. They also suggested that national societies with their more heavily diversified product portfolios were much more reliant on fee based income than the other categories of societies. Banks in turn were more heavily dependent than national societies.

Cost levels of building societies were also examined. The picture which emerged was one of a general rise in cost to income ratios. For national societies this rise was expected because diversification has placed them under additional cost pressures. Local societies over the period did nevertheless experience much faster increases in their cost to income ratios and now operate at much higher absolute levels than either national or regional societies. While this may in part be due to size reducing their ability to capture economies of scale, an additional factor is that a number of local societies have entered into significant refurbishment programmes which have temporarily increased their cost to income ratios and have introduced a bias into the aggregate statistics.

Overall, building societies did have much lower cost to income ratios than banks and in consequence remain highly competitive in the market place. Cost to income ratios are currently under much scrutiny by both banks and building societies. Banks in particular have been engaged in heavy cost cutting programmes both in terms of branch rationalisation and staff redundancies. Given the highly competitive nature of the financial services industry plus the present economic downturn the expectation must be that banks and building societies will continue to pare away at their cost to income ratios.

Differences in bad debt provision levels were a further area explored in this chapter. Unfortunately the discussion was considerably hampered due to non-uniformity in the accounting treatment of bad debt by the respective building societies and banks. As a consequence the discussion was limited to a review of the position of national societies *vis a vis* banks. Very much as expected the retail banks were found to have significantly higher provision levels. Corporate lending and exposure to third country debt were the main problem areas for the retail banks.

To complete the analysis two measures of profit were computed. They were return on mean reserves, (shareholders' funds for banks), and return on mean total assets. Both statistics identified building societies as having a superior and more consistent profit performance than that of banks. Where slight ambiguity did emerge was in the performance of the respective society classes. On the basis of pre-tax profits as a percentage of mean reserves national societies were ranked as the top performers for each of the years 1989 through to 1991. In contrast pre-tax profits as a percentage of mean total assets saw local and regional societies out perform national societies in 1989 and 1990 with national societies only moving to the lead position in 1991. Pre-tax profits as a percentage of mean total assets probably gave the more accurate profit assessment, as the reserve base measure suffered from the problem that local societies operate higher reserve ratios than their national counterparts.

In summary therefore, building societies with their more limited product portfolios consistently outperformed the retail banks over the period 1989 to 1991. A large part of societies' success was due to their much lower cost to income ratios and relatively insignificant bad debt problems.

For the future it is difficult to envisage building societies maintaining their superior position. Banks have now started to tackle their cost problems through branch and staff rationalisation programmes. They can also be assumed to have taken on board some hard lending lessons as a consequence of their bad debt exposures during this current recession. If these two factors are taken in conjunction with the fact that banks have a much greater product and market choice in the establishment of their optimal portfolio mix it becomes clear why building societies may be hard-pressed to hold onto their lead position.

Notes

[1]Gross capital ratios are reported for each society in the Data Appendix.

[2]Tier 1 risk asset ratios are reported for each society in the Data Appendix.

[3]Non-Interest income as a proportion of total income is computed for each society in the Data Appendix.

[4]Cost to income ratios are documented for each society in the Data Appendix.

[5]Bad debt levels are documented for each society in the Data Appendix.

[6]Pre-tax profits as a percentage of mean reserves are detailed for each society in the Data Appendix.

[7]Pre-tax profits as a percentage of mean total assets are documented for each society in the Data Appendix.

5. Cost Efficiency and Structure

(prepared in conjunction with J.C. Glass)[1]

Introduction

In chapter 2 it was demonstrated that the deregulatory process has permitted building societies to both expand and diversify across a range of financial markets. In chapter 3 it emerged that the expansion programmes have not solely been constrained to product expansion but in addition a selection of societies have engaged in geographic market expansion. This movement by building societies into new geographic areas has been characterised primarily by branch openings but in addition by a process of transfer of engagements from smaller to larger societies.

Although the above noted changes have obviously created new opportunities for individual building societies they also raise important questions about the future structure of the UK building society industry. As institutions expand, and as competitive pressures intensify it is likely that the current process of concentration will become ever more pronounced. This tendency towards concentration may be exacerbated even further if the long awaited wave of building society takeovers by banks, including foreign institutions seeking to expand their retail banking networks, eventually occurs. In the final analysis whether the broad national, regional and local building society structure continues to hold good, although in a more concentrate form, or whether the industry becomes dominated by a small number of very large multibranch firms depends on which societies can remain profitable in the face of increasing competitive pressures. The question of building society profitability, in turn, hinges crucially on the cost efficiency of societies. Consequently, an assessment of the possibility of change in the structure of the sector necessitates that empirical evidence is available on the cost efficiency of individual societies and on the industry as a whole.

Theoretical Underpinnings

Two types of economies in the production of outputs may be achieved by individual firms in any industry. The first is economies of scale which are associated primarily with the size of an individual firm. The second is economies of scope which relate to the joint production of two or more products. Consider first of all an analysis of economies of scale.

There are two kinds of economies of scale. Economies that arise from increases in the production of individual products are called production specific economies of scale. Economies associated with increases in all of a firm's outputs are referred to as overall economies of scale. These two forms of scale economies are synonymous for a firm producing simply one product, as would have been the case for building societies pre-deregulation when their sole output was that of mortgages. For multiproduct firms, such as the case with building societies at present, overall economies of scale occur if total costs increase proportionately less than output when there is a simultaneous and equal percentage increase in each of the firm's products. In essence if there are economies of scale the firm can become more efficient by increasing the quantity of its outputs. Of course if there are diseconomies of scale the firm in this instance can become more efficient through output reduction. If constant returns to scale pertain the firm is producing an efficient quantity of the outputs.

Product specific economies of scale are present if a decline in the per unit cost of producing a specific product occurs as the output of that product increases with all other products held constant. If economies of scale exist with respect to a specific product the firm can increase efficiency through an expansion in the output of that particular product. Again, however, if there are product specific diseconomies of scale increased efficiency will result through a cutback in the output of the product in question. If returns to scale specific to the product are said to be constant then a variation in the output of that product will have a neutral impact upon cost.

Economies of scope were identified as a second way in which economies in the production of output can be achieved. Since financial firms now have the opportunity to offer a range of products, they must select not only the scale of operation but in addition which products they will supply. In essence cost savings can be obtained through the production of an appropriate mix of financial products. Economies of scope occur if it is cheaper to produce a group of outputs together in a single firm rather than separately in specialised firms.

Sources of Economies of Scale and Scope

The spreading of fixed costs over greater output levels and making better use of specialised labour and capital are usually identified as the prime sources of scale economies. A number of specific examples may help to clarify how these scale economies occur. In the financial services industry computers can be employed to service many of the aspects of business on both the asset and liability sides of the balance sheet. The fixed cost of computer installation is, however, high. Therefore the larger the customer base of the financial firm which instals the computer equipment the more fixed costs will be spread and the greater will be the fall in per unit costs of production. Automated teller machines, (ATMs) are another example of the effect of technology on the cost of production. The cost per transaction is much lower for an ATM than a human teller but the establishment costs for the ATM are high. A large customer base is again necessary for the financial institution to be able to lower its average cost by using the ATM.

Economies of scope, in contrast, are viewed to arise primarily through the joint usage of some fixed input. If an input is not fully employed in the production of one output it might be used to produce a second output. Mester (1987) cited information as one input which lends itself to the generation of scope economies. Once information on credit for an individual or business is gathered to enable the provision of a mortgage advance that information can then be used for other forms of loan advance to that individual or business. In this instance it is less expensive for the same financial institution to provide the loans than for a different bank to provide the subsequent loans.

An Overview of the Literature

In recent years there has been a selection of studies which have examined the structure of the UK building society industry. These include Gough (1979), Cooper (1980), Barnes and Dodds (1983), Hardwick (1989) and Hardwick (1990). The respective studies utilised a range of competing methodologies and yielded a range of conflicting findings.

Gough employing data for 1972 and 1976, and Barnes and Dodds using data for 1970 and 1978, estimated linear average cost functions and concluded that there was no evidence of economies of scale in the industry. Cooper on the basis of the Cobb-Douglas total cost function applied to 1977 cross-section data found that while there were significant scale economies for societies with assets less than £100m, larger societies were subject to diseconomies.

Hardwick's (1989) cross section study which utilised a single output translog cost function examined a sample of 97 societies for the year 1985. This study concluded that societies with assets of less than £280m could achieve statistically significant economies of scale but that there were no significant economies to be achieved by the growth of larger societies. Hardwick (1990) utilised the same data base to examine building societies as multiproduct producers. In this analysis the production approach was employed to classify outputs, with the relevant outputs those of the number of outstanding mortgage accounts and those of the number of outstanding deposit and share accounts. The primary finding of this study suggested that there were statistically significant economies of scale for societies with assets of up to £5,500m. There was also evidence of product specific economies of scale in the production of the mortgage output for societies with assets of up to £1,500m. Furthermore, Hardwick also found diseconomies of scope for societies with assets up to £1,500m.

All the above studies were conducted at a stage prior to the freeing up of financial services when building societies were essentially constrained in their operations to the provision of mortgages and related products. In addition, these studies failed to recognise that the ability to successfully undertake expansion programmes is likely to some degree to be influenced by the structure of the society. More specifically, output growth is likely to be a function of whether the society is national, regional or local in form.

In this chapter a multi-input multi-output hybrid translog cost function is employed to model the UK building society industry. The primary objective being to analyse in today's changed market environment the impact which the different structural characteristics of national, regional and local societies have on cost efficiencies. The sector is modelled for the financial reporting year 1991 with the discussion presented following and building upon that of McKillop and Glass (forthcoming 1994).

Methodology and Data

The study utilises a two-output, three-input cost function to provide empirical answers as to the efficiency or otherwise of UK building societies. As earlier documented the analysis focuses upon economies of scale, product specific economies of scale and economies of scope. In addition this particular cost function analysis also permits the computation of two other empirical measures which have not so far been discussed. These measures are augmented economies of scale and input specific economies of scale.

The rationale behind the augmented economies of scale measure is that it takes account of the fact that branch numbers are likely to vary with output. In short the augmented economies of scale measure encompasses the indirect effect on total cost of the induced change in the number of branches. In the case of input specific scale economies, the source of any economies or diseconomies of scale can be identified. More specifically this measure enables the disaggregation of the impact that labour and capital have upon economies of scale.

Given that the econometric analysis of economies of scope and product specific economies of scale require a cost function which is defined wherever one of the outputs is zero, the hybrid translog specification, proposed by Fuss and Waverman (1981) was utilised. The form of the hybrid translog specification, the constraints imposed on the function, the system of equations estimated, the estimation technique employed plus the equations used to obtain the scale and scope measures are all detailed in Appendix 5:I.

The approach adopted in the classification of the inputs and outputs is termed the intermediation approach. This approach views the building society as seeking out deposits from the personal sector and wholesale money markets which are subsequently intermediated into mortgages and other revenue-earning assets.

The general form of the cost function can be written as

$$C = f(P_1, P_2, P_3, Q_1, Q_2, B)$$

Total cost, C includes both operating and interest costs and is measured as the sum of all labour, capital and interest expenses. The two outputs are Q_1 which is defined as mortgage type products and Q_2 which for simplicity is classified as non-mortgage products. In more detail Q_1 consists of class 1 assets which are basically first mortgages to owner-occupiers. In contrast Q_2 consists of the sum of class 2 plus 3 assets, namely advances secured on land, unsecured advances, investment in land and investment in subsidiaries which in turn encompasses credit cards and money transaction accounts with overdraft facilities. P_1, P_2, and P_3 are respectively the labour input price, the capital input price and the price of borrowed funds. Following Hardwick (1989, 1990), the rental price of capital is computed by dividing total annual expenditure on premises and equipment (plus depreciation) by the value of mean assets for the financial year in question. The price of labour is measured by the average wage per employee calculated by the ratio of labour expenses to employee numbers. While the price of borrowed funds is measured by the total interest paid on borrowed funds divided by the total value of borrowed funds. B represents branch numbers.

The data base upon which the analysis is built is that of the 1991 statement of accounts of the 89 societies which as of August 1992 were authorised to take deposits from the public.

Empirical Results

Scale economies

For the multiproduct firm overall economies of scale ($\epsilon < 1$) occur if total costs increase proportionately less than output when there is a simultaneous and equal percentage increase in each of the firm's products. On the basis of equation 5, Appendix 5:I, average overall economies of scale values were computed for societies in total plus the national, regional and local subcategorisations. These estimates are reported in Table 5:I. Reported also in Table 5:I are the average augmented economies of scale measures, which take account of the indirect effect on total cost of induced changes in branch numbers[2].

Table 5:I
Economies and Augmented Economies of Scale

Building Society Groupings	Economies of Scale	Augmented Economies of Scale
National Societies	1.01	0.94*
Regional Societies	1.00	1.01
Local Societies	0.92*	0.96*
All Societies	0.96	0.97*

*significantly different from one at the 5% level

Depending upon the society grouping under consideration, the average economies of scale value is either marginally less or marginally greater than one. Only the value for local societies is, however, significantly different from one at the 5% level. This indicates that increasing returns to scale pertain and consequently if input prices and the number of branches remain unchanged, expansion will lead to a reduction in per unit costs. In contrast the values for national and regional societies are not significantly different from one which implies that expansion will leave per unit costs unchanged.

Measuring economies of scale in this manner fails to take account of the induced change in the number of branch offices as output expands. Consequently average augmented scale measures based on equation 7, Appendix 5:I were estimated. In nominal terms all the augmented scale measures reported in Table 5:I are less than 1 with the exception of the estimate for regional societies. All estimates obtained are significantly different from one with the exception again, that of regional societies. The fact that, for example, national societies can reap scale economies while regional societies may not be able to is due to the fact that the large scale asset base of national societies coupled with an extensive branch network system heightens customer awareness making it easier to expand mortgage business. The large mortgage customer base then makes it easier and more efficient for national societies than for regional societies to diversify into products such as money transmission, estate agency and insurance services through simply the cross-selling of these products.

Such an explanation then of course immediately raises the question, why are local societies able to reap scale economies when regional societies are not? The likely explanation is that local societies, unlike the other society groupings, have availed of very few of the avenues open to them for diversification under the 1986 Act and have simply continued to concentrate on the provision of mortgage and related products. It is clear from the augmented economies of scale estimate for local societies, and indeed the economies of scale estimate that further expansion of mortgage and related business by local societies would result in a fall in per unit costs. It is perhaps the case that local societies are at a point in their evolution where increased critical mass would now justify the adoption of more efficient production technology. Amalgamations between local societies would be one way of achieving this enhanced critical mass.

Input-specific economies of scale

Computation of input specific measures permit the identification of the source of economies or diseconomies of scale. Input specific economies of scale pertain if ($\epsilon_i < 1$) while diseconomies of scale hold if ($\epsilon_i > 1$). Equation 10, Appendix 5:I was employed to estimate average input specific scale economies with the results for the various classes of societies detailed in Table 5:IIA. Equation 12, Appendix 5:I was utilised in the computation of the augmented version of these input economies, with these results presented in Table 5:IIB. It is clear from a comparison of Table 5:IIA and 5:IIB that the trend movement of the input economies is similar in fashion, with the exception of slight variations for the capital input estimates, to that for the augmented input economies. Given the nature of these results and given that it has already been argued that the augmented measures are more appropriate, the analysis of results therefore concentrates, primarily for ease of exposition, upon augmented input-specific economies of scale.

Table 5:IIA
Input Specific Scale Economies

Building Society Groupings	Capital Input	Labour Input	Borrowed Funds Input
National Societies	0.93	1.62*	1.0
Regional Societies	0.94	1.25*	0.99
Local Societies	0.90	1.07	0.93*
All Societies	0.92	1.19	0.96

Table 5:IIB
Augmented Input Specific Scale Economies

Building Society Groupings	Capital Input	Labour Input	Borrowed Funds Input
National Societies	0.69*	1.74*	0.92*
Regional Societies	1.46*	1.40*	0.99
Local Societies	0.90	1.07	0.92*
All Societies	1.05	1.35*	0.96

*significantly different from one at the 5% level

If the labour input is initially considered it is evident that for national, regional and indeed societies as a whole that this input gives rise to significant augmented input diseconomies with the effect most pronounced for national societies. As indicated in chapter 3 employment levels within building societies have steadily risen in recent years. This to a large extent has been due to the requirement by societies for employees with new skills to accomodate their diversification strategies. Given that much of this diversification is still in its infancy and has not as yet reached its full profit potential this may explain diseconomies stemming from the labour input.

In the case of the capital input a non-uniform picture emerges. While capital gives rise to significant input economies for national societies, it in contrast gives rise to significant diseconomies for regional societies. The difference between these two society groupings, in the case of the contribution of capital, no doubt reflects the fact that size coupled with an extensive branch network system confers greater flexibility on national societies. At the moment, for example, national societies have been very much involved in the removal of many back-office functions out of head-office and the branches to specialised computerised sub-units. Such back-office work encompasses loan and mortgage processing, accounting records and passbook entries, credit card accounting, cheque card processing and fraud monitoring plus customer databases. The net effect for these societies which have engaged in relocation has been a more specialised and effective usage of capital in its form of information technology. In contrast the relatively smaller regional societies do not appear to have the requisite critical mass to enter into relocation programmes which permit the more efficient adoption and usage of capital investment. The issue of relocation is examined further in chapter 10.

In the case of borrowed funds significant input economies occur for both national and indeed local societies. Relative to regional societies the result for national societies may be a consequence of their better credit ratings which permit them to access the wholesale money markets at relatively cheaper rates. This, nevertheless, does not explain why local societies are also able to obtain input economies from borrowed funds. Although refering back to Table 3:V in chapter 3 it is clear that wholesale funds as a proportion of total funds are much lower for local societies than for national or regional societies and in consequence wholesale funding costs are not really a problem for local societies.

Product-specific economies of scale

Product-specific scale economies for both classes of financial products were estimated using equation 13, Appendix 5:I and are reported in Table 5:III[3]. In addition also detailed in Table 5:III are estimates of the change in the marginal cost of each class of financial product.

Table 5:III
Product Specific Scale Economies and Marginal Cost Variations

Building Society Groupings	Product-specific		Δ in Marginal Cost	
	Mortgage Products	Non-Mortgage Products	Mortgage Products	Non-Mortgage Products
National Societies	1.11*	6.54	-0.02	-0.03
Regional Societies	1.07*	8.01	-0.17	-1.35
Local Societies	1.16*	7.99	-1.13	-1.19
All Societies	1.12*	7.84	-1.09	-1.24

*significantly different from one at the 5% level

In contrast to the previous analysis of input specific and overall scale economies, a product specific estimate which is greater than one is indicative of product specific economies of scale while a value less than one reflects product specific diseconomies of scale. Although the nominal values for product specific economies indicate increasing returns to scale in the use of both mortgage products and non-mortgage products, the results across all classifications for non-mortage products are not significantly different from one and indicate that constant returns to scale cannot be ruled out. The implication therefore is that from the standpoint of costs alone neither national, regional or local building societies would benefit from altering their present provision levels of non-mortgage products. In contrast an examination of the scale economies estimates with respect to mortgage products indicates that for all society groups significant product-specific economies of scale can be achieved through the increase in the output level of this financial product.

Information on the change in marginal cost with respect to the respective products is also detailed in Table 5:III. On the basis of the negative sign across all estimates the picture which again emerges is that product-specific increasing returns to scale pertain. In this instance, however, the estimates obtained do not turn out to be significant.

Economies of scope

Equation 15, Appendix 5:I was employed to obtain an estimate of the degree of economies of scope $\hat{S}\hat{C}_{12}$ over the production of the two products with the relevant estimates detailed in Table 5:IV. Included also in Table 5:IV are estimates of cost complementarity based on equation 16, Appendix 5:I.[4]

Table 5:IV
Economies of Scope and Cost Complementarity

Building Society Groupings	Economies of Scope	Cost Complementarity
National Societies	-0.73	0.03
Regional Societies	-0.55	0.57*
Local Societies	-0.46	0.91*
All Societies	-0.52	0.73*

*significantly different from zero at the 5% level

The nominal values reported in Table 5:IV depict a relatively consistent picture in that they indicate both diseconomies of scope over the production of the two outputs and also that the cost function does not exhibit cost complementarity. Only in the case of the cost complementarity estimates do values emerge which are significantly different from zero, with the significance of the estimates holding for regional, local and societies as a whole but not for national societies. The fact that in terms of the cost complementarity estimates both regional and local societies, in the financial year 1991, were faced with production cost disadvantages in producing mortgage products and non-mortgage products jointly may as earlier indicated be a consequence of size limiting their ability to adopt the most efficient production techniques. This is particularly pertinent when it comes to the adoption of up-to-date information technology where systems can now be utilised in the production of a range of products and services,(see chapter 6 for details on differences in information technology adoption between societies).

For national societies although their is no evidence of significant cost disadvantages in producing the two products jointly neither is their evidence of a cost advantage. It should be noted nevertheless that the absence of scope economies and cost complementarity does not imply that joint production is not profitable. The ability of a society not only to capture market share but also to maintain its market position in the face of stiff competition from other societies as well as from other financial intermediaries is crucially linked to it being able to offer current and potential customers a diverse range of financial products. In addition, such joint production across different classes of earning assets can reduce risk for a society from the perspective of risk reduction through portfolio diversification.

At this juncture it may be of interest to note that Hardwick (1990) in his pre-deregulation study of UK building societies obtained statistically significant diseconomies of scope for building societies with assets up to £150m. In contrast, and in line with our study, he found no evidence of economies or diseconomies of scope for larger societies. Although the outputs under consideration in the Hardwick study were as earlier documented, the average number of outstanding mortgage accounts and the average number of outstanding share and deposit accounts, he utilised the result for "smaller" societies to intimate that

> "the existence of diseconomies of scope across the full range of services would mean that .... diversification (unless accompanied by the creation of separate specialist departments) would raise the average operating costs of building societies."

The findings of our study which explicitly considers as an output classification those financial products which societies have diversified into since 1986 would tend to reinforce such a conclusion but our results also indicate, from the perspective of the cost complementarity estimate, that the larger asset based regional societies face a similar problem.

Summary

In this chapter the impact upon cost efficiencies of the structural characteristics of building societies has been examined. A key part of the analysis has been that societies are viewed as multiproduct firms which produce both mortgage and non-mortgage products.

The empirical analysis offered three key insights into the industry. The first was that there is evidence of significant augmented economies of scale for both national and regional societies. This finding augurs well for the expansion programmes through transfer of engagements currently being pursued particularly by national societies. A good case in point is that of the Cheltenham and Gloucester and the Bradford and Bingley. From the start of 1991 to August 1992 these two societies have been involved in a total of 9 transfer of engagements, mostly from local societies. The analysis also suggested that local societies, in terms of cost per unit of output, would also benefit from amalgamations. What this part of the analysis did call into question, at least from a cost efficiency perspective, was the dash for asset growth policy which many regional societies pursued in the post 1986 period.

The second area of interest to emerge from the discussion was that in terms of augmented input-specific economies of scale cost savings are attributable to the employment of the capital input for national societies but not for regional societies. The difference between these two society groupings in all probability reflects the fact that the larger capital base and extensive branch network system of national societies enables them to follow more radical changes in the use of the capital input in the pursuit of efficiency. One example of such a change is the situation where a number of national societies have shifted some back-office functions from their head-office and their branches to specialised computerised sub-units.

The third area of note to emerge from the analysis was that for regional and local societies cost inefficiencies emerge in the production of mortgage and non-mortgage products. National societies, in contrast, do not appear to exhibit either cost efficiencies or inefficiencies over the production of the two output classes. Although there does not appear to be cost savings for national societies due to joint production of different outputs, it should be said that this does not imply that they should concentrate on one product and become in Mester's (1987), terminology a "financial boutique" as opposed to a "financial supermarket". There are other motives for joint production such as customer convenience and diversification to reduce risk. In addition it must also be recognised that when it comes to the introduction of new financial products building societies are very much at the start point of the learning curve. It is therefore likely to be a number of years before many of the initial teething problems involved in the introduction of new products are eliminated. The issue of diversification into new product ranges is explored in detail in chapter 7.

Notes

[1]J.C. Glass is a Senior Lecturer in Financial Economics in the Department of Banking and Commerce at the University of Ulster.

[2]Augmented economies of scale measures are reported for each society in the Data Appendix.

[3]Product specific economies of scale measures for both mortgage and non-mortgage products are reported for each society in the Data Appendix.

[4]Cost complementarity measures are detailed for each society in the Data Appendix.

APPENDIX 5:I

Model and Equation Specification

The hybrid translog cost function employed in the study is given as:

$$
\begin{aligned}
lnC &= a_o + \sum_{k=1}^{2} a_k Q_k^* + \sum_{i=1}^{3} b_i \ln P_i \\
&+ \frac{1}{2}\sum_{k=1}^{2}\sum_{m=1}^{2} d_{km} Q_k^* Q_m^* + \frac{1}{2}\sum_{i=1}^{3}\sum_{j=1}^{3} f_{ij} \ln P_i \ln P_j \\
&+ \sum_{i=1}^{3}\sum_{k=1}^{2} g_{ik} \ln P_i Q_k^* + m_b lnB + \frac{1}{2} m_{bb}(lnB)^2 \\
&+ \sum_{k=1}^{2} n_{kb} Q_k^* \, lnB + \sum_{i=1}^{3} W_{ib} lnP_i lnB
\end{aligned} \quad (1)
$$

$Q_k^* = (Q_k^\theta - 1)/\Theta$ with $\Theta \neq 0$ and $k = 1,2$ denotes the Box-Cox transformation of the two outputs. As the hybrid translog cost function (1) is viewed as a second-order logarithmic approximation to an arbitrary twice-differentiable cost function, the cross partial derivatives of the cost function must be equal. This implies the symmetry restrictions

$$d_{km} = d_{mk} \text{ and } f_{ij} = f_{ji} \quad (2)$$

In addition, in this approximation, all variables are normalised (and scaled to unity) around their means, the implication being that the expansion point is where $P_i = Q_k = B = 1$.

The cost function is constrained to be homogeneous of degree one in input prices. For (1) this requires the restrictions:

$$
\begin{aligned}
&\sum_{i=1}^{3} b_i = 1; \quad \sum_{i=1}^{3} f_{ij} = 0 \\
&\sum_{i=1}^{3} g_{ik} = 0; \quad \sum_{i=1}^{3} W_{ib} = 0 \\
&\qquad\qquad [j = 1,2,3] \\
&\qquad\qquad [k = 1,2]
\end{aligned} \quad (3)
$$

If (1) is estimated on its own, it is likely that parameter estimates will not be efficient due to the high correlation between many of the cross-products among explanatory variables. Hence, to reduce this problem and to use additional information without introducing new parameters, the cost function is estimated jointly with the cost-share equations for each input.

The set of cost-share equations associated with the hybrid translog cost function, is obtained via Shephard's lemma as:

$$S_i = b_i + \sum_{j=1}^{3} f_{ij} lnP_j + \sum_{k=1}^{2} g_{ik} Q_k^* + w_{ib} lnB \quad (i = 1,2,3) \tag{4}$$

where $S_i = \partial lnC/\partial lnP_i$. Since $\sum_i S_i = 1$, this requires the same

restrictions as given above in (3) and implies that only two of the three cost-share equations are linearly independent.

Overall economies of scale

Overall scale economies are measured by the sum of cost elasticities with respect to outputs, see Hanoch (1975). For the hybrid translog cost function, this scale elasticity ϵ, is given by:

$$\epsilon = \sum_{k=1}^{2} \{Q_k^\theta (a_k + \sum_{m=1}^{2} d_{km} Q_m^* + \sum_{i=1}^{3} g_{ik} lnP_i + n_{kb} lnB))\} \tag{5}$$

Overall economies (diseconomies) of scale are said to be present when $\epsilon < 1$ ($\epsilon > 1$), with constant returns to scale being said to exist when $\epsilon = 1$.

Augmented economies of scale

Equation (5) gives an appropriate measure of economies of scale in so far as the other explanatory variables in the cost function hold constant as output changes. To take account of the fact that branch numbers are likely to vary with output, an augmented economies of scale measure is computed which encompasses the indirect effect on total cost of the induced change in the number of branches.

$$\text{Augmented } \epsilon = \sum_{k=1}^{2} (\partial lnC/\partial lnQ_k) + (\partial lnC/\partial lnB) \left(\sum_{k=1}^{2} \partial lnB/\partial lnQ_k\right) \tag{6}$$

The estimate of

$$\sum_{k=1}^{2} \partial lnB/\partial lnQ_k$$

was obtained separately by regressing lnB on lnQ_1 plus lnQ_2. For the cost function in (1) the augmented value is given by:

$$\text{Augmented } \epsilon = \epsilon + [m_b + m_{bb} lnB + \sum_{k=1}^{2} n_{kb} Q_k^* + \sum_{k=1}^{3} W_{ib} lnP_i] \ (h+r) \tag{7}$$

where h and r are obtained from the regression

$$lnB = C + h lnQ_1 + r lnQ_2 \tag{8}$$

Input specific scale economies

Input-specific economies of scale ϵ_i relate to the cost-savings attributable to the employment of the ith input as the firm expands and are computed so that the source of any economies or diseconomies of scale can be identified. Since $C = \Sigma_i C_i$ then ϵ_i can be defined as:

$$\epsilon_i = \sum_{k=1}^{2} \partial lnC_i / \partial lnQ_k = \epsilon + \sum_{k=1}^{2} \partial lnS_i / \partial lnQ_k \quad (i = 1, 2\ 3) \tag{9}$$

For the hybrid cost function ϵ_i then becomes:

$$\epsilon_i = \epsilon + [S_i]^{-1} [\sum_{k=1}^{2} g_{ik} Q_k^*] \quad (i = 1, 2\ 3) \tag{10}$$

Input specific economies (diseconomies) of scale are said to be present when $\epsilon_i < 1$, ($\epsilon_i > 1$), with constant return to scale being said to exist when $\epsilon_i = 1$.

Augmented input specific scale economies

To accommodate the fact that output variability is likely to lead to shifts in branch numbers, augmented input specific scale economy values are also estimated with the appropriate measure given by:

$$\text{Augmented } \epsilon_i = \epsilon_i + (\partial lnC/\partial lnB)(\sum_{k=1}^{2} \partial lnB/\partial lnQ_k) + (\partial lnS_i/\partial lnB)(\sum_{k=1}^{2} \partial lnB/\partial lnQ_k) \quad (i=1,2,3) \tag{11}$$

The final term in equation (11) represents the proportionate change in the ith input's cost share resulting from the induced change in the number of branch offices. For the hybrid translog cost function (11) becomes:

$$\text{Augmented } \epsilon_i = \text{augmented } \epsilon + \epsilon_i - \epsilon + [\hat{S}_i]^{-1}.(w_{ib})(h+r) \quad (i=1,2,3) \qquad (12)$$

with h and r obtained as in equation (8).

Product specific scale economies

Baumol et al (1982) demonstrated that the degree of scale economies specific to product k is measured by the ratio of the average incremental cost of the product (AIC_k) to its marginal cost ($\partial C/\partial Q_k$), that is:

$$PS_k = AIC_k/(\partial C/\partial Q_k) = [IC_k/C]/ECQ_k \qquad (13)$$

where IC_k is the incremental cost of product k defined as the firm's total cost with the given vector of outputs, minus what the total cost would be if the product k was zero, all other output levels remaining unchanged. Returns to scale specific to product k are said to be increasing, decreasing or constant as PS_k is greater than, less than, or equal to unity, respectively.

While the hybrid translog cost function enables measurement of product-specific economies of scale, the estimates obtained must be treated cautiously as they are the result of extrapolating the cost function into the region of zero outputs. In this respect a useful additional investigation involves checking the direction of change of marginal cost with respect to product k, where

$$\frac{\partial^2 C}{\partial Q_k^2} = \frac{C}{Q_k^2}\left[\frac{\partial^2 lnC}{\partial lnQ_k^2} + \left(\frac{\partial lnC}{\partial lnQ_k}\right)\left(\frac{\partial lnc}{\partial lnQ_k} - 1\right)\right] \qquad (14)$$

Economies of scope

Again, following the work of Baumol et al (1982), the degree of economies of scope is measured by the relative increase in cost that would result from producing the two products separately rather than jointly and is given by:

$$SC_{12} = [C(Q_1, 0) + C(0, Q_2) - C(Q_1, Q_2)]/C(Q_1, Q_2) \qquad (15)$$

with $SC_{12} > 0$ ($SC_{12} < 0$) implying economies (diseconomies) of scope over the production of the two goods.

As with product-specific scale economies estimates, the economies of scope estimate must be treated with care as it is the result of extrapolating the cost function into the region of zero outputs. A cross check can, however, be made by computing cost complementarity, denoted by $\partial^2 C/\partial Q_1 \partial Q_2 < 0$, given that a multiproduct cost function which exhibits cost complementarity exhibits economies of scope.

$$\frac{\partial^2 C}{\partial Q_1, \partial Q_2} = \frac{C}{Q_1 Q_2}\left[d_{12}Q_1^{\theta}Q_2^{\theta} + \left(\frac{\partial lnC}{\partial lnQ_1}\right)\left(\frac{\partial lnC}{\partial lnQ_2}\right)\right] \tag{16}$$

with $\partial^2C/\partial Q_1\partial Q_2 < 0$ indicating that an increase (decrease) in the output level of one product leads to a decrease (increase) in the marginal cost of the other product.

Estimation procedure

The hybrid translog cost function (1) is jointly estimated with the cost-share equations (4) with the restrictions (2) and (3) imposed across equations and error terms added for empirical implementation. Since the cost shares in (4) sum to unity, one of the cost-share equations (the borrowed funds cost share) is omitted from the estimated model to avoid the problem of singular contemporary covariance matrices of disturbances. Moreover, as the equations in the estimated model have a set of parameters in common the iterative Zellner estimation procedure is utilised.

6. Information Technology

Introduction

The purpose of this chapter is to examine the significance of the changing role of information technology applications within building societies. The rationale for investment in information technology is closely connected to the search for competitive advantage in the marketplace. In evaluating the use of information technology, a key reference point is that of competitive advantage. Currently, there is a huge investment differential between banks and building societies in the area of information technology which gives an added impetus to the examination of the appropriateness of the current developments in information technology within the building society sector. An effective information technology strategy is not, however, simply determined by the aggregate level of financial investment. Rather, the starting point lies in formulating a viable business strategy which addresses the threats and opportunities of the competitive environment within the financial services sector, where information technology is used to achieve distinctive competence for building societies *vis a vis* their main competitors the banks. Identifying where building societies are using information technology in a distinctive way is therefore an important concern of this chapter. Revealing the degree of commonality and diversity in the application of information technology by national, regional and local societies provides another important element in the analysis. Empirical evidence on the use of information technology is thus provided throughout this chapter by using the results of a telephone survey conducted by the authors in

September, 1992. The survey response was good, 7 of the 10 national societies participated in the survey as did 26 of the 33 regional societies and 33 of the 46 local societies.

A further theme explored in this chapter is the fundamental change taking place in the role of information technology in the financial services sector. Here, technical developments have led to assertions that a systems revolution is now emerging with the advent of architected and open systems, and the widespread development of customer relational databases. Document image processing represents a further technological development that can be expected to contribute to this revolutionary change. In addition to considering these new developments the discussion also concentrates upon more familiar information technology applications. The current and future use of both ATM and debit card networks are considered alongside telephone and home banking applications. Particular attention is also given to the more marketing driven application of information technology. Finally, key elements of the management of information technology projects are examined and comment is made on the issue of systems compatibility and its effect on building society mergers.

Competitive Advantage

The role of information technology in securing and sustaining competitive advantage has been increasingly the focus of academic debate. One of the best known formulations of the relative competitive advantage to be gained from technological innovation is that of Porter (1985). Here, technology strategy is about exploiting innovations. Broadly, three strategy imperatives are identified. Firstly, where technological innovation is unequivocally the key to survival; secondly, where technology buttresses a competitive strategy of low cost leadership or specialisation, and thirdly, where technology offers a first mover advantage to early innovators. Ford (1989) distinguishes between the basic technologies necessary for competitive survival but which do not necessarily confer competitive advantage with those technologies where the organisation has a distinctive competence and where competitive advantage is conferred. The same author also stresses the linkage between technological competence and broader management and organisational competencies in realising this competitive advantage. Steel (1983) also points out that the profile of a successful, technologically adaptive organisation may be a reflection of its ability to deflect or absorb the cost of technology failures as much as its ability to reap the benefits of technological advances. In examining the use of information technology within the building society sector, an attempt is made to provide a perspective which assesses the use of information technology in terms of competitive advantage. Before pursuing this theme the evolution of information technology in the financial services sector generally, should briefly be considered.

Early Developments in Information Technology

The financial services sector has been the largest user of information technology since the early years of mainframe computing. Banks and building societies were at the forefront in the creation of batch accounting systems, and both institutions pioneered the use of information technology for back-office accounting. These early computer systems were designed to handle large volumes of transactions and were optimised for throughput and accuracy. They were established primarily to reduce the volume of paperwork and the growth of staff during a period of increasing levels of business. The banks particularly, are now faced with problems associated with these first generation ageing systems which have been constantly repaired and modified since the 1960s. Similar problems, although on a reduced scale, exist in the building society sector where a priority is also being given to revitalising ageing head-office accounting and branch office systems. Table 6:I presents details on the number of societies which reported an upgrade or replacement of their branch accounting system and mortgage system in the last three years.

Table 6:1
Upgrade or Replacement of Existing Systems

Systems Type	National Building Societies n=7	Regional Building Societies n=26	Local Building Societies n=33
Branch Accounting System	4	15	17
Mortgage System	6	13	12

Viewed from the 1990s, the limitations of the early computer systems are now apparent. Designed on the basis of an overly technical systems analysis and design methodology, the focus of the early systems was at the account or product level and often merely automated previous manual systems. Thus, their major drawback stems from the fact that they are poorly matched to the demands of the market; account driven systems are simply not sophisticated enough to serve the needs of the more marketing driven financial services sector of the 1990s. To an extent, building societies are fortunate to be late-comers to personal banking since they are not encumbered by outdated automated processing systems to the same magnitude as the banks.

Investment Differential

Investment in the financial services sector in information technology is estimated at 12-20 percent of non-interest costs in the banking sector and 15 percent of non-interest costs in the building society sector. Of course, the difference in the scale of the two sectors means that the differential in the monetary amounts spent on information technology is huge. For instance, despite the fact that building societies have quadrupled their spending on information technology between 1985 and 1990 from £69m to £240m (Barchard,1991b), this remains well below the levels of investment taking place in the banking sector. For example, the National Westminster is alone reported to have committed itself to investing £3bn in information technology for the period 1989 to 1993 while the Halifax, the UK's largest society, spends less than £100m a year on information technology (Cane,1989b). Much of the investment in the banking sector is necessary, as was already pointed out, to make good the deficiencies of early computer systems. However, to simply draw the conclusion that size of investment alone automatically confers competitive advantage for the banks deserves a degree of caution.

> "The race between the banks and building societies to develop computer systems equal to the needs of the markets in the 1990s is something of a David and Goliath contest. The advantage might seem to lie with the banks - but building societies, even small ones, seem to be holding their own. The large clearers tend to argue that their vastly larger systems have to be superior, though there are some areas - mortgage processing is one - where the building societies' more customer-focused approach seems to have given them the advantage." (Barchard,1991b).

Changing Role of Information Technology and the Systems Revolution

Looking at recent developments in information technology, it can be seen that its role in the financial services sector is undergoing fundamental change. Traditionally, information technology was seen largely as a means of improving efficiency. Increasingly, it is being seen as the key to effectiveness and a pre-requisite for survival. To evaluate its role in conferring competitive advantage, it is necessary to consider the interaction between business strategy, industry competition and the rate and direction of technical change. It should also be recognised that within the financial services arena there has been a growth in co-operation with rivals, primarily in terms of shared ATM networks. It is, nevertheless, the case that the major purpose of information technology developments in the 1990s relates to improving the responsiveness of financial institutions to customer needs in an increasingly competitive and dynamic marketplace.

It is clear that institutions in the financial services sector share a common goal of making the transition from functional, but monolithic account-based systems, to customer relationship systems based on a more flexible information technology infrastructure capable of adaption within an ever changing business environment. At the heart of this systems revolution lie developments in architected and open systems. Architected systems, for instance, provide users with a development toolbox to make future changes within a computer system. Based on more intuitive fourth generation languages, architected systems are built on a data model which allows systems designers to create the applications structure. Such systems require extensive user participation in the analysis and design process and result, supporters claim, in better quality systems. Essentially, architected systems define the environment in which computer applications may be introduced rather than the applications themselves. In other words, as one commentator put it,

> "Architected systems seem to be an attempt to come to terms with the fact that the life cycle of a typical large IT project would be a decade, while business planning horizons are only two or three years." (Cane,1989a).

An architected system therefore takes account of the need to incorporate a change capability since future business applications remain uncertain.

The National Westminster Bank's current project with IBM aimed at developing an architected system is an example of one of the most ambitious moves towards new generation systems. This initiative includes implementation of the largest DB2 relational database applications in the world which aims to give the bank a state-of-the-art customer relational database. Since banks make most of their profit from domestic retail banking, a customer relational database is seen as a key requirement in a high volume, low cost, environment.

Building societies similarly see customer relational databases as a priority development in their information technology capabilities. For instance, the Leeds Permanent has recently spent £15m on a new customer information system. The Abbey National is currently spending large amounts to build an integrated customer database. The emphasis within the building societies sector is for integrated customer information and even for the smaller regional and local societies this is possible. Typically, they acquire a commercially available package rather than attempt to build a bespoke customer relational database from scratch. Where local and regional societies do develop new systems from scratch, this is done on the basis of a consortium arrangement. It is interesting to note that the Halifax has had an operational database on its customers for over ten years and this was developed using in-house expertise. As is discussed more fully in chapter 8, customer relational databases are seen by retail financial institutions as a key marketing tool to more effectively engage in cross selling to existing customers. Reported in Table 6:II is the current and intended use of customer relational databases by national, regional and local societies.

Table 6:II
Customer Relational Databases

Usage of Customer Relational Databases	National Building Societies n=7	Regional Building Societies n=26	Local Building Societies n=33
Current Use	5	17	17
Intended Future Use	2	5	7

Financial institutions are also increasingly preoccupied with open systems issues as they try to distribute computing to their branches. Open systems in effect allow the same programmes to be run on hardware supplied by different manufacturers. One concern, for example, with IBM's project with the National Westminster Bank is the extent to which this new architected system can support an open systems environment. Open systems offer more cost effective computing with greater competition between hardware and software suppliers since users are not tied to a particular supplier. Thus, by using open systems, both banks and building societies can buy the most effective hardware and software for their needs and keep pace with technological improvements without having always to scrap existing systems. Increased competition amongst suppliers should lead to greater availability of lower cost specialist software, particularly for the *niche* market applications typical of the financial services sector. Similarly, open systems should help in the transferability of information technology skills across functional areas. A further important feature of these new generation systems is an on-line real time availability, although it is the banks that require to make up ground here as many building societies have had real time counter-top branch terminals in place since the early 1980s. Most banks, in contrast, operate their current systems on batch and query processing, mostly on an overnight basis. In view of their importance as key components of the systems revolution, the survey of information technology across building societies sought to establish the current take-up of architected and open systems. Table 6:III summarises the position with regard to these applications in relation to national, regional and local societies. Furthermore, the future intention to develop these same applications is documented.

Table 6:III
Architected and Open Systems

Use of Architected and Open Systems	National Building Societies n=7	Regional Building Societies n=26	Local Building Societies n=33
Current Use of Architected Systems	5	7	0
Intended Future Use	2	7	0
Current Use of Open Systems	2	11	10
Intended Future Use	3	11	6

Telecommunications and Data Networks

The financial services sector is one of the largest users of telecommunications and data networking. The use of local area networks (LANs) for local office computing and wide area data networks (WANs) between geographically separate locations is highly developed in the financial services sector. In keeping with a policy of distributed processing, and a recognition of the centrality of the branch as the focus for marketing activities, networks give expression to the reality of devolved decision-making to branch level. Whilst the national societies have sophisticated network systems, many of the smaller regional and local societies also regard a network system as a priority as, for example, the Portsmouth building society did when it installed a network link connecting its head-office to its twenty branches in 1990. Allied to this increased usage of a network link between head-office and branches is the whole question of using information more effectively, mainly through the development of management and executive information systems aimed at better co-ordination and management of a society's business. This theme of organisational decentralisation within the building society sector is examined more fully in chapter 9.

Document Image Processing

The traditional concept of a building society is one of a paperbound organisation where original documents such as those related to say mortgage or insurance business, need to be available at short notice. There is also the requirement, which adds to this paperbound image, of the handwritten signature being the basis for authorisation. Storage of original documents can pose particular problems where this entails centralised document archives and can also involve considerable cost. Generally, the reliance on the paper media leads to delays in administration, both in the time taken to file and retrieve documents and in the lost time in transmitting documents from one part of the organisation to another. Banks suffer similar problems associated with the storage and use of paper documents. Document Image Processing (DIP) is a technological innovation that only now has begun to be commercially viable on a wide scale due to reducing costs and improvements in technical quality - although it still remains relatively expensive. DIP allows original documents to be electronically scanned at high speed then indexed and stored. When required, documents copied this way can be immediately retrieved. By linking DIP to a network, documents can be electronically distributed to locations throughout the organisation. One major difficulty with DIP concerns the legal status of scanned documents and this issue requires legal clarification. Until this happens, organisations using DIP are really obliged to ensure the continued safekeeping of all original documents. When the full potential of this technology can be realised, it will be possible to dispense with the need to keep these original documents. The Britannia has pioneered the use of DIP since 1987 and has developed the largest installation of its kind in Europe, scanning over 27,000 documents a day. This technology is also being treated with great interest in the banking sector, and the National Westminster, for example, has begun to use DIP in its credit card processing operations. It is important to recognise that DIP is not simply a systems add-on but also provides a new impetus for organisations to understand the operational flow of their business. Often, there are delays dealing with important documents because they pass between too many people or departments. Approaches such as business process redesign (BPR) promise to impact on office procedures by simplifying work flow and reducing the number of stages involved in document handling. It is the combination of DIP and BPR techniques therefore, that hold the promise of significant productivity gains in office work within the financial services sector. Summarised in Table 6:IV are the survey results showing the current and intended use of DIP and workflow changes in office procedures prior to its introduction.

Table 6:IV
Current and Intended Usage of Document Image Processing and Intended Workflow Changes prior to Introduction

Usage of DIP and Workflow Changes	National Building Societies n=7	Regional Building Societies n=26	Local Building Societies n=33
Current Use of DIP	2	1	0
Intended Use of DIP	1	7	3
Future Workflow Changes	1	1	1

Although the results show a modest interest in this technology, its significance is likely to be far greater once the legal status of scanned documents is clarified. The proportion of societies reporting consideration of workflow changes prior to any introduction of DIP is surprisingly low.

Automated Teller Machines

Perhaps one of the most dramatic developments in the use of information technology, certainly from a customer's view point, has been the development over the past two decades, of the Automated Teller Machine (ATM). An ATM allows customers to access their bank or building society account electronically in order to make withdrawals, undertake balance enquiries or make transfers among accounts. With some systems, it is also possible to make deposits and pay bills. There are two distinct types of ATM - intelligent ATMs which control their own functionality and dumb ATM terminals where all functionality is controlled from the centre. Currently, both types of ATM are fairly evenly distributed, but given that it is easier to change facilities at the centre, it is anticipated that dumb ATMs may eventually predominate. There are three large ATM networks. LINK - the network established primarily by building societies; MINTLINK - the network serving the National Westminster, Midland and TSB Group; and 4-ATM which serves Lloyds, Barclays, the Royal Bank of Scotland and other smaller banks. Being a late entrant, LINK was able to provide a competing ATM service at a quarter of the investment made by the banks for their earlier networks. In the UK, it is estimated that the banks have 14,700 ATMs. At present 34 banks and building societies belong to the LINK network, with the Halifax having the largest number of ATMs with 1,581 machines out of a total of 5,500 ATMs in the network. According to the Association for Payment and Clearing Services (APCS) figures, ATM withdrawals were 820m in 1989 and are expected to reach 1.4bn by the year 2000. Table 6:V details building society membership of LINK and the ATM coverage by national, regional and local societies.

Table 6:V
LINK Network - Building Society ATM Coverage

Building Societies	Number of ATMs
National Societies	
Alliance and Leicester	254
Bradford and Bingley	59
Bristol and West	60
Britannia	50
Halifax	1,581
Leeds Permanent	96
National and Provincial	56
Nationwide	650
Woolwich	336
Regional Societies	
Birmingham Midshire	27
Chelsea	6
Coventry	36
Cumberland	3
Derbyshire	24
Dunfermline	5
Furness	2
North of England	6
Northern Rock	30
Norwich and Peterborough	9
Portman	5
Yorkshire	51
Local Societies	
Market Harborough	2

The survey revealed that 4 regional societies and 1 local society intended to offer an ATM service in the future. Although the survey also attempted to ascertain the state of play regarding charges for ATM transactions, the majority of societies declined to provide data on this. In particular, the study sought to determine whether those societies with a small number of ATMs were being disadvantaged by the imposition of charges where their customers used foreign machines. It would have been interesting in turn to know if any charges incurred in this way were passed on to customers. This issue is an important one and, if charges of the kind described do exist, it is possible to speculate that this could influence potential entrants to the ATM network. The issue of charges for foreign transactions apart, shared networks represent co-operation between competing institutions and this has been primarily motivated by the efficiency gains of lower unit costs and enhanced customer convenience made possible by these arrangements. It seems likely that the three large networks that currently exist may combine to make up a single, national, shared network. It has been the economies of scale resulting from shared networks that has helped to support the deployment of ATMs at off premise locations such as supermarkets, garages and factory locations. For the future that there is unlikely to be further dramatic growth in the numbers of ATMs seems to be accepted by most commentators. Rather, what is more likely to happen, is a change in the way that this technology is used in the future. For instance, it is probable that ATMs will be situated more inside lobbies rather than outside in a hole-in-the-wall as institutions attempt deliberately to entice customers back into their branches.

> "Banks and building societies which spent the 1970s and 1980s pushing their customers out into the high street will spend the 1990s trying to entice them back into the shop." (Black,1990).

With the move to shift ATMs inside banks and building societies lobby machines are likely to be more dedicated to the provision of a wider range of customer services, with high street machines being used mainly as cash dispensers. Technologically, there is no reason why ATMs cannot be adapted to offer a wider range of functions, particularly when it is viewed that UK machines lag behind those in Europe and the US in terms of the facilities offered to customers. It would also appear likely that the next generation of ATMs will accept SMART cards. The building society network, LINK, is currently exploring connections with European cashpoints and already has a gateway into PLUS System, an American network. At present, LINK is the only ATM network that can offer balance enquiries across a network of institutions. The requirement to be more customer responsive imposed by an increasingly competitive retail market suggests that, for many institutions, competitive advantage in the use of ATMs will mostly consist of differentiating the services provided from those of their competitors.

Debit Card Networks

The proprietorial nature of ATMs in the retail financial sector may be dented somewhat by the rise of the debit card. Data provided by the Association of Payment and Clearing Services indicate that debit card usage leapt from 67m transactions in 1989 to 192m transactions in 1990, and is projected to top 3bn by the year 2000. This is double the projected ATM transactions figure for the year 2000 quoted earlier. Thus, despite the collapse of the EFTPOS initiative, debit card transactions, particularly through SWITCH and VISA DELTA, have risen spectacularly.

The survey revealed that four national societies have a debit card operation. The Halifax and the Britannia both belong to SWITCH, while the Nationwide and the Alliance and Leicester belong to VISA. The Woolwich indicated its intention to join the VISA network in the future. Two regional societies provide debit cards, the Dunfermline and the Cumberland, both belonging to SWITCH, while the Yorkshire, the West Bromwich and the Chelsea indicated their intention to join a debit card network in the future. It is interesting to speculate about the attractions of a debit card operation as a means of allowing the regional societies in particular the medium whereby they could break into money transmission. Given the anticipated significance of debit card transactions, it is perhaps surprising that so few regional societies have admitted to plans for entering this arena.

Telephone and Home Banking

If debit cards are likely to become an increasingly important innovation, equally probable is that telephone banking will also become more prevalent. Some commentators claim that telephone banking will be in the 1990s what ATMs were to retail banking in the 1980s. When Firstdirect, a subsidiary of the Midland Bank, was launched in 1989, it became the first UK bank that could only be contacted by telephone. Open for business twenty-fours a day, Firstdirect offers a person-to-person service which obviates the need for any form of branch structure. Firstdirect remains unique in its format. Telephone banking more usually is offered as an additional service by institutions. The method usually adopted in telephone banking is for customers to be answered by a recorded voice when they access their bank or building society computer, for instance, as is the case at the Northern Rock and the National and Provincial. Some building societies have been particularly anxious to exploit the potential of telephone banking as an additional marketing tool as they fight for market share for their new products. This explains why, for instance, the Halifax introduced in 1989 its telephone banking service as part of its MAXIM cheque account offering. Furthermore, for some of the smaller building societies, telephone banking has the potential for overcoming their limited geographical coverage. Technically, the introduction of telephone banking is a relatively straightforward matter for those institutions already serviced by an ATM network. By installing a voice response unit which responds to the bleeps made by touchtone telephones, the computer system in turn responds to the voice response unit as though it were an ATM, thus giving access to the customer to services provided by the system. For customers lacking modern touchtone telephones, some institutions offering telephone banking supply tone pads to overcome this difficulty. Some banks have installed voice recognition units which actually listen and respond to callers, although there can be difficulties with this technology in those instances where these systems fail to recognise voice instructions. Nevertheless, with improvements being made to this type of technology, voice recognition units could perhaps become more common.

The survey on information technology attempted to uncover the future plans to introduce telephone banking within the sector. Many societies admitted that they are looking at the feasibility of this, although only one regional society declared its intent to introduce telephone banking in the immediate future. It seems improbable that this use of information technology will not develop as commentators predict, particularly as we enter an era of increasing cost consciousness within the building society sector. Since telephone banking obviates reliance on an expensive branch network, it is an option that societies are no doubt considering carefully. In addition, as those financial institutions that have already ventured into telephone banking report favourably on its impact, interest in this innovation should heighten further.

Home banking, which has been pioneered by the Bank of Scotland, has not as yet made a tremendous impact in the UK financial services sector. Here, customers are connected via personal computers to their bank's computer and can directly access services. No building society, apart from the Nottingham in the early 1980s, has ventured into the realms of home banking, preferring as was noted earlier, to take the telephone banking route as the most appropriate for exploiting the potential offered by information technology to improve the access of customers to services. In the case of the Bank of Scotland initiative in home banking, its value seems to be restricted to only a small proportion of their customers. In contrast, telephone banking appears to be appropriate to a much wider range of customers.

Information Technology Support for Customer Contact

The drive towards increasing the effectiveness of financial intermediaries has led to an awareness of the enormous potential of information technology in the marketing field. Attention has already been drawn to the almost universal concern in financial institutions with customer relational databases. Ultimately, these customer database applications are designed to support customer contacts, and this is being linked to complementary investment in information technology sales applications for use by sales people at the point of contact. In order to more effectively sell complex financial services products, increasing use is being made of PC/notebook based packages which provide expert system guidance for a sales force. Using communication links between mainframe customer databases and PC/notebooks means the sales force has immediate information on customer profiles which can assist in targeting cross-selling. Pioneered by Allied Dunbar (which now has 3,500 portable PCs in the field) face-to-face sales contact in the financial services sector may increasingly be typified by the use of information technology as a support mechanism for sales people. Given the wider range of financial services products offered by the larger building societies, the survey results confirm that sales support systems will be utilised more in the future.

Other Features within the Sector

The survey on information technology not only looked at technical applications, but also considered aspects of the management of information technology projects. In this instance formalisation relates to the use by management of investment appraisal techniques, such as net present value, payback and internal rate of return, to evaluate the likely returns to be gained from technology before adoption. The effectiveness of information technology investment is a matter of central concern, and the survey attempted to uncover the extent to which investment decisions are formalised. Table 6:VI summarises the results in respect of the degree of formalisation of investment decisions. In addition, also reported in Table 6:VI is the number of societies which reported that they had abandoned an IT project.

Table 6:VI
Formalisation of Investment Decisions/IT Project Abandonment

Investment Decision/ Project Abandonment	**National Building Societies n=6**	**Regional Building Societies n=22**	**Local Building Societies n=33**
Formalised Investment Decision for IT Projects	6	13	5
Abandonment of an IT Project	3	5	1

The reported lack of formalisation of investment decisions for regional and local societies is somewhat surprising. Taking the incidence of abandoned projects as an indicator, where less formalised projects would perhaps be expected to be more at risk of collapse, there is no evidence that regional and local societies suffer more failures than national societies where formalisation of investment decision-making is universal. Only 5 regional societies and 1 local society reported the abandonment of an information technology project in the last three years. Whereas, of the 6 national societies which responded to this particular question in the survey, 3 reported that they had abandoned projects in the last three years. Whether this should be regarded as a problem depends on the ability of any given society to absorb the cost of a project failure, and many successful, technologically adaptive organisations have only become so through their willingness to accept the risk of failure as a necessary aspect of technological innovation.

The risks associated with technological innovation may be unavoidable, especially if the project offers first mover advantage and the project is at the envelope of technological developments. The pressure to ensure that information technology investment is effective is not diminished by this point. Across the sector, information technology investment constitutes approximately 15 percent of non-interest costs and the formalisation of investment decision-making that does take place consists mainly of cost benefit analysis and value for money evaluations. Nevertheless, measuring the effectiveness of information technology investments is no easy matter given the problems of quantification, so that a major decision criterion for information technology projects is the extent to which competitive advantage is anticipated to be the outcome.

Societies were asked to identify the information technology application that gave them most competitive advantage. Of those societies that were willing to answer this question, the majority referred to applications that related to their core business, namely mortgage and investment systems. Perhaps as a sign of the times, one national society reported the development of a new arrears system as being likely to give competitive advantage. The general emphasis on traditional core activities, where building societies have a distinctive competence, is clearly where building societies see competitive advantage, and this is obviously reflected in the priority given to the continual upgrading of investment and mortgage systems described earlier.

The survey results also confirmed that national and regional societies generally possess an in-house software development capability. In contrast, only 4 local societies reported expertise in this area. Unlike the banks, national and regional building societies have displayed a do-it-yourself approach to information technology projects and have not relied on outside expertise. Not surprisingly, local societies are more reliant on external help. The current consortia arrangement which exists in respect of the "foresight project", being developed by Omnia ICL, is no doubt a reflection of this. Membership of this consortia comprises of 21 regional and local societies and the project aims to provide computerised back-office administration and accounts which is interfaced with front-office applications.

In chapter 3, the significance of merger activity within the building society sector was discussed. Given the fundamental place of information technology in the business operations of a building society, an important consideration in the viability of any proposed merger is the question of systems compatibility. For instance, technological compatibility proved to be an important inducement in the merger between the Alliance and the Leicester. Equally, the Woolwich and the Nationwide abandoned a proposed merger on the grounds of incompatibility between their information technology systems. The commonality established by the Omnia ICL project is interesting when considered in the light of information technology compatibility and mergers. Especially where there is involvement by both regional and local societies, we can at least speculate that one barrier to the absorption by regional societies of local societies has been removed. Of course, future merger decisions would be based on other criteria in addition to information technology compatibility.

Summary

This chapter has attempted to document recent developments in the use of information technology within the building societies sector. Although building societies cannot match the banks in terms of the huge monetary sums invested in computer systems, it has perhaps been established that building societies are concentrating a lot of their information technology investment in upgrading mortgage and branch systems, thus focusing investment in areas best suited to sustaining their competitive advantage. The kinds of technological innovation within the sector equals that of the banking sector, and evidence has been provided that the sector is beginning to incorporate state of the art developments, such as architected and open systems technology. A major feature of information technology strategy across all segments of the building society sector is the continued evolution of customer relational database applications, which serves to attest to the increased importance of information technology in marketing building society products. Similarly, the existence of sophisticated data networks is helping to transform the role of the building society branch where there is increasing emphasis on devolved decision making and an underscoring of the branch as a future focus for marketing activities.

Building societies have the only nationally branded ATM network LINK, although the survey results revealed that only five societies showed interest in joining an ATM network in the future. Improving the range of functions available from ATMs appears to be inevitable as the networks attempt to differentiate themselves from competitors. LINK is the only ATM network that can offer balance enquiries across a network of institutions, and is very active in establishing European and American connections. We counterposed ATMs and debit card networks and concluded that debit card operations are set to rise spectacularly. Already, national building societies are showing a presence in both the SWITCH and VISA networks, although the entry of regional societies appears to be more cautious. The take-up of telephone banking, with a few notable exceptions, appears more limited than anticipated given the predictions of the future importance of this application made by industry commentators. Again with notable exceptions, the take-up of Document Image Processing is limited although this can be partly explained by the current problems associated with the legal status of scanned documents. Nevertheless, all three developments, debit cards, telephone banking and document image processing are likely to take-off in the future within the sector and the current proponents of these innovations are likely to provide a demonstration effect of their benefits.

Pressures are likely to continue to mount for value for money and effectiveness from information technology investments, and this will lead to greater emphasis on formalisation of investment decisions. Despite the evident absence of formalised investment techniques by local societies in particular, the incidence of abandoned projects is low. National societies have a higher rate of abandoned projects although this result was interpreted as a reflection of the unavoidable risks associated with their often pioneer role in developing new applications. The major emphasis throughout the sector is clearly on refinement and development of computer systems that relate to the core business of investments and mortgages where building societies have competitive advantage.

Self-reliance in information technology appears to be a hallmark of the sector, and many national and regional societies have well developed in-house expertise for handling their own computer developments. In general terms, building societies are less dependent on external help than are the banks. Consortia arrangements do, however, exist for some regional and local societies as in the case of a project managed by Omnia ICL. Since systems compatibility has influenced merger activity in the past, we might speculate about the future influence of consortia arrangements of this kind which generate systems compatibility in a sector that most commentators agree will concentrate rapidly in the future.

7. Product Diversification

Introduction

In chapter 2 the salient characteristics of the 1986 Building Societies Act plus subsequent changes within the Act, which have extended societies' range of activities, were documented. It was emphasised that a central feature of the Act was that societies were offered both enhanced flexibility in terms of the products they could offer on each side of the balance sheet and in addition the opportunity to diversify into other activities. Most societies have availed of the opportunity to expand their product portfolios. What has differed between societies has been the extent of their diversification programmes and indeed the manner in which this diversification has been undertaken. This latter point refers to the fact that some societies have preferred to provide new product ranges in-house while others, in the provision of their new products, have simply acted as agents for other financial institutions.

On the basis of survey work an attempt is made in this chapter to provide a rounded picture of the manner in which societies have expanded their product portfolios. In addition, emphasis is also placed on identifying product lines which initially formed part of societies' diversification programmes but from which they subsequently found it necessary to withdraw. The fact that societies having diversified have found it necessary to fine tune and indeed prune their product portfolios has been due to the prolonged duration of the current economic downturn.

In this chapter an effort is also made to provide insight into the factors which influence the extent of the diversification programmes undertaken by societies. A simple correlation analysis is utilised to determine whether factors such as size, risk, and profit performance, amongst other variables, are of importance in the decision by societies to diversify. Embedded also within this part of the discussion is an attempt to discover whether the strong profit performers are those societies which have undertaken extensive diversification or whether in fact the top performers are those which are narrowly focused in their product range.

Product and Service Developments

Information on the financial products and services on offer from societies was obtained from a telephone survey carried out by the authors during May 1992. Seven societies failed to respond in full to the telephone survey, (five local societies and two regional societies) and were therefore omitted from the analysis. The survey results are detailed in Table 7:I with the information provided on the basis of the national, regional and local society classifications. It is of course virtually impossible to gather information on all services and products on offer from societies, in particular, the various loan subcomponents classified as advances secured on land. At times therefore the discussion is interspersed with a broad based analysis of developments and trends in the holdings of class 2 and class 3 assets by societies.

Two financial product areas stand out in terms of their omission from Table 7:I. They are mortgage advances and savings accounts. It is with these two product lines, where much development and innovation has occurred in recent years, that the discussion commences.

Mortgage advances

The endowment mortgage and the repayment mortgage are the traditional form of the mortgage product. The endowment mortgage is still the most popular of all mortgages. Monthly payments to the building society pay the interest on the loan while the proceeds of a life assurance policy go towards repaying the mortgage at the end of the term in addition to providing life cover. Repayment mortgages in contrast repay both the interest and capital by monthly repayment. A more recent entrant into the market is that of the pension linked mortgage which operates along similar lines to the endowment mortgage. Interest only is paid to the building society during the term of the mortgage, but at the end of the term some of the accrued funds in the linked pension plan go to pay off the mortgage in full. The advantage of this scheme is that the borrower receives tax relief on his pension premiums. A further development is that of the fixed-rate mortgage where the interest rate on the loan is held constant over an agreed period of time. In most instances the time period is between 1 and 5 years.

Capped mortgages are somewhat similar, except that instead of the interest rate remaining the same, the interest rate levied can go down if market rates generally go down but it is guaranteed not to go above the capped rate. Some societies also offer low-start mortgages on which repayments are scheduled so that the burden is lighter in the early years. Many societies offer temporary discounts on larger loans and also to first time buyers. Another mortgage similar in form to the endowment mortgage is that of the personal equity plan, PEP, mortgage. The PEP mortgage is free from capital gains and income tax. A PEP mortgage operates quite simply. The borrowers' contributions are invested through the PEP in either a unit trust or shares. The Halifax, for example arranges most of its PEP mortgages through the Global Advantage PEP-linked unit trust, which is managed by Halifax Standard Trust Management, a joint venture with Standard Life.

Savings accounts

Product development has also been a feature of the savings market. Until the early 1970s ordinary share accounts made up approximately 90 percent of the funds invested in building societies. These accounts were such that savings could be paid in or withdrawn without notice with the interest rate paid moving in line with market rates, (see Kaye, 1989). In the mid 1970s, spurred by large swings in the volume of funds moving in and out of accounts, societies began to offer term share accounts. These accounts offer a fixed rate above the ordinary share rate in return for the funds being left with the society for a fixed term. The length of this term is usually between one and five years. In the early 1980s societies also started to offer short notice high interest accounts. The period of notice was usually between seven days and three months. No notice accounts followed shortly after, although most of these accounts required a minimum balance. Many of these no notice accounts, as well as the term accounts, now adopt a tiered interest rate approach whereby the interest rate paid is dependent upon the amount invested. One savings account which is documented in Table 7:I is that of the Tax-exempt Special Savings Account, (TESSA).

The introduction of TESSA in 1991 has made it possible for everyone to enjoy tax-free savings whatever their individual tax position. From Table 7:I it is clear that almost all societies now provide, through TESSA, a range of tax efficient products. The abolition of composite rate tax on building societies savings accounts has resulted in all accounts now paying interest either gross or net according to the tax status of the recipient. Gross interest accounts have proved particularly valuable to non-working wives.

Societies which have entered into the provision of money transmission services have recently begun to withdraw a limited number of their short and no-notice savings accounts. In addition the Halifax for one has introduced a system of charges for low balance high activity accounts. The obvious implication of such a change is that the Halifax is attempting to encourage customers to avail of their purpose built money transmission account.

Table 7:I
Product Profile

Product Range	National Building Societies n=10	Regional Building Societies n=31	Local Building Societies n=41
Secured Loans	10	29	26
Unsecured Loans	9	23	16
Cheque Book Account and Cheque Card	6	6	1
ATMs	9	11	1
Credit Cards	4	2	0
General Insurance	10	21	24
Investment Advice	10	28	35
Unit Trusts	7	11	12
Pension Plans	9	23	28
Personal Equity Plans	7	21	17
TESSA's	10	31	39
Share Service	1	4	2
Estate Agencies	7	12	5
Property Development	7	5	0
Off-Shore Foreign Services	10	4	0

Money transmission

So far it has been mainly the larger societies which have availed of the opportunity to offer an extensive money transmission service. Six of the ten national societies now offer an interest bearing current account with cheque book. The Nationwide, in May 1987, was the first to introduce this current account service, the Woolwich followed suit in early 1989 and the Halifax in Autumn 1989. Initially the Halifax wanted to provide an electronic banking service. It was forced instead, through customer pressure, to introduce a paper based system. The acquisition of Girobank by the Alliance and Leicester provided the society with ready made expertise in personal banking, in particular a well developed cheque book backed by an efficient postal and telephone banking service. In May 1991 the Britannia launched a multi-function card combining SWITCH debit, a £100 cheque guarantee and ATM facilities. Customers receive a cheque book only if they request one. At present some 80 percent of customers have requested this additional facility. Cheque clearing for the Britannia is carried out through the Co-op bank which also provides a clearing facility for Northern Rock, one of the regional societies to offer a current account and cheque book service. Bristol and West is the other national society which provides a cheque book service.

The Halifax also became a member of the SWITCH debit card payment system in 1991. They indicate encouraging growth in the use of SWITCH with transactions trending around 500,000 a month. Three other national societies offer debit cards. Britannia which is a member of the SWITCH system, the Alliance and Leicester a member of VISA and the Nationwide which belongs to VISA/DELTA. Wyllie (1992) reports that most banks already have debit cards attached to their current accounts. Abbey National, for example, in December 1991 launched a VISA/DELTA debit card, with cheque guarantee and ATM functions, on its current account. During one six week period, the bank had 100,000 customers applying for the card. Wyllie further adds that by the end of the century debit cards are likely to be used in preference to cheques for the majority of retail purchases with cheque volumes falling to around two thirds of current levels. If there is a shift in customer preference away from expensive to offer paper based systems and towards electronic substitutes this is in turn likely to encourage more societies to provide an extensive money transmission service. Nevertheless, even with reduced operational expenses, the cost of operating a money transmission service is likely to rule out all but the national societies and the more single minded of the regional societies. Among the regional societies determined to offer an all-round banking service are the Northern Rock, the Portman, the Chelsea, the Norwich and Peterborough, the North of England and the Cumberland. Although as with the first rush of national societies into cheque books, personal loans and credit cards, many of the banking products sold by these regional societies are not their own products but those of a bank. While the adoption of such a policy saves upon product development costs, which are likely to be high given the investment in information technology required to launch such banking products, it nevertheless effectively reduces the society to a sales outlet for somebody else. Relatively new advances in money transmission which rely heavily on information technology, such as telephone banking and debit cards, are examined in more detail in chapter 6. Information technology adoption by building societies is the subject area under scrutiny in chapter 6.

Another aspect of the money transmission mechanism documented in Table 7:I is that of credit card operations. Only a very limited number of societies offer such a service and for the most part they are the larger of the national societies, the Halifax, the Alliance and Leicester, the Leeds Permanent and the National and Provincial. One surprise here is the decision of the Leeds Permanent to offer a credit card service given that it alone among the top five societies decided not to enter into transactional retail banking. Of the regional societies the Northern Rock and the Norwich and Peterborough also offer a credit card facility. There are a number of reasons why societies have been and are likely to remain reluctant to issue credit cards. These include the substantial launch costs; the saturation of the market; the threat of retailers levying a surcharge for purchase by credit card; the increasing displacement of credit cards by charge cards; plus the fact that societies initially have lost money on credit card operations. A good example of this latter point is that of the Leeds Permanent VISA card which only moved into profit in 1991 having made substantial losses in the first two years of operation. The shift in profitability is in part due to Leeds VISA being the UK's most successful affinity card, but also and perhaps of even more importance is that the Leeds, in conjunction with the Halifax and a number of the banks, have introduced a charge fee for their credit cards.

Crucial in the ability of societies to issue credit cards and provide money transaction accounts with overdraft facilities is that they are permitted to engage in unsecured lending. Under the 1988 review of Schedule 8, societies which meet the qualifying commercial asset criteria are able to offer unsecured loans up to £10,000 (at present, November 1992, proposals are before parliament to raise this limit to £25,000). Initially the majority of societies which provided unsecured lending acted as an agent for a finance house or other specialist provider of consumer loans. The three main providers of finance for societies were, and still are, Chartered Trust, Standard Trust and Mercantile Credit. The larger societies have, however, increasingly started to provide unsecured lending from their own funds. At present the top five societies all offer own-money unsecured loans.

Investment advice

The Financial Services Act which came into force in 1987 formed part of long-term government policy to provide protection for the consumer under the auspices of self-regulatory bodies. The legislation itself covers an extensive range of activities. Drake (1987) succinctly summarised its coverage for building societies as all areas of building society business other than deposit taking, mortgage and commercial lending, wholesale fund raising and deposit based personal pension schemes. The latter are outside the scope of the Act as deposits are not viewed to be investments.

The concept of polarisation was also introduced under the Act. Under polarisation societies had to choose between either giving independent financial advice or becoming tied to one company and its financial products, (see chapter 2 for more details on the Financial Services Act).

Many societies initially opted to provide independent financial advice in the belief that this would fit in best with customer requirements. Very quickly most of these societies formed the opinion that offering independent financial advice was expensive and that customers appeared not to unduly require best advice. The tied option also allows staff to concentrate upon a restricted range of products which reduces training and administration costs and in addition offers higher commission fees.

The Bradford and Bingley now stands alone among national building societies in offering independent financial advice. Indeed its position became even more marked in 1991 when the National Westminster announced that from January 1993 it would no longer provide independent financial advice. The National Westminster is the last of the major banks to abandon independent status. This of course must be set against the fact that most of the larger institutions also have subsidiaries which give independent advice. The Nationwide is, for example, tied to Guardian Royal Exchange. If a customer enters one of the Nationwide's branches and requests advice on endowment mortgages, life assurance or pensions they will be told that advise can only be given on Guardian Royal Exchange products. If the customer insists on independent financial advice they will be referred to Nationwide's subsidiary company Nationwide Independent Financial Services.

Of the regional societies, most now operate on a tied basis. The Birmingham Midshires, for example, relinquished its independent status in January 1992 when it tied to Sun Life Corporation. The society also formed an independent arm for customers requiring independent advice. The largest regional society still to retain its independent status is the Yorkshire. Murray (1992) stated that independent status for the Yorkshire has helped to differentiate the society from other organisations and has proved its worth financially.

Life assurance

Although not explicitly detailed in Table 7:I all societies offer life assurance. The key feature in life assurance in recent times is not that more societies are switching ties from one life company to another but rather that societies are increasingly looking into the viability of setting up their own life company.

Following the review of building society powers in 1987 societies since 1988 have had the option subject to qualifying asset limits to own up to 100 percent of the equity of a life assurance company. Murray (1992) argued that the advantages of the adoption of such a course of action are enormous.

> "It gives societies control over the manufacture of products as well as their distribution; it keeps costs and expenses down; and it gives them a new profit centre. It also keeps other organisations away from their customer base."

To date three national societies have established life subsidiaries, either by buying a life company or forming a joint venture with a life company. The National and Provincial launched National and Provincial Life Assurance Ltd during 1990. It was a joint venture with General Accident which in addition to providing a range of insurance products also provides investment and pension products. On January 1, 1990 Britannia Life commenced operations following the acquisition by the Britannia of FS Assurance Ltd. During 1991 Britannia Life acquired Crusader Insurance from Cigna. As well as bringing on board an additional 200,000 policy holders the acquisition has permitted Britannia Life to extend further the services on offer, particularly in the area of unit linked life assurance and pension business. The Woolwich established Woolwich Life Assurance in October 1991 to offer mortgage-related life assurance products. The expectation must be that societies, particularly those with an extensive network system through which products can be sold, will increasingly move into the production and sale of their own life and related products.

General insurance

General insurance is another product area which societies have entered *en masse*, either through teaming up with an established insurance company or through operating as a fully fledged broker of general insurance. Many societies considered general insurance as a natural extension of their product range particularly home and contents insurance and sickness, accident and redundancy cover for mortgage repayments. The sales potential of societies through their branch network and customer bases has also encouraged many societies to enter into the provision of other aspects of general insurance. These have included motor, health and travel insurance.

In terms of underwriting general insurance scope is limited in that societies are permitted to hold no more than 15 percent of the equity of a general insurance company. This is in part a consequence of the fact that the risks involved in underwriting general insurance are much more pronounced. Given the adverse conditions faced by many insurance companies in recent years this equity limitation appears to have been farsighted. Lloyds of London, in the middle of 1992, declared losses of over £2bn for the 1989 three year account. The companies which make up the membership of the Association of British Insurers also posted a loss for 1991. Their aggregate trading loss for 1991 on general insurance was some £3.3bn. Norwich Union, the mutually-owned insurer, suffered an 81 percent increase in pre-tax losses on its general insurance business in 1991, from £147.7m to £267.7m. Prudential, the UK's largest life insurer, announced in March 1992 that it would no longer sell general insurance in the UK through brokers after losses of £77m from general business in 1991. The Prudential is retaining some presence in home-related general insurance primarily because they view there to be a natural synergy between home insurance and their life, pensions and savings products. Legal and General are also in the process of considering the viability of broker based general insurance. In the main these sharp rises in underwriting losses have occurred as a consequence of the recession; adverse weather conditions; and crime related losses, most notably theft. This has resulted in an upward spiral in premiums levied, particularly in the areas of motor insurance, legal protection and home and contents policies. Insurance companies are also placing a squeeze on commission. One example is that of Sun Alliance which early in 1992 refused to accept commission terms offered to it for block business by Abbey National. The position faced by many societies involved in general insurance can be summarised by a quotation from the 1991 annual report and accounts of the Yorkshire building society

> "General insurance earnings have held up well during 1991, although current claims experience on many types of risk is likely to put pressure on levels of commission in future, as the society tries to restrain the level of premium increases."

Equity based products

Equity related products, such as unit trusts and PEPs as well as stockbroking activities are another area of diversification open to societies. From Table 7:I it is clear that societies, across groupings, are highly involved in unit trust and PEP business but are much less involved in stockbroking. As described earlier, the extension of societies' activities into PEPs and unit trusts relates in large part to the fact that they can be utilized for mortgage repayment. A number of societies have also entered these markets in a more fundamental way.

Own brand unit trusts are offered by a number of the large societies. These societies have either purchased a unit trust subsidiary which is what the Britannia and the National and Provincial have done, or they have entered into the market in the form of a joint venture as has the Halifax in conjunction with Standard Life, or they have set up unit trusts and farmed out the management as has the Woolwich. This latter fund deserves special mention as it was set up in 1991 to specifically offer straightforward unit trusts to a wider market of potential investors. The trust also offers a PEP option. The fund is managed by Mercury Asset Management and is sold through the society's branch network. As of August 1992 the fund had £58m under management, 24,000 investors and was ranked 16th out of 98 in the UK general equity sector. Given that over two-thirds of the investors in the Woolwich Stockmarket Fund are new to unit trust investment this vehicle appears already to be a successful market and investment tool for the Woolwich.

PEPs have been available from the beginning of 1987. It was not until 1989, when the terms upon which money could be invested in PEPs were improved, that money began to flow into these vehicles in substantial amounts. The tax shield, in terms of the amount which can now be invested in a general PEP stands at £6,000 but, in addition, at the start of 1992, the single company PEP was introduced with a tax shield allowance of £3,000, although it should be said that self-select PEPs could also be single company in form. In theory therefore, an investor can now combine these two allowances and put £9,000 into a PEP-sheltered single share. Earlier it was noted that most building societies are happy to accept PEPs as a means of building up a fund to pay back the capital element of a house loan. Some societies have developed specialised *niches* for themselves in the PEP market. A good case in point is the Bradford and Bingley which is now one of the main players in the PEP market, particularly corporate PEPs. In the case of corporate PEPs, an individual company's shares are traded by an administrator under a sponsoring agreement between the company and the administrator. Through the Bradford and Bingley it is possible to purchase PEP sheltered shares in a number of leading companies including BP, Glaxo, Beecham, Tate and Lyle, Christian Salvesen, First Leisure, BAT and Whitbread. More generally societies involved in PEPs have designed these products to ensure that they maintain their customer base. Essentially PEPs are targeted at the customer who has built up savings through a traditional building society account and is now considering branching into equity based savings.

A stockbroking service is also on offer from a number of societies. The Yorkshire holds a minority stake, (19.1 percent), in BWD Securities of Huddersfield. The Norwich and Peterborough has a stockbroking subsidiary, Waters Lunniss. Again the branch network of these societies make it a convenient option for customers wishing to buy or sell shares. Other societies which offer a share dealing service invariably do so in conjunction with an outside stockbroker. A case in point is the National and Provincial's telephone share dealing and advice service which is operated in conjunction with Capel-Cure Myers Capital Management Limited.

A number of banks also offer a share-dealing service. Abbey National joined their number in early 1992 when it announced that for Abbey National shares it was bringing in-house both telephone and postal share-dealing which had previously been farmed out to other companies and also Abbey's share register which had been run by Lloyds bank.

Share-dealing is likely to remain an interest of only a minority of societies. In part this is due to the fact that the market for share services aimed at small investor is already well served but also, as argued in the Investors Chronicle (Feb 1992), the number of people holding shares in the future is anticipated to decline. Indeed a number of societies having entered the share-dealing market have subsequently withdrawn. The most notable was the Cheltenham and Gloucester which introduced a share-dealing service in 1988 and withdrew in 1989. The reason put forward for withdrawal was that

> "the profitability of the service could no longer be sustained against the background of escalating costs, in particular those relating to compliance with the Financial Services Act." (C and G Annual Report, 1989).

Estate agencies

Estate agency was one of the earliest areas of strategic diversification for societies. Snowball (1992) cited a range of reasons for the entry of societies into estate agency. A number of these reasons stand out as more important than the others. They are that entry would help take away market share from banks and insurance companies, it would enable the client base of societies to grow and widen and it would enable them to capture additional mortgage business and cross sell other financial products.

While from a strategic perspective the purchase of estate agencies by many of the national and larger regional societies may have been theoretically correct it nevertheless proved in the majority of instances to be a costly venture. Snowball (1992) stated that

> "When in mid-1988, the residential property market virtually collapsed with drops of up to 50% in trading volume and revenue in parts of the country, the new entrants to the industry were badly caught, badly stretched, incurred heavy losses and, in consequence, suffered major problems of organisation, confidence and stability."

In consequence most societies have considerably pruned their estate agency outlets while others have opted to withdraw from this market. For example the Cheltenham and Gloucester, in December 1991, sold off its estate agency business to Hambro Countrywide.

Off-shore activity

A number of societies have also established off-shore subsidiaries, (see Table 7:I). For the most part these are located in either the Channel Islands or the Isle of Man. The rush to establish these subsidiaries occurred towards the end of 1989 and the start of 1990. At that juncture societies were of the opinion that with the introduction of independent taxation from April 1990 many investors would want to switch money from building society accounts, liable to composite rate tax, to accounts paying interest gross. The objective of the subsidiaries was therefore to attract high balance investments from UK and expatriate accounts. In the final event the 1990 budget actually proposed the abolition of the composite rate tax system and since April 1991 societies have been able to pay interest gross. There still remains a benefit for the taxpayer because with the offshore account interest is paid gross with tax paid at a later date, while in the UK interest is received after the deduction of basic rate tax. There is also a European dimension to off-shore activity. This is explored in detail in chapters 11 and 12.

Advances secured on land

Although not explicitly detailed in Table 7:I all societies have been involved, in some cases quite extensively, in the provision of advances secured on property other than owner-occupied houses. Such advances are defined as class 2 assets, (see chapter 2). The BSC Annual Report, 1989-90 provides a useful summary of the various forms that such loans have taken in recent years. They indicate that class 2 lending has focused upon small scale loans secured on owner-occupied commercial premises, particularly shops with living accommodation; loans to housing associations; loans secured on tenanted income producing commercial property; loans to developers secured on residential developments; and loans on commercial developments.

In an effort to gain insight into the extent of class 2 lending the opportunity is taken in Table 7:II to subdivide commercial assets into its three components, class 1, class 2 and class 3 assets, for societies at the aggregate level and across the respective groupings.

Table 7:II
Asset Class as a Proportion of Commercial Assets (%)

Table 7:IIA Class 3 Assets

Building Society Groupings	Class 3 Assets/Commercial Assets		
	1989	1990	1991
National Societies	0.82	1.1	1.15
Regional Societies	0.23	0.28	0.32
Local Societies	0.0	0.0	0.0
All Societies	0.72	0.95	1.0

Table 7:IIB Class 2 Assets

Building Society Groupings	Class 2 Assets/Commercial Assets		
	1989	1990	1991
National Societies	2.73	3.22	2.96
Regional Societies	3.41	4.4	4.66
Local Societies	4.41	5.88	6.66
All Societies	2.86	3.45	3.28

Table 7:IIC Class 1 Assets

Building Society Groupings	Class 1 Assets/Commercial Assets		
	1989	1990	1991
National Societies	96.45	95.68	95.89
Regional Societies	93.36	95.32	95.02
Local Societies	95.59	94.12	93.34
All Societies	96.42	95.6	95.72

The picture which emerges from Table 7:IIB is that class 2 lending is of much more importance for regional and local societies than it is for national societies. Indeed it transpires that the importance of class 2 assets is most pronounced for the local society classification. This reflects two factors. First that many regional and local societies had class 2 type assets before the 1986 Act. Second, for many local societies class 2 diversification is the only option as the qualifying commercial asset size of £100m restricts many of them from engaging in class 3 lending, (the zero percentage figures quoted in Table 7:IIA for local societies belie the fact that a very small number are involved in class 3 lending).

Although the various society groupings in Table 7:IIB are well beneath their prescribed limits for class 2 loans this does mask the fact that a number of societies have specialised quite heavily in this category of asset. For example, for the end year 1991 a total of 15 societies had more than 10 percent of their commercial assets in the form of class 2 loans. Of that number, 5 were regional societies, whilst the remainder were local societies. The Manchester building society with almost 16 percent of its commercial assets tied up in class 2 advances is the society which has ventured the most into this loan category. The regional societies strong in this lending field are the Skipton, the Stroud and Swindon, the Kent Reliance,the North of England and the Progressive.

Class 2 assets more than doubled between 1988 and 1989, thereafter the rate of growth slowed down considerably. Between 1989 and 1990 the growth rate was approximately 50 percent before falling off to less than 10 percent between 1990 and 1991. The slowdown in the growth of class 2 lending is partly a result of the bad experiences of a number of societies over the past couple of years, (see BSC Annual Report, 1991-1992). This bad experience has stemmed not only from the general downturn in the commercial property market but also from the financial difficulties which many house builders have found themselves in due to the continued fall off in house turnovers. An increase in provisions for losses against other advances secured on land has led many societies to seriously review their class 2 lending policies and in certain instances curtail aspects of business within this asset category. A case in point is the National and Provincial. In their 1991 annual report they stated

"We have maintained a prudent balance within our loan portfolio with no new housing development lending during 1991 .... ."

Other examples of major societies which have cut back considerably on their class 2 exposure are the Alliance and Leicester and the Skipton. Profit performance at the Alliance and Leicester fell by some 50 percent during 1991. This in the main was due to bad debt provisions emanating from its large portfolio of commercial lending. The Alliance and Leicester subsequently withdrew from this market. Profits at the Skipton fell by over 60 percent during 1991. Again the problem centred upon heavy bad debt provisions for commercial lending. They also stopped lending in this market.

Property development and management

Societies have also been involved in the establishment of subsidiaries to enable them to become more directly involved in property development and management. These societies are either the national or the larger regional societies, (see Table 7:I). The investment undertaken by societies in property development can be viewed as a

"mixture of commercial acumen with a dose of philanthropy." (Kallas, 1990).

The Woolwich, for example, through its subsidiary Woolwich Assured Homes has attempted to bring flexibility to the housing market by creating homes for rent and targeting them at groups in need: those waiting to sell; the divorced partner with nowhere to live; the elderly who have to sell in order to avoid the cost of house repairs; and those locating to new areas. Nationwide through its associated company Quality Street has invested heavily in rented housing. While approximately 50 percent of these funds are invested in top-quality homes for executives and holiday home owners, a sizeable proportion is also targeted at providing rented accommodation for the homeless, waiting-list applicants and special needs groups.

For the same reasons that societies have felt it necessary to cut back upon their commercial property lending to other parties they have also reviewed the exposure limits of their own subsidiaries involved in property development. The experience of the Cheltenham and Gloucester with its property development subsidiary is broadly representative of the situation faced by most other societies with exposure in this market.

"Although two of C and G Homes's total of 14 sites were built out to completion during the course of the year, sales everywhere were slow. This has naturally lengthened the expected duration of the company's projects and has led to losses during the year. Given the state of the UK house-building market in 1991 no new projects were started." (C and G Annual Report, 1991).

The financing of property development via a subsidiary as with other investments through subsidiaries plus loans on an unsecured basis are all classified as class 3 assets. From Table 7:IIA it can be seen that national and regional societies have been involved in the creation of such assets. Local societies in the main are barred from involvement in class 3 lending due to the qualifying commercial asset limit on societies of £100m.

In aggregate terms class 3 assets grew by a factor of 2 both between 1988 and 1989 and between 1989 and 1990 but the growth rate reduced to approximately 25 percent between 1990 and 1991. Much of the initial growth in class 3 lending can be ascribed to societies investing in appropriate mortgage companies. These companies are subsidiaries which were established to purchase mortgage books from other lenders and then to administer them. Direct involvement in housing development, estate agency and unsecured lending were also key factors in the initial sharp growth of class 3 lending. While over the period there has been a continued steady upward growth in unsecured lending these other areas have been subject to a pronounced decline. Indeed, as earlier indicated, retrenchment and disinvestment have become a much more common occurrence. Out of the top six national societies, for example, three have experienced a reduction in their weighted holding of class 3 assets during the period 1989 to 1991. While in part a bias is introduced into the inter-temporal comparison due to transfer of engagements of smaller societies, not involved in class 3 lending, to some of these larger societies, there nevertheless appears to be some evidence of a cut back on diversification.

From the analysis to date it is clear that diversification has come in many guises. At one end of the spectrum there are the larger national societies which have endeavoured, through the provision of as wide a range of financial services and products as possible, to compete on all fronts with the retail banks. At the other end of the scale local and smaller regional societies have tended to diversify into those areas which are heavily tied in with their core mortgage and savings business. What has not emerged from the discussion is the factors of influence in determining the extent of diversification by individual societies. Another key question which has as yet remained unanswered is whether societies engaged in more extensive diversification programmes have experienced enhanced profit performance. In the remainder of this chapter an attempt is made to provide answers to both these questions.

Diversification : The Factors of Influence

Most of the available literature on the diversification strategies of financial intermediaries concentrates on US banking institutions. In this part of the analysis a broad overview of this and related literature on diversification is undertaken. From this overview potential determinants of diversification are identified and their relevance, or otherwise, as factors of influence in the diversification strategies of UK building societies is then assessed.

A useful place to start when attempting to isolate factors influencing diversification is in the area of strategic management. Within this general discipline there is a proliferation of models which purport to demonstrate the conditions under which a product diversification programme may be pursued. Examples of two such models may be found in the work of Ansoff (1965) and Ramanujam and Varadarajan (1989). Drawing from these two works and others a broad array of factors can be identified as potential diversification influences. The first is that of external conditions. Under this heading product obsolescence, new opportunities for profit and growth plus shifts in the economic environment all come to the fore as factors of relevance. The second generic classification is that of internal conditions. This refers to organisational features internal to the institution. In this instance, factors such as excess resources or perhaps even the existence of a skills base which can be easily adapted in the introduction of new product ranges are viewed as important. The third and final group of factors perceived to be relevant can be broadly categorised as management objectives. Factors considered to be of importance in this case include the risk attitudes of the main decision makers within the organisation and indeed their attitude towards company growth and enhanced company profitability.

What then of the relevance of these factors for UK building societies? Perhaps the factor most likely to be of relevance is that of asset size. The hypothesis is that the smaller the asset base of a society the less likely it is to engage in diversification. This is of course true for societies with an asset base of £100m or less in that their diversification options are limited under the 1986 Act. Even without this restriction local societies, in general, plus many of the smaller regional societies, are likely to be constrained in their diversification plans by their asset size. Most of these societies, for example, only have a small number of individuals in a managerial position, consequently demands on their time are such that a diversification programme is well down the list of priorities. Coupled with this the investment required to finance diversification, when taken as a proportion of total assets, is likely to be so large that the risk of the diversification programme in all probability outweighs its perceived advantages. The impact of asset size on diversification can to some extent be validated through the findings reported in Table 7:I which indicated that the more exhaustive diversification programmes have been carried out by national societies. Further supporting evidence for the positive relationship between size and diversification can be found in Table 7:III. In Table 7:III correlation coefficients are provided both for class 3 assets as a proportion of commercial assets against total asset size and for the sum of class 2 and class 3 assets as a proportion of commercial assets again against total asset size. The computed values are provided for the years 1989 through to 1991 and also for each of the society groupings.

Table 7:III
Correlation Between Asset Size and Diversification

Building Society Groupings	Correlation Coefficients: Class 3 Assets/ Asset Size			Class 2 + Class 3 Assets/Asset Size		
	1989	1990	1991	1989	1990	1991
National Societies	0.67	0.37	-0.08	0.67	-0.27	-0.32
Regional Societies	-0.24	0.39	0.31	0.23	-0.12	-0.11
Local Societies*	-	-	-	0.26	0.01	-0.1
All Societies	-	-	-	0.74	-0.07	-0.13

*Omitted from the analysis given the limited number of local societies engaged in class 3 lending.

First of all taking class 3 assets as the proxy for diversification a positive relationship does indeed emerge between size and diversification during 1989 and 1990 for both national and regional societies. While this positive correlation still holds firm during 1991 for regional societies a weakly negative value emerges for national societies. The turnaround in the value for national societies is no doubt a function of the fact that larger national societies, having undertaken much broader diversification programmes, are more likely to have entered into unprofitable product lines from which they subsequently have found it necessary to withdraw. This disinvestment activity has consequently placed downward pressure upon their weighted holding of class 3 assets relative to other societies in the group.

Tacit support for this analysis also emerges from the computed correlation coefficients between the sum of class 2 and class 3 assets and asset size. For 1989, across each of the society subcategories and for societies as a whole, there is a strong positive correlation between asset size and diversification. Thereafter the correlation for the most part becomes negative, with the relationship much more pronounced for 1991. Again the negative values are not taken to imply that recently smaller societies have, in absolute terms, been involved in relatively greater levels of diversification. Rather the belief is that the more diversified societies have placed a significant break on their diversification resulting in either a very marginal increase or a fall in the sum of class 2 plus class 3 assets as a percentage of total commercial assets.

One additional feature of note in Table 7:III is the more acute nature of the negative relationship for 1990 and 1991 when class 2 assets are introduced into the equation. This suggests that larger societies have curtailed advances secured on land and accords well with the analysis earlier in this chapter which found societies retreating from aspects of commercial property lending.

Market threat is a concept which appears with significant frequency in many of the strategic management models devoted to diversification. For an undiversified institution it is not unrealistic to assume that the advent of new market competitors, raising the prospects of reduced profitability, provides a strong rationale for product diversification. The relevance of market threat is quite pertinent for building societies. From market share statistics it is clear that at certain times societies have faced major competition from other lending institutions for their traditional mortgage business. Towards the end of 1987, for example, the market share of institutions other than building societies stood at marginally over 50 percent. It could therefore be argued that during such periods of threat building societies are likely to be encouraged to implement product diversification strategies. Support for the hypothesis of market threat, leading to an increased propensity to diversify can be found in Silverman and Castaldi (1992). On the basis of a survey of small banks in the US the authors concluded that those institutions which anticipated the greatest increases in competitive intensity were the most interested in diversification options.

Closely linked to the concept of market threat is that of profitability. There are, however, competing forces at work when it comes to profitability. At one level it could be argued that those institutions with higher levels of profits have greater resources with which to undertake investment in new products. Yet at the same time high returns in core business could negate against diversification to the extent that the institution is encouraged to reinvest in its mainstream business. In such a situation if an institution does undertake diversification it is more than likely to be in product areas which are only marginally tangential to its main product line. From the perspective of building societies an obvious example would be insurance products tied into mortgage business. Limited related diversification has indeed proved itself to be very successful in other industry sectors. Miles (1982) provided a detailed analysis of limited diversification in the tobacco industry and concluded that it proved to be a highly successful option. In a broader based non-industry specific study, Rumelt (1982), reached similar conclusions as to the benefit of highly focused diversification. This may also hold true for building societies. Among national societies, for example, it appears that societies which have undertaken extensive diversification programmes have to date fared less well than those which have been more circumspect in their diversification plans. Prime examples of societies which have suffered a profit downturn as a consequence of diversification are the Nationwide, the Alliance and Leicester and the Woolwich. In contrast societies such as the Cheltenham and Gloucester and the Leeds Permanent which have undertaken more limited diversification are among the top profit performers.

Support for the hypothesis of an inverse relationship between profit and diversification can also be obtained from Table 7:IV. Presented in Table 7:IV are correlation coefficients for profit against diversification for each of the society classifications. Profit is measured as end year total profits divided by mean total assets, while diversification is measured as before.

Table 7:IV
Correlation Between Profit and Diversification

Building Society Groupings	Correlation Coefficients: Class 3 Assets/Profit 1989	1990	1991	Class 2 + Class 3 Assets/Profit 1989	1990	1991
National Societies	-0.54	-0.14	-0.39	-0.54	-0.08	-0.55
Regional Societies	0.01	-0.33	0.01	-0.01	-0.29	-0.23
Local Societies*	-		-	0.11	-0.01	0.19
All Societies	-		-	-0.16	-0.13	-0.01

*Omitted from the analysis given the limited number of local societies engaged in class 3 lending.

The broad overall picture from Table 7:IV is one of negative correlations between profit and diversification with the effect most pronounced in the case of national societies. Where positive coefficients result they tend to be close to zero which suggests that if a relationship does exist it is extremely weak in form. A degree of caution must nevertheless be exercised in interpreting these figures. The negative values should not be taken to imply that broad based diversification is necessarily unwise. It must be recognised that the coefficients are computed at a point in time and if and when market conditions improve the more extensively diversified societies may be better placed to take advantage of the upturn. In addition, diversification requires considerable investment capital which itself initially imparts a downward bias into the profit figures of the society.

Risk, where risk is measured in terms of the variability of profits over time, could be viewed as a further influence in the decision to diversify. Silverman and Castaldi (1992) in their study of small US banks found a positive correlation between past variations in profit and diversification. Profit variation in their model was computed as the standard deviation of profits over a prior 3 year period. Silverman and Castaldi (1992) suggested that there were two primary reasons for the said relationship between diversification and risk. The first is that institutions with higher profit variability may consider diversification as a means of stabilising earnings. This is akin to the old adage of not placing all one's eggs in the same basket. The second argument put forward by the authors, and one which is somewhat at odds with the first, starts with the supposition that diversification itself is risky. They then argued that those institutions which have taken greater risks in the past, as indicated by their profit variability, may have higher risk tolerance levels and as a consequence are more favourably disposed to diversification strategies which others would view as too risky.

Correlations between risk and diversification are reported in Table 7:V. The risk measure employed was that of the variability in profits as a percentage of mean total assets over the period 1989 to 1991.

Table 7:V
Correlation Between Risk and Diversification

Building Society Groupings	Correlation Coefficients: Class 3 Assets/Risk			Class 2 + Class 3 Assets/Risk		
	1989	1990	1991	1989	1990	1991
National Societies	-0.43	-0.32	0.26	-0.42	0.62	0.39
Regional Societies	0.38	0.22	0.0	0.39	0.16	0.05
Local Societies*	-	-	-	0.11	-0.06	-0.06
All Societies	-	-	-	-0.09	0.04	0.02

*Omitted from the analysis given the limited number of local societies engaged in class 3 lending.

With the exception of the 1989 values for national societies the general picture to emerge is one of a positive correlation between risk and diversification. While this lends support to the arguments put forward by Silverman and Castaldi (1992) a degree of caution should be exercised. The main problem is that the risk proxy is computed over the same period as the correlation analysis is performed. The positive relationship may therefore simply be a consequence of the fact that diversification itself is giving rise to profit variability as opposed to past variability driving diversification programmes aimed at stabilising earnings.

Summary

The discussion in this chapter has hopefully demonstrated the varied nature of the diversification programmes undertaken by societies. At one end of the scale there are the large national players which have aspirations to compete on an equal footing with the retail banks through the provision of as wide a range of products and services as possible. At present, it is perhaps only the top five societies which have the resource base to easily pursue such a course of action.

For the remainder of the national societies and the larger regional societies the tendency has been to initially diversify into product lines complementary to their core savings and mortgage business and thereafter to diversify into a subset of the other available product areas. Some societies perhaps spread themselves a little too thinly in that they attempted to cover too many of the available options. In contrast others took a more focused approach and targeted only a limited number of the available avenues. At the other end of the scale there are the local and smaller regional societies. Diversification for these societies has simply meant moving into product lines which are heavily tied into their core mortgage and savings business. This refers to areas such as life assurance, pension plans, personal equity plans, TESSA's and advances secured on land, (class 2 assets).

As would no doubt be expected a number of diversification strategies have not worked out as planned and certain societies have found it necessary to withdraw from specific product lines. Share dealing, estate agency, commercial property lending and property development are all areas which have seen significant retrenchment by societies. This retrenchment has tended to be more common place among those national and regional societies which have attempted to provide a broad based platform of products and services.

At present diversification amongst societies has slowed almost to a halt and is unlikely to pick up significant pace at least in the short-term. The shape of the sector is therefore likely to remain one of where larger national societies offer an extensive product portfolio; smaller regional and local societies provide mortgages, savings and related products; and the larger regional and smaller national societies offer the core product lines coupled with a limited number of the other available product and service options.

A final feature of the discussion in this chapter was an analysis of the factors of influence in the diversification decision. On the basis of a literature overview a selection of factors were highlighted as of potential importance. The factors to emerge were asset size, market threat, risk as measured by profit variability and profit performance itself. For the three year period 1989 to 1991 a correlation analysis, where possible, was then utilised to test the relevance of these factors for building societies. Asset size and risk were both viewed to be positively correlated with diversification. Market threat was also considered to have a positive influence on diversification. In the case of profit performance a negative correlation tended to emerge. Perhaps the most surprising result is that of the inverse correlation between profit and diversification. While this suggested that relatively undiversified societies outperformed the more extensively diversified societies it was emphasised that the analysis was undertaken only over a very limited time period and a time period during which market conditions have been extremely unfavourable. When economic conditions pick up it may well be the case that a positive relationship emerges between profit and diversification because the more diversified societies are better placed to take advantage of an upswing.

More generally, it must be emphasised that the correlation analysis suffered from a number of weaknesses not least the limited time period under scrutiny and the fact that interrelationships between many of the factors of influence themselves were not fully explored. To overcome these weaknesses one area for future research would be the construction of a multivariate model to capture differences in diversification between societies. Regression analysis based upon pooled time series and cross section data could then be utilised to identify relevant explanatory variables.

8. Marketing

Introduction

The factors leading to greater emphasis on a marketing approach by building societies are easily discerned. For instance, increased competition has introduced new threats and opportunities which can only be managed through marketing strategies designed to protect and preferably enhance the market position of any given society. Taking advantage of the new market opportunities provided by legislative changes in the regulatory framework has also provided impetus to the development of a more rigorous marketing approach. Similarly, as technology developments are increasingly harnessed to the creation of a more customer focused framework throughout the financial services sector, the pressure to match best practice in the marketing application of technology is immense. Finally, consumer sovereignty requires a responsiveness to the changing needs of customers and this provides an imperative for a marketing approach in a sector that has witnessed an unprecedented rate of change in its business environment in recent years.

In a sector traditionally dominated by a concern for prudent risk management it should not be expected that the transition to a marketing approach will have occurred without difficulties. Similarly, for a sector that has also previously enjoyed a monopoly position in the mortgage market, the shift to the new competitive environment has not been without event and building societies have been seen to be vulnerable in the recent past to concerted competitive onslaught by the banks and other financial institutions. Increasingly, as the previous chapter demonstrated, it is possible to think of building societies as multi-product institutions, engaged in markets which are new to them and which involve greater risk than their traditional savings and loans markets. Although, as was indicated in chapter 7, there has recently been a degree of retrenchment in the diversification process initially fostered by deregulation. Despite this, however, the changes that have taken place in the business environment clearly pose for building societies a requirement to be more market demand led as opposed to supply led, as in the past. The current adverse economic conditions only add to the pressures to find effective marketing strategies, and competitive pressures are likely to intensify in the future rather than diminish. The future profitability of the sector will no doubt owe much to the success of marketing strategies and this chapter attempts to assess how well the marketing function has developed at national, regional and local society level in the context of a deregulated business environment. In this chapter consideration is also given to the nature of the marketing strategies employed by different society types and major differences in marketing practice are highlighted where these exist. By conducting an audit of the marketing function, the data obtained also contains pointers to the future direction that marketing in the different segments of the sector might take.

The empirical evidence used for the analysis offered in this chapter was obtained from a postal survey of all building societies and was conducted by the authors in December, 1992. The returns obtained for this survey comprised 8 national societies, 26 regional societies and 29 local societies. In certain instances some societies failed to provide answers to all questions. Consequently where survey material is referred to the number of societies which responded to the particular aspect under scrutiny is also documented. The survey was targeted at those officers who had responsibility for the marketing function. At appropriate points, reference is made to earlier survey work on the role of marketing within building societies, Morgan (1989), Ennew et al. (1989), and Edgett and Thwaites (1990) and where substantive differences exist to the findings of the earlier surveys these are commented upon in detail. Given the continued downturn in the economy, and the fact that societies have now more experience of a deregulated environment, an audit of current marketing strategy and practice is, at this juncture, both timely and relevant.

The Rise of the Marketing Function

Traditionally, building societies have engaged in a product orientated approach to their business activities (Hooley and Mann, 1988) and until recently there may have been a belief that a good product sold itself. As institutions that have long been dominated by finance and operations, the development of a marketing approach based on consumer needs and market segmentation is a relatively recent feature for many societies. Whereas, in other commercial sectors, marketing achieves corporate dominance because of its direct link with revenue generation, it is perhaps necessary to be circumspect about the primacy of revenue generation in the building society sector. The implication here is that any *a priori* ascribed status for marketing as the champion of revenue generation should perhaps be treated with caution. As Table 8:I clearly shows, the dominant corporate concern of most societies still lies with prudent risk management.

Table 8:I
Corporate Concern of Building Societies*

Corporate Concerns	National Building Societies n=8	Regional Building Societies n=25	Local Building Societies n=27
Prudent risk management	4	16	17
Increase revenue	4	8	5
Reduce costs	4	5	5

*2 national societies and 2 regional societies identified all 3 concerns as being equally important

Since there has been a growth in the establishment of specialist marketing departments within the building society sector this tends to indicate an acceptance of the benefits of applying specialist marketing expertise. It should be made clear though that many of these departments were only established in the past decade, primarily as a response to changes in the competitive environment. Whilst the coverage by specialist marketing departments found at national and regional society level is virtually universal, local societies have preferred to retain chief executive responsibility for marketing. Tables 8:IIA and 8:IIB illustrate the survey results in respect of both the position of specialist marketing departments throughout the industry, and also where responsibility for the marketing function is located in organisational terms within different society types.

Table 8:IIA
Existence of Specialist Marketing Department

Specialist Marketing Department	National Building Societies n=7	Regional Building Societies n=26	Local Building Societies n=29
Specialist Marketing Dept	6	22	5
Absence of Marketing Dept	1	4	24

Table 8:IIB
Responsibility for Marketing Planning

Responsibility	National Building Societies n=8	Regional Building Societies n=24	Local Building Societies n=22
Head Office Specialist	8	20	2
Chief Executive	0	4	19
Product Manager	0	0	1

Although it is useful to know the degree to which specialist marketing services have developed within the building society sector, it is perhaps more interesting to evaluate perceptions from within the sector as to the effectiveness of such developments. In order to gain a qualitative appreciation of this point, respondents to the survey were asked to rate their societies use of marketing. Table 8:III documents the results obtained.

Table 8:III
Rating of Society's Use of Marketing

Rating	National Building Societies n=8	Regional Building Societies n=24	Local Building Societies n=27
Highly sophisticated	0	0	0
Sophisticated	4	10	0
Adequate	2	1	19
Ineffective in Some Respects	2	13	5
Weak	0	0	3

Since these results are based on the perception of respondents, (those with responsibility for the marketing function), this should be taken into consideration when interpreting the survey findings. In the case of regional societies, an interesting dichotomy emerges where 10 societies perceive their marketing effort as sophisticated while 13 others report the view that their marketing is ineffective in some respects. Local societies report that at best their marketing is adequate, whilst a significant number fall into the categories of ineffective and weak. The perception of marketing within the national societies grouping appears to be quite mixed and 2 societies reported the use of marketing to be ineffective in some respects. Any interpretation of the results for regional societies should consider two important factors. The first relates to the relatively recent origin of specialist marketing departments in this segment of the building society sector and the second to the particular position of regional societies in attempting to diversify and compete in markets that local societies for instance cannot. National societies have had longer established marketing departments and their asset size gives them a market assurance that regional societies cannot easily match. The fact that many regional societies perceive their marketing to be ineffective in some respects may be a reflection of an honest appraisal of the challenges they have faced in diversification programmes. Similarly, the results obtained for local societies may also be a reflection of their particular characteristics and it should be recalled that in this segment responsibility for marketing lay in the hands of a chief executive rather than a dedicated, marketing specialist.

Marketing Strategies

Utilising the typology of competitive strategy developed by Porter (1980), the marketing strategy of building societies can be classified in terms of both competitive scope and competitive advantage. Where a society is active in a large number of market segments it displays a broad competitive scope, whilst a narrow competitive scope is typified by activity in only a few market segments. Competitive advantage strategies consist of a number of variants. Either the strategy is aimed at a cost competitive advantage which is typified by a strategy which offers a narrow range of products, or alternatively, the strategy consists of a decision to offer a wide range of differentiated products. Whether to operate on an industry wide basis or opt to be involved only in particular segments introduces the concept of focus as a viable competitive strategy. Thus, in Porter's typology, (see Porter, 1990), a number of generic strategies for competitive advantage exist, and these are illustrated in Figure I.

Competitive Advantage

		Lower Cost	Differentiation
Competitive Scope	Broad Target	Cost Leadership	Differentiation
	Narrow Target	Cost Focus	Focused Differentiation

Figure I

A society can aim to achieve competitive advantage through cost leadership. Here, competitive advantage would accrue from having the lowest costs and therefore the largest profit margins rather than through offering the lowest price. A cost leadership strategy is viable where a high market share exists which in turn allows for the maximisation of economies of scale and experience. Ultimately there can only be one cost leader in any given market. The second generic strategy available to a society is that of differentiation. Here, competitive strategy is based on offering products that are unique in the marketplace and easily differentiated from those of competitors. One device employed with strategies based on this approach is the use of branding.

The third generic strategy involves a focus strategy where a product is designed to meet the needs of a particular segment of the market. By focusing on one segment of the market, it is likely that a society might better achieve differentiation or low cost in that segment.

In a previous survey of building society competitive strategy, conducted by Ennew et al. (1989), it was reported that the majority of societies were utilising a cost focus strategy, (43.5 percent) or cost-led strategy, (30.4 percent). The remaining societies reported the use of a differential lead strategy, (8.7 percent) and a differential focus strategy, (17.4 percent). A later survey conducted by Edgett and Thwaites (1990), identified that a shift had taken place in the competitive strategy of building societies where 21.4 percent of societies sought a differential lead as opposed to the 8.7 percent reported in the earlier study. Although a trend was identified that building societies were moving away from cost strategies to more differentiated strategies, the Edgett and Thwaites study cautioned that the movement in this direction was unlikely to be as strong as indicated in the earlier study where it was reported that over 60 percent of building societies intended to adopt a differentiation strategy in the future, with 37 percent aiming to achieve a differentiated lead. Table 8:IVA summarises the most recent findings on building society competitive strategy derived from the survey results obtained as part of the examination of marketing within the building society sector. The current position concerning competitive strategy can also be compared to Table 8:IVB which summarises the future direction of competitive strategy as identified by respondents.

Table 8:IVA
Current Competitive Strategy

Competitive Strategy	National Building Societies n=8	Regional Building Societies n=25	Local Building Societies n=28
Cost Focus (Few Products, Few Segments)	2	11	15
Cost Lead (Few Products, Many Segments)	1	6	7
Differential Focus (Many Products, Few Segments)	2	3	4
Differential Lead (Many Products, Many Segments)	3	5	2

Table 8:IVB
Future Competitive Strategy

Competitive Strategy	National Building Societies n=8	Regional Building Societies n=25	Local Building Societies n=28
Cost Focus (Few Products, Few Segments)	4	7	13
Cost Lead (Few Products, Many Segments)	0	11	10
Differential Focus (Many Products, Few Segments)	0	3	3
Differential Lead (Many Products, Many Segments)	4	4	2

It has been suggested that within the financial services sector there is a trend towards differential focus, in other words broad product lines in narrow market segments (Brooks,1987). The emphasis on expanded product offerings within financial services involves particular difficulties. There are no product patents in financial services, and even with the use of branding, products can easily be copied. An obvious problem with a differentiated focus strategy also emerges where different institutions target the same customers within a segment. These difficulties apart, differentiation strategies are evidently important in the financial services sector and can yield first mover advantage to those institutions that engage in this approach. It is perhaps paradoxical that as the distinctions between different types of institutions in the financial services sector are eroded, it is possible to point to an increase in the individuality of particular institutions. Whether building societies have, however, been as successful as they would like in the creation of differentiated corporate identities has been questioned (Balmer,1990). Nevertheless it is the case that to talk in terms of homogeneous groups where, for instance, all the banks do one thing and the building societies do something else is no longer possible. Rather, individual banks and building societies are often pursuing their own line of development, actively striving to stand out from the rest of the crowd. As was indicated earlier, first movers will undoubtedly come under competitive pressure, but the initial lead gained may be sufficient to prove unassailable.

From the data contained in Tables 8:IVA and 8:IVB it is possible to gain an indication of a shift in the competitive strategy by societies within different segments of the sector. For instance, it can be seen that in the case of national societies that cost focus and differential lead strategies are the preferred competitive strategies. In the case of regional and local societies, it can be seen that they predominantly engage in cost-focus and cost-led strategies. Any movement planned for the future is in terms of a shift to greater emphasis on cost leadership by both society types, and a slight reduction in the prevalence of differential strategies. The adoption of a cost leadership strategy by regional and local societies should be considered in the light of the analysis offered on cost/income ratios provided in chapters 4 and economies of scale in chapter 5. The viability of a cost leadership strategy is dependent on economies of scale and control of costs. In chapter 4 attention was drawn to the favourable cost/income ratios of building societies in comparison to banks, but the increase in recent years of cost/income ratios for regional and particularly local societies was also highlighted. Since a cost leadership strategy is dependent on control of costs, plus maximisation of market share and a high level of management expertise, it has been suggested that this is a viable strategy only for the larger societies (Speed,1990).

Building societies do not appear to have aggressive growth plans in respect of winning market share, but seem more inclined to aim for a steady increase in market share. Table 8:V illustrates this point.

Table 8:V
Market Share Objectives

Objectives	National Building Societies n=8	Regional Building Societies n=26	Local Building Societies n=29
Maintain Share	1	3	4
Steadily Increase Share	6	22	25
Rapidly Increase Share	1	1	0

Whilst it has been reported in the survey by Edgett and Thwaites (1990) that 23% of societies categorised their market share objectives as aggressive, this current survey indicates that there has been a move away from this stance. This shift is perhaps understandable in the context of the less favourable economic conditions of the early 1990s. An appreciation of the emphasis placed by different society types on the different ways to achieve their growth in market share ambitions is provided in Table 8:VI. The scale 1-3 is used to denote the following range: 1, very important; 2, important; and 3, either not very important or not important at all.

Table 8:VI
Techniques Employed to Achieve a Growth in Market Share

Techniques	National Building Societies n=8			Regional Building Societies n=26			Local Building Societies n=27		
	1	2	3	1	2	3	1	2	3
Cost Reduction and Increased Productivity	5	2	1	18	8	0	15	12	0
Win Market Share from Competitors	5	3	0	14	11	1	6	16	5
Enter Emerging New Segments	2	2	4	3	12	11	0	10	17
Expand Total Markets	1	5	2	2	16	8	2	14	11

There appears to be a preference amongst all society types for cost reduction and increased productivity as the means of achieving their objectives, although in the case of national and regional societies, in particular, a degree of emphasis is also placed on winning market share from competitors. Perhaps as a reflection of current economic conditions, entering new markets and expanding the total market do not have the same degree of importance for societies in comparison to cost reduction and increased productivity. These results are broadly consistent with the cost focus approach to competitive strategy identified earlier across society types. The emphasis placed on winning market share from competitors by regional societies is congruent with the aspiration identified earlier of competitive advantage being sought through cost leadership by some regional societies.

Marketing Practice

The defining characteristics of a genuine marketing approach by building societies can be thought of in terms of three major attributes. Firstly, the society sees itself as satisfying a defined set of wants for a defined set of customers. Secondly, the society accepts that this requires market research. Thirdly, the society recognises that all activities that relate more or less to customer satisfaction should be placed under integrated marketing control. Using this definition, the starting point for a marketing approach is therefore bound up with effective market segmentation. The purpose of market segmentation is to subdivide the market into appropriate divisions and thereby optimise marketing strategy by dividing the market into homogeneous sectors allowing a society to relate its marketing effort to the needs of these sectors. Table 8:VII itemises the incidence of the use of market segmentation by the different society types.

Table 8:VII
Use of Market Segmentation

Market Segmentation	**National Building Societies n=8**	**Regional Building Societies n=26**	**Local Building Societies n=27**
Use Market Segmentation	8	20	6
Do Not Use Market Segmentation	0	6	21

It should be stated that although 21 local societies reported that they did not use market segmentation they clearly do segment the market, by default, on a geographical basis. For those societies that reported the application of segmentation techniques, a breakdown of the methods of segmentation that they find useful is provided in Table 8:VIII.

Table 8:VIII
Methods of segmentation

Methods of Segmentation	National Building Societies n=8	Regional Building Societies n=20	Local Building Societies n=6
Product Category	2	7	4
Customer Needs/Benefits	6	16	3
Volume	0	4	1
Demographic	4	6	0

Although a number of societies obviously utilise more than one method it can be seen that the dominant segmentation method employed by national and regional societies is in terms of customer needs/benefits, which accords with the definition of a marketing approach provided earlier. The skill with which financial intermediaries segment markets can be identified as a key requirement for survival, (Brooks,1987). The results for local societies should be treated with some caution because, as will become apparent when promotional practice is examined, it can be argued that local societies do in fact segment markets. The results may be due to a lack of familiarity by chief executives with the concept of segmentation. It is chief executives who have responsibility for marketing in local societies.

Since effective segmentation of markets is dependent on market research, this dimension of a society's marketing effort is a good indicator of how rigorous or otherwise the approach to marketing is within a given society. Table 8:IX summarises the views of respondents on the usefulness of the market research undertaken by their society.

Table 8:IX
Usefulness of the Society's Market Research

Usefulness of Market Research	National Building Societies n=8	Regional Building Societies n=24	Local Building Societies n=25
Very Useful	6	12	9
Moderately useful	1	9	5
Limited use	1	3	11

In all segments of the industry, although to a lesser degree within local societies, the output of the marketing research department is regarded as being very or moderately useful. It should be noted that a survey carried out in 1987 revealed that building societies compared unfavourably with banks and insurance companies in terms of in-house market research capability, (Morgan,1989). The evidence from this survey suggests that the growth in the utilisation of market research has been a major feature in recent years and reflects greater awareness by regional societies in particular of the value of market research.

The survey by Edgett and Thwaites (1990) considered the variety of market research techniques employed by societies and found that, with the exception of *ad hoc* surveys, utilisation of other market research techniques was low. Using the same categories of research technique as Edgett and Thwaites, plus the addition of sales forecasting, market research techniques were again examined to see if societies had become more sophisticated in their application of market research techniques. Table 8:X contains the survey results on this issue. The scale 1-3 is employed to denote frequency of use; 1 for often; 2 for sometimes; and 3 for never.

Table 8:X
Market Research Techniques

Categories	National Building Societies n=8			Regional Building Societies n=26			Local Building Societies n=29		
	1	2	3	1	2	3	1	2	3
Qualitative Research	6	2	0	7	13	6	0	10	19
Continuous Surveys	6	2	0	9	8	9	2	3	24
Ad hoc Surveys	5	3	0	9	15	2	1	18	10
Tracking Studies	5	3	0	10	10	6	2	7	20
Industry Audits	3	2	3	7	8	11	2	5	22
Consumer Panels	4	2	2	4	7	15	0	2	27
Field Experiments	0	4	4	3	8	15	1	8	20
Sales Forecasting	2	5	1	10	10	6	3	13	13

The survey results clearly indicate that the range of market research techniques employed, particularly by national and regional societies, has been expanded in recent years. This, however, is not the only dimension where advances in marketing practice can be identified. In chapter 6 importance was attached to the increasing significance of computerised customer database applications as a central feature of building society marketing activity. Confirmation that the majority of national and regional societies now make use of a customer relational database was obtained in the survey results. For those societies that did not currently have a customer relational database, the majority saw it as a priority for future development. Beyond better access to customer information via customer databases, the existence of a marketing information system (MIS) can be viewed as a further important dimension of the marketing planning capability of societies. Table 8:XI contains the results relating to this issue.

Table 8:XI
Use of a Marketing Information System

Marketing Information Systems	National Building Societies n=7	Regional Building Societies n=25	Local Building Societies n=27
Use MIS	4	13	0
Do Not Use MIS	3	12	27

Those societies that utilise a marketing information system regard it as an essential tool for monitoring marketing performance against stated objectives. Furthermore in terms of marketing planning it offers benefits in modelling market trends and the targeting of product development. Interestingly, a few societies reported the use of geographic information systems as part of their armoury in the use of information for marketing planning.

New Product Development

A hallmark of the sector in recent years has been the level of new product development, on this count the point of interest relates to the extent to which societies see new product development being the result of go-it-alone innovative development or more fruitfully arising from joint ventures and strategic alliances. Of course, new product development may in fact be a mix of both approaches, but when asked to identify the most important future method of new product development, the following results, which are documented in Table 8:XII, were obtained.

Table 8:XII
Most Important Method of New Product Development

Product Development	National Building Societies* n=8	Regional Building Societies n=26	Local Building Societies n=24
Go-it-alone strategy	5	13	17
Joint ventures	4	2	6
Strategic alliances	3	11	1

*2 national societies reported all methods of product development as important

The use of joint ventures and strategic alliances does not appear to be as important a concern for local societies as for national and regional societies. Joint ventures and strategic alliances are useful in more quickly developing commercial know-how in new product areas than is perhaps possible through a go-it-alone strategy, and the incidence of their intended use can be taken as a reflection of the intent of national and regional societies to perhaps by-pass any limitations of in-house experience in particular product areas and gain directly from the expertise that association with other organisations provides. In chapter 9, the impact of joint ventures and strategic alliances is considered in the wider context of organisational change within the building society sector.

Advertising and Promotional Practice

A core component of marketing practice is advertising and promotional activity and there is a trend for societies to increase the resources devoted to this. Particularly where a differentiation strategy is being pursued it is apparent that advertising and promotional activity serves to distinguish a society's products and corporate image. The issue of branding is considered separately later in this chapter. The concern of the survey was to both document the range of advertising media employed and identify the main types of promotional activity undertaken. Table 8:XIII contains the results obtained. The following numerical keys were employed to denote frequency of use; 1 for often; 2 for sometimes; and 3 for never.

Table 8:XIII
Advertising and Promotional Practice

Categories	National Building Societies n=8			Regional Building Societies n=26			Local Building Societies n=29		
	1	2	3	1	2	3	1	2	3
T.V. Adverts	3	4	1	3	12	11	0	3	26
Press Adverts	6	2	0	21	5	0	20	9	0
Displays	8	0	0	21	5	0	20	7	2
Mailshots	7	1	0	10	13	3	2	23	4
Children/Youth	3	2	3	4	14	8	6	14	9
Retired	3	4	1	3	16	7	0	17	12
Families	3	3	2	5	15	6	0	16	13
Exhibitions/ Sponsorship	1	7	0	9	15	2	5	20	4

As has been stated, much of the advertising activity undertaken in the sector, particularly TV advertising, has been targeted at differentiating societies from each other and promoting a distinctive corporate image for individual societies. The campaigns by the Nationwide, the Alliance and Leicester and the Halifax are good examples of this generic form of advertising aimed at promoting the corporate image of these particular societies. Earlier, the difficulties associated with differentiating products within the financial services sector were discussed, and the emphasis placed on corporate image should be understood in the light of this. Clearly, the TV advertising conducted by building societies is aimed at making them stand out from the crowd.

The most used media for advertising for all types of society are press adverts and display media. Mailshots are predominantly used by national and regional societies, although a significant proportion of local societies report their occasional use. The development of computer-based customer relational databases will no doubt assist societies to undertake more accurate, targeted mailshots aimed at improving cross selling to existing customers. Whilst earlier in this chapter it was reported that local societies did not utilise market segmentation techniques, their promotional efforts in respect of children, families and the retired seems to suggest that this may not entirely be the case.

Branding

Operating in markets where there are many competing products with very similar characteristics, the attraction of branding for building societies lies in the fact that it supports the process of differentiation. The logic behind branding is perhaps obvious, in that ultimately it is bound up with creating brand loyalty to particular products or to a particular society itself. It can be argued that branding of financial products is important simply because customers often find such products difficult to appraise and can approach them with a degree of confusion. Much of the focus of branding in the building society sector can be seen to be at the level of corporate image where the qualities promoted are service, product quality and trustworthiness. One obvious difficulty is that all societies would make a claim to these particular attributes. Whether a society should brand its products or its name is an important question. Some evidence exists for instance that in terms of transaction accounts customers prefer to deal with a name that they trust and are less interested in the small print of the product. When it comes to savings, however, the opposite is the case and the product matters more than the institution that sells it. Branding within the building society sector can therefore legitimately involve different approaches even within the same society, although there is a risk that confusing messages may be sent to customers if both product and corporate branding are not congruent with each other. Table 8:XIV details the generic use of branding within the sector, and the variations in its prevalence within the different segments of the industry.

Table 8:XIV
Use of Branding

Branding	National Building Societies n=8	Regional Building Societies n=26	Local Building Societies n=26
Extensive Use	6	13	8
Some Use	2	10	13
Not Relevant	0	3	5

Customer Service as the Key to Competitive Advantage

The components of the marketing mix are being re-evaluated in the financial services sector. Whilst institutions make every effort to differentiate their product offerings, it is recognised that customers in fact often find it difficult to distinguish between them. Although it is also possible to differentiate on the basis of price, the experience of recent years shows that this is not an approach that appeals to the seller. Therefore, a view exists that dissatisfaction with an over concentration on price, product and promotion has resulted in an emphasis throughout the financial services sector on customer service as the key to competitive advantage (de Moubray,1989). Traditionally, building societies have had a favourable reputation compared to the banks for the provision of a friendly, convenient and uncomplicated service, (Bradley,1987). It is indisputable that all the advertising and promotion in the world will not disguise poor service. In attempting to measure this dimension of a society's marketing activity, sales and customer care training was taken as a surrogate measure of customer service on the grounds that investment in such training represented a corporate commitment to a quality service approach. Table 8:XV contains the survey findings in respect of this issue.

Table 8:XV
Sales/Customer Care Training

Training	National Building Societies n=8	Regional Building Societies n=26	Local Building Societies n=27
Very Good	2	9	6
Good	0	12	10
Moderate	5	4	9
Poor	1	1	2
Very poor	0	0	0

Surprisingly, 5 national societies reported their sales/customer care training as being moderate and 1 other national society categorised sales/customer training as poor. Of course this may be a reflection of the standards that they have set themselves in this area. There appears to be satisfaction in both the regional and local society segments about the provision of training in these areas, and in this issue local societies do not appear to differ from the other segments.

Summary

This chapter has confirmed the trend by building societies towards a more rigorous approach to marketing. Inherently, some tension may exist between an overriding obligation for prudent risk management and unmitigated marketing led policies. Nevertheless within this constraint, and also the limitations of the regulatory framework, building societies are generally becoming more sophisticated in the application of a marketing approach to their business. If competitive pressures initially led to the need for such an approach, this will be strongly reinforced as competitive pressure intensifies in the 1990s.

Comparisons were made with previous survey work of the building society sector in 1989 and 1990 which revealed that strategies for competitive advantage had not developed in the way suggested by these earlier studies.

Although both these earlier studies reported that building societies predominantly operated cost strategies, there was some evidence of a shift towards differentiation strategies. Both studies, albeit to differing degrees, suggested that the future preference of an increasing proportion of the building society sector would be to desert cost strategies in favour of differential lead or differential focus strategies.

The empirical work undertaken for this chapter suggests that this has not happened in any dramatic form, and that clearly the majority of building societies see competitive advantage to be served by cost strategies. A realignment of future competitive strategy was reported by regional societies, where cost lead strategies might replace cost focus as the dominant strategy in this sector. Similarly, cost lead strategies might also strengthen in the local society sector, where again future realignment was identified in these terms. The consequences of such a shift would of course result in an intensification of competition, and it was regional societies that placed most emphasis on winning market share from competitors to achieve their growth plans. It should be noted that most societies, including regional societies, reported that they were aiming for a steady increase in market share. It should also be acknowledged that a cost leadership strategy involves the introduction of new business, which contains risks and could adversely affect costs if sufficient volume is not achieved. Given that the prerequisites of a successful cost leadership strategy include economies of scale and control of costs, conventional wisdom would suggest that this is a strategy more appropriate for national and regional societies.

The inherent difficulties of differentiation strategies were also discussed in this chapter, particularly in relation to product differentiation where competitors can easily copy products. Much of the advertising and promotional effort undertaken in the building society sector is focused on creating a unique image for a particular society, although inevitably, societies run the risk of promoting the same set of desirable attributes that most societies would claim to possess. Brand loyalty, to both products and institutions, may not be easily achieved, but when successful the rewards can be lucrative, especially if it confers first mover advantage in building up a market lead.

The practice of marketing was examined in some detail, and national and regional societies were seen to have embraced marketing as a recognised function with specialist staff employing the full range of marketing techniques. Local societies tended to lag somewhat in the range of techniques employed, and control of marketing lay typically with the chief executive. All society types recognised the importance of a computer customer database, given its potential for cross selling.

It was suggested that, despite its undoubted increased importance in the sector over recent years, the conventional marketing mix of price, product and promotion alone may not ensure competitive advantage. Rather, customer service is increasingly seen as the ultimate differentiator and the key to competitive advantage. Traditionally, building societies have had a favourable reputation for friendly, convenient and accessible service. Currently, within most of the financial services sector, standards are being established for quality customer service, as institutions focus sharply on this issue. For building societies improving customer service in the 1990s is a priority.

9. Organisational Change

Introduction

Building societies conjure in the mind connotations of stability and traditionalism, and for most of their long history, they have indeed, in important respects, been remarkable for their lack of profound organisational change. As was documented in chapter 3, this is not to deny that through mergers, transfers of engagements and terminations that there has been an unrelenting evolution of an increasingly concentrated structure for the building society sector throughout most of its history. Rather, what remained constant until the 1980s was the preservation of a relatively simple unitary organisational structure for most building societies. Thus, traditionally, organisational design within the building society sector was based on a functional approach to departmentalisation. For instance, in the 1970s the typical structure of a building society consisted of a head-office containing a mortgage department responsible for the administration of lending, a savings department responsible for deposit taking, and a personnel department. The remaining staff were located in the branch network which, in turn, was supported by a number of small regional offices providing a personnel function.

Chapter 2 illustrated how the reforms introduced by the Building Societies Act of 1986 have placed building societies in a highly competitive and dynamic business environment where they compete more directly with banks and other financial institutions. In adapting to the opportunities and threats posed by increased competition and financial deregulation, it is not surprising to find that building societies have been engaged in a process of organisational change in order to better orientate themselves to the demands of a changing market place.

Building societies have increasingly adopted a more complex quasi-divisional organisational structure. Consequently, whilst the strategic functions for divisions are located within head-office, there is increased emphasis on autonomy for their operation within the divisions themselves. Adapting organisational structure to changed market conditions has not been the only impetus for organisational change. Reducing costs, for instance, has led to a trend towards establishing new administrative centres dedicated to back-office operations. Recently, it is possible to point to a reduction in the number of regional offices, whilst those remaining have been given greater autonomy in monitoring the performance of the branch network.

The increasing complexity of business and the intensification of competition during the 1980s exposed the weaknesses of traditionally centralised and hierarchically organised structures to match the requirements of the changed business environment within the financial services sector. Here the literature on business organisation provides a reference point for our analysis, (Miles and Snow, 1986, Drucker, 1988 and Martin, 1990). These writers suggest that the key imperatives in organisational design in the 1990s relate to a flattening of management hierarchies of control, decentralisation of management decision-making and the disintegration of corporate operations. According to this perspective on organisational design, the challenge for building societies in devising new organisational structures lies in achieving the benefits of loose-tight properties, (Peters and Waterman, 1982), where there is both purposeful corporate direction from head-office and maximum devolved decision-making within divisions and branches. In this chapter, structure is broadly defined to include integrating devices such as corporate culture and strategic planning since both are important elements in resolving the organisational dilemma posed by loose-tight properties in organisational design. Similarly, the impact of information technology developments on organisational change is considered to be an important element within the analysis, particularly in the potential it provides for the more efficient and effective management of organisations.

Much of the material in this chapter is based on a postal survey of building societies undertaken in 1991. The survey covered the period July 1988 to July 1991. Questionnaires were sent to 89 building societies. In total 70 societies replied, giving a response rate of 79 percent. The breakdown of those societies which responded to the survey request comprised all 10 national societies, 30 regional societies and 30 local societies. At appropriate points in this chapter, reference is made to a survey conducted by (Nellis and Litt, 1990) which examined branch managers' views of organisational change within societies.

Product Diversification, Joint Ventures and Acquisitions

That business organisation should be altered to suit a multi-product portfolio is perhaps self-evident. As a starting point, an attempt was therefore made to gauge the strength of new product development across all segments of the building society sector to verify the view that societies were indeed becoming multi-product providers of financial services. Because of the constraints imposed by the regulatory regime and also the limitations of size and resources, the expectation was that the ability to engage in new product development would not be entirely constant throughout the sector, with local societies in particular facing the most barriers in this area. Whilst the results provided in Table 9:I confirm that a high proportion of national and regional societies have been engaged in new product development, the involvement of local societies is also quite significant. Obviously, these aggregate results need to be considered against the more detailed analysis provided in chapter 7 where the scale and scope of product diversification is more fully elaborated.

Table 9:1
New Products

New Products	National Building Societies n=10	Regional Building Societies n=30	Local Building Societies n=30
Increase	10	27	26
Decrease	0	3	1
Constant	0	0	3

In terms of engaging in product diversification, both joint ventures and acquisitions help reduce the time required to develop and introduce new products. The diversity of new product development described in chapter 7 gives credence to the view that building society joint venture and acquisition strategies originate from a desire to more quickly develop commercial know-how in new product areas than would be possible through a go-it-alone strategy. For instance, most commentators would accept that joint ventures can provide a speedy channel acceptance, reduce marketing costs, increase sales volume and provide important production cost savings. Acquisitions, motivated by the benefits ascribed to synergy, again provide a vehicle for quickly developing a more wide ranging product portfolio, although the difficulties involved in combining disparate organisations are sometimes underestimated. Typically, difficulties revolve around culture clash which can mitigate against achieving the corporate benefits sought from an acquisition. Gauging the economic efficacy of joint ventures and acquisitions should be done in the context of the analysis of economies of scale and scope provided in chapter 5 and building society performance provided in chapter 4. Tables 9:IIA and 9:IIB summarise the survey results in respect of the levels of reported joint venture and acquisition activity within the building society sector.

Table 9:IIA
Joint Ventures

Joint Ventures	**National Building Societies n=10**	**Regional Building Societies n=30**	**Local Building Societies n=30**
Increase	6	13	9
Decrease	3	16	12
Constant	1	1	9

Table 9:IIB
Acquisitions

Acquisitions	**National Building Societies n=10**	**Regional Building Societies n=30**	**Local Building Societies n=30**
Increase	7	7	3
Decrease	3	23	27
Constant	0	0	0

Since the Building Societies Act came into effect in January 1987, there is a lag of a year between this and the period covered by the survey. The reported decreases in joint ventures and acquisitions in the results may be a reflection of the fact that most societies acted quickly in these areas immediately the Act came into effect. For the period covered by the survey, acquisition and joint venture activity is most pronounced in the national segment, with 6 national societies reporting an increase in the use of joint ventures and 7 national societies reporting acquisitions. Interestingly, over a third of regional societies and just under a third of local societies reported an increase in the use of joint ventures over the period. Positing a link between product diversification and the increased use of acquisitions and joint ventures within the sector appears to be justified. The growth in the use of subsidiaries since deregulation can also be taken as an indicator of the dynamic link between product diversification and changing organisational forms. Clearly, across building societies, more complex organisational forms are emerging than the one described earlier for the traditional concept of a building society.

Empirical Evidence for Changes in Organisational Structure

Recent literature on business organisation (Aksoy and Marshall, 1992, Kanter, 1989 and Peters and Waterman, 1982) tends to support the view that for many large scale organisations there is an increasing tendency to engage in a downsizing of the corporate head-office and to rationalise the functions carried out at head-office level. For example, in the study conducted by Aksoy and Marshall, the example is cited of a UK clearing bank which has reduced its headquarters staff from 2,500 to 250 people. Intensification of competition throughout most sectors of the economy has encouraged the adoption of leaner head-offices, where improved productivity is sought through less bureaucratic forms of administration. Also associated with the leaner head-office is an attempt to reduce the number of management levels in the organisation. Although downsizing is regarded as desirable, the role of the head-office should not, however, be regarded as being diminished. Rather, a qualitative change of role, involving a concentration at the head-office level on strategic and integrative functions, enhances its importance.

The survey results reveal that most national, regional and local societies have experienced an increase in staff numbers at both head-office and branch level. Table 9:III summarises the results obtained.

Table 9:III
Staff Numbers at Head-Office and Branches

Staff Numbers	National Building Societies n=10	Regional Building Societies n=30	Local Building Societies n=30
Head Office			
Increase	8	30	28
Decrease	1	0	0
Constant	1	0	2
Branches			
Increase	9	26	20
Decrease	1	3	2
Constant	0	1	8

It is interesting to compare the above figures on the growth in staff to the data obtained by the survey *vis a vis* changes in branch numbers. A comparison of Table 9:III with that of Table 9:IV reveals, for instance, that whilst 9 national societies reported an increase in staff numbers at branch level, 6 national societies also reported a decrease in the number of branch offices. The explanation for this seemingly contradictory result relates to the growth of decentralised administration centres and back-office operations now being favoured by national societies.

Table 9:IV
Branch Numbers

Branch Numbers	**National Building Societies n=10**	**Regional Building Societies n=30**	**Local Building Societies n=30**
Increase	4	20	12
Decrease	6	4	0
Constant	0	6	18

Earlier in this chapter attention was drawn, in broad terms, to the evolution within the sector of quasi-divisional organisational structures in place of the traditional functional, departmental structures. Confirmation that a more divisionalised type structure is evident within the sector, was provided by the survey results and is illustrated in Table 9:V.

Table 9:V
Number of Sub-Units and Delegation to Sub-Units

Sub-Units	**National Building Societies n=10**	**Regional Building Societies n=30**	**Local Building Societies n=30**
Number of Sub-Units			
Increase	6	26	20
Decrease	2	0	0
Constant	2	4	10
Delegation to Sub-Units			
Increase	8	26	22
Decrease	0	0	0
Constant	2	4	8

It can be seen that increased use of sub-units is pronounced throughout the sector. Similarly, the increased incidence of delegation to sub-units is consistent throughout the sector. Both these results corroborate a shift to a more divisional type structure by building societies.

At this point, it is useful to refer to a survey conducted by Nellis and Litt (1990) which documents branch managers' views of change in building societies, since it confirms the increased significance of delegation, in this case, to branch level. This particular survey, based on data obtained from 3,456 building society branches, confirms that over 80 percent of branch managers claim to enjoy greater authority and responsibility since deregulation. It would appear from this particular survey that the scope for delegation appears to be related to branch size. Thus, 94 percent of managers in branches employing over 50 staff, compared to 69 percent of managers with less than 5 staff, reported an increase in delegation.

That the role of the branch manager presents greater managerial challenge since deregulation is again confirmed by Nellis and Litt (1990) when 90 percent of respondents reported that they faced greater pressures because of increased competition, greater diversity of operations, the need for more skills and product knowledge and higher expectations from head-office about their level of performance. Similarly, the greater emphasis on responsibility at branch level is further confirmed, for example when 85 percent of respondents stated that they have more flexibility to make decisions on such matters as mortgage limits.

Returning to the broad theme of quasi-divisionalisation, it is perhaps self evident that the attractions of a more divisionalised type structure are in keeping with the changes that have taken place within the business environment of building societies. Clearly, this type of organisational structure is better suited to the flexible response to new product developments and it can also facilitate growth through the addition of new divisions. The introduction of a divisional type structure is, however, not entirely without difficulties. An obvious point relates to cost, in that most commentators would accept that a divisional structure can be more expensive to initiate and maintain and that increases in operating, administrative and capital costs can result. Whether this actually happens or not is, in reality, related to sales volumes. If these are large enough to fully utilize the duplicated resources implied by a divisional form of structure, it is possible to gain an advantage from a divisional format. If volumes are too low, the cost of a divisional format may be lost economies of scale. With this point in mind, consider the survey results in respect of administration costs which are presented in Table 9:VI.

Table 9:VI
Administration Costs

Administration Costs	National Building Societies n=10	Regional Building Societies n=30	Local Building Societies n=30
Increase	5	29	25
Decrease	4	1	3
Constant	1	0	2

Whilst Table 9:VI confirms the general trend of increases in administration costs, caution does need to be exercised since it would be unsafe to assume that these reported increases can be attributed solely to organisational re-structuring. The definition of administration costs used by building societies covers a range of factors, therefore it is difficult to sustain any direct causal link between organisational restructuring and increases in administration costs. What might be seen as significant from the survey results is the fact that 4 national societies reported decreases in administration costs, although whether this can be linked to organisational restructuring may again be contentious. However, as will be illustrated in chapter 10, the logic of building society relocation policy, and the creation of specialist regional administration centres by national societies particularly, is bound up with the pursuit of cost efficiency.

Although the survey revealed evidence of more divisionalised type organisational structures, where there was increased emphasis on delegation to sub-units, it also revealed that generally this was not accompanied by any move towards producing flatter organisational structures through reductions in the levels of management hierarchy. The exception to this though, was in the case of 5 national societies which reported decreases in the levels of hierarchy within their organisation. The survey results relating to this issue are contained in Table 9:VII.

Table 9:VII
Hierarchical Levels

Hierarchical Levels	National Building Societies n=10	Regional Building Societies n=30	Local Building Societies n=30
Increase	2	26	18
Decrease	5	0	1
Constant	3	4	11

Comparing the results to the reference points discussed earlier in respect of the key imperatives of organisational design for the 1990s that have been identified by the academic literature, evidence emerges from the survey results that only in the case of some national societies is there the combined use of delegated authority to sub-units and reductions in the levels of management hierarchy. It is also possible to speculate that the reductions in administration costs for some national societies relate to the disintegration of corporate operations where there has been spatial relocation of head-office functions into specialist regional administration centres. When it comes to the issue of downsizing head-office, there, however, appears to be little evidence that national societies are engaging in this particular aspect of organisational restructuring.

Overwhelming evidence across national, regional and local societies did emerge in respect of one key issue relating to the emergence of new organisational forms. Earlier it was stated that structure would be broadly defined, and the universal increase in the formalisation of planning and resource allocation can be properly associated with the changes in organisational structure so far described. Table 9:VIII illustrates the results obtained for this feature of organisational change.

Table 9:VIII
Formalisation of Planning and Resource Allocation

Formalisation of Planning	National Building Societies n=10	Regional Building Societies n=30	Local Building Societies n=30
Increase	10	27	23
Decrease	0	1	0
Constant	0	2	7

The results here are no doubt a reflection of the fact that building societies find themselves in a more competitive and turbulent business environment since deregulation. The business affairs of all types of society have become more complex and, in the case of societies which have undertaken diversification, more risky. With the move towards more complex organisational structures for many societies, greater attention requires to be given to integrating a more divisionalised organisational form at the corporate level. Therefore, the universal increase in the use of formalisation of planning and resource allocation can be viewed as a means of better managing organisational complexity and risk. Before deregulation, building society planning concentrated on ensuring an adequate flow of investment funds to service mortgage lending and tended to display a relatively short-term horizon

(Macey and Wells, 1987). Planning in building societies has now adopted a more long term horizon and, in view of the factors associated with a more turbulent, unpredictable business environment, has taken on the breadth and scope of more genuine strategic planning.

It is also not surprising to find that the results in Table 9:IX show an almost universal increase in the use of information technology by all types of building societies. Chapter 6 provides a detailed account of the key developments in the application of information technology by building societies. It is clear that information technology is regarded as a critical factor in improving both a society's efficiency and effectiveness. The shift towards a more profit-related, market driven stance by building societies has placed information technology to the forefront, especially in respect of adopting marketing principles and practice. Therefore much of the innovation in the use of information technology relates to improving the marketing capabilities of societies and this theme is explored fully in chapter 8. There are also important connections between the increased use of information technology and the increased emphasis on the formalisation of planning and resource allocation identified earlier. For instance, the large amounts of capital investment associated with information technology projects creates, in itself, a planning imperative. A major benefit of information technology lies also in the contribution it can make to the establishment of a management information system essential to the monitoring and control of strategic plans. Information technology is therefore an important element in managing at the corporate level the seeming paradox of loose-tight properties in organisational design. For example, not only is information technology a powerful decision support tool which permits greater emphasis to be placed on decentralisation to sub-units and devolution of responsibility to lower organisational levels, it offers at the same time head-office the means to better manage the strategic integration of business planning activities for the whole organisation through the effective use of timely and relevant data on organisational performance. Similarly, the modelling and simulation capabilities of information technology offers an invaluable planning aid to corporate planners at head-office level. For the reasons given, it can be appreciated that the increased use of information technology should be viewed as central to the current organisational change process being undertaken by building societies.

Table 9:IX
Information Technology

Information Technology	National Building Societies n=10	Regional Building Societies n=30	Local Building Societies n=30
Increase	10	30	30
Decrease	0	0	0
Constant	0	0	0

Re-designing organisational structures to match a changed environmental context, obviously lies at the heart of recent changes in building societies' structures and this is being done in the belief that these structural changes will contribute to improved organisational performance. Consideration has also been given to the part that existing internal features of building societies play in the probability of organisational restructuring (Ferguson and McKillop, 1992). Whilst there is no doubt that the major determinant of organisational change relates to the force of a competitive business environment, Ferguson and McKillop *op. cit.*, provide an additional dimension on organisational change within this sector which is worth briefly outlining.

Using an econometric methodology, the analysis of internal features of building societies revealed a number of positive and negative factors which impacted on the statistical probability of a given building society adopting a new form of organisational structure. The defining characteristics of the new form organisational structure in this particular study was where a society was active in new product development, had increased the number of organisational sub-units and the use of delegation, and had also decreased the number of hierarchical levels. The study found that the higher the relative price of labour, profit growth, absolute administrative costs and asset size, the greater the probability that a building society would adopt the kind of organisational structure just described. Intuitively, these results make sense from an organisational slack and efficiency perspective. Profit growth, which was the dominant positive statistical influence, creates the resources and confidence to engage in organisational restructuring, whilst both the relative price of labour, absolute administrative costs and asset size, provide an efficiency rationale justifying a move to a new organisational form. Three factors were identified in the study that impacted negatively on the likelihood of organisational restructuring, these were the growth in employee numbers, the ratio of management expenses to branch numbers and staff costs. These negative factors were taken to indicate the force of bureaucratic inertia, a feature reinforced by the constant pursuit of growth *per se*.

The results of this study provide a force field analysis, where the stronger the positive factors, the greater is the probable impetus towards organisational change. Ferguson and McKillop *op. cit.*, conclude by stressing that while it is useful to examine the force of internal features in this way, organisational structures have to be designed, that is, deliberately chosen. Even where strong positive factors of the kind identified exist, it is not automatically assured that a new organisational form will be the outcome. There is a high probability only. The actual organisational outcome is a matter of strategic choice, where as a matter of policy new organisational structures are created.

Culture Change, Performance-based Management and Human Resource Issues

It is important to recognise that the nature of organisational change within the building society sector has as much to do with new values and beliefs as it does with concerns about business strategy and organisational structure. The following comment by Iles (1992) graphically illustrates the realities involved in transforming the traditional culture of a building society.

> "Change is difficult at the best of times but when it affects underlying values it is particularly hard. The branch manager is caught between a number of rocks and hard places. Accepting change means that most branch managers will have to change underlying traditional values, acknowledge that a large portion of their accumulated experience is no longer relevant, recognise that many of the skills they possess are not as highly valued as was originally assumed and that they need, rapidly, to acquire new ones. A number of institutions are experiencing requests for early retirement from branch managers which is possibly a symptom of resistance to change."

Perhaps the most significant change in values for building societies is reflected in the transition from social objectives to more overtly commercial ones. Chapter 4 pointed to the effect of the rules on capital adequacy in bringing about the need for a more profit orientated approach in building societies. Increasingly, the main indicator of building society organisational performance is the profit and loss account. The traditional emphasis on the value of investment business and the value of mortgage lending is still important, especially the latter, but as was illustrated in chapter 4, commission income has become a major performance indicator. Despite this transition to a more profit orientated approach, some commentators argue that this does not fundamentally change the basic objectives of a building society. For instance, one view taken is that

> "Managers are required to act in the interests of the generality of members. A clear interpretation of this is that they must minimise the spread between rates offered to depositors and the rates charged to those with mortgages without taking excessive risks. The way to do this is to be as efficient and profitable as possible." (BSA, 1991).

In reality, however, the switch from social to commercial objectives may not be so simple as to be subsumed under the banner of acting in the generality of members as the following comments make clear,

> "[Building Societies] are finding that many of the changes are very difficult to implement. Commercial objectives are laudable until the societies introduce a reduced lending rate for a group of new borrowers, to the chagrin of their millions of existing borrowers. In addition, insistence on a linked endowment policy with the commission going to the society is likely to bring protest if the applicant is an investor, or if the insurance intermediary is an agent of the society." (Macey and Wells, 1987).

The difficulties of reconciling the divergent interests of an ever complex constituency may, as the above quotation suggests, result in building society objectives being multiple and conflictive at the operational level, even if there is clarity about acting in the overall interest of the members at the level of corporate policy. This issue of building society objectives is further considered in chapter 13 when the plc conversion and mutual bank route for the future evolution of building societies are examined.

The nature of objectives apart, the impact of a more profit orientated approach can be seen to have permeated most building society cultures. Perhaps the change that has taken place can best be described in terms of the creation of an overtly performance based culture. For instance, Nellis and Litt *op. cit.*, confirm that, particularly in the case of national and regional societies, performance related pay schemes are common. Promotion prospects in building societies are less likely to be based on seniority and increasingly new blood is being introduced through external recruitment. The demands of new business development also appear to be favouring specialists and there is a high demand for expertise as opposed to generalist skills. More than ever, building societies are reliant on the quality of their staff in order to achieve a competitive edge. Interestingly, Nellis and Litt *op. cit.*, reported that, in the case of branch managers, the factor which they perceived to be their own greatest weakness was that of a lack of knowledge and expertise in new fields. Therefore in describing organisational change within building societies, it is important to recognise that it is not organisations that change, but rather the people within them. It is not surprising to find, as a consequence of this, that building societies of all types see investment in training and development as a key factor in creating a new business culture based on new expertise and high performance.

In chapter 2, the sector was described as being in a state of unstable equilibrium and, in this situation, (the limited number of external appointments apart), the stability of the current strategic leadership in shaping the direction and development of societies long term business plans is a feature worth examining. Whilst the rate of change may be high in the sector, the management of the process of change may require a degree of stability and this will be provided by chief executives. In Table 9:X consideration is given to the current (1992) age profile of chief executives for the sector in order to see if there is a high projected wastage rate for chief executives and hence a succession planning issue. The information was obtained from the annual report and accounts of individual societies. Unfortunately not all societies included such data in their accounts and in consequence 11 societies were omitted from the analysis, 1 national society, 1 regional society and 9 local societies.

Table 9:X
Age Profile of Chief Executives

Building Society			**Age Range**		
Groupings	**<40**	**41-43**	**44-46**	**47-49**	**50-52**
National Societies	0	0	0	1	3
Regional Societies	1	0	7	7	9
Local Societies	4	5	3	7	8
			Age Range		
	53-55	**56-58**	**59-61**	**62-64**	**65>**
National Societies	2	2	1	0	0
Regional Societies	3	1	2	2	0
Local Societies	3	2	2	1	2

Assuming a normal retirement age of 65, only 2 chief executives are due to retire. If retirements were to take place in advance of the statutory age, say at either 60 or 55, then the wastage would be 10 and 15 respectively. From the above figures, it can be seen that the chief executive population displays a fairly balanced profile with the majority of chief executives under the age of 50. The age profile of chief executives is important in one other respect, and this relates to the likelihood of transfers of engagements occurring. It was suggested during the course of research that the likelihood of transfers of engagements may be positively linked to the age profile of the chief executive. This is an interesting perspective when it is considered that, for instance, 18 chief executives in the local society sector are over the age of 50. This factor could, given the propensity to concentration in the sector, be of more significance to chief executive wastage than the effect of wastage through retirements.

A recent consultants report (Merton Associates,1990) indicated that salary levels for building society chief executives were anomalous when taken on an inter-society basis. Moreover, it was claimed that there were instances where salary bore little relationship to society performance. Given the comments made earlier about building societies as performance based organisations it is appropriate to examine this issue in some detail. A correlation analysis was therefore undertaken to examine whether a relationship existed between the salary level of the chief executive and the asset size of the society and also between the salary level of the chief executive and the profit performance of the society. Profit performance was measured as profits as a percentage of mean reserves. This analysis considered the national, regional and local society groupings and also all societies as an aggregate group.

Before considering the detailed results of the correlation analysis, data is initially provided on the monetary value of salary levels for chief executives for the years 1989 and 1991 in Table 9:XI.

Table 9:XI
Salary Levels of Chief Executives, 1989 and 1991

Building Society Groups	Salary, 1989, £ Highest/Average/Lowest			Salary, 1991, £ Highest/Average/Lowest		
National Societies	178,600	135,570	82,800	306,040	209,190	132,000
Regional Societies	126,300	70,160	25,800	161,200	94,785	47,350
Local Societies*	51,000	35,737	20,400	63,200	46,266	25,000
All Societies	178,600	62,089	20,400	306,040	86,147	25,000

*The smallest 7 local societies were not included in the analysis since chief executive salary levels were not available from the annual report and accounts.

Table 9:XII provides correlation coefficients for the relationship between the chief executive's salary level and the asset size of the building society.

Table 9:XII
Correlation between the Salary of the Chief Executive and the Asset Size of the Society

Building Society Groupings	Correlation Coefficients 1989	1990	1991
National Societies	0.39	0.24	0.25
Regional Societies	0.75	0.78	0.79
Local Societies*	0.40	0.68	0.58
All Societies	0.66	0.67	0.71

*The 7 smallest local societies were not included in the analysis since chief executive salary levels were not available from the annual report and accounts.

It can be seen that in the case of regional and local societies there is a strong positive correlation between the salary of the chief executive and the asset size of the society. This is also the case when all societies are considered. Whilst there is a positive correlation in the case of the national societies grouping it is only moderately so.

The correlation between chief executive's salary level and profit performance of the society is perhaps a more relevant measure than the correlation between asset size and salary level. The results of the correlation analysis for this is contained in Table 9:XIII.

Table 9:XIII
Correlation between the Salary of the Chief Executive and the Profit Performance of the Society

Building Society Groupings	Correlation Coefficients 1989	1990	1991
National Societies	0.27	0.06	0.16
Regional Societies	0.20	-0.08	-0.21
Local Societies*	0.09	0.05	-0.10
All Societies	0.41	0.33	0.29

*The smallest 7 local societies were not included in the analysis since chief executive salary levels were not available from the annual report and accounts.

It is apparent, taking the results for all societies, that although there is a positive correlation between chief executive's salary level and profits as a percentage of mean reserves, this has been declining during the period 1989 to 1991. For national societies the relationship is moderately positive, whilst in the case of regional and local societies there are instances when the relationship is actually negative. Consequently, the results of the correlation analysis are somewhat inconclusive, although for building societies in aggregate terms there appears to be a more pronounced positive correlation.

Summary

Clearly, the issues that face building societies in terms of the organisational change described in this chapter involve both opportunities and challenges that are critical to future organisational success. The analysis of organisational change has been grounded in empirical evidence concerning a shift from a simple, unitary organisational structure to a more divisionalised type organisational structure throughout most of the sector. The major impetus for this structural change has been the demands placed on all types of building society by a more dynamic, competitive business environment. The use of joint ventures and acquisitions within the sector is an indicator of the kind of structural changes occurring, where more complex organisational forms are the result. In terms of the key imperatives of organisational design for the 1990s identified by the academic literature, all building society types show a strong move towards delegation of management decision-making. Evidence of a flattening of management hierarchies is, however, much weaker, occurring only in the case of a few national societies. The disintegration of head-office functions has occurred to a limited extent mainly through the establishment of specialist regional administration centres. There is no evidence supporting a trend toward the leaner head-offices favoured in many other corporate sectors.

Not surprisingly, both the increased use of formalised planning and resource allocation and information technology were universal across the sector. Formalised planning can be viewed as an integrative device to better manage the complexity and risk associated with the new business environment. Similarly, information technology makes the task of planning and integrating at the corporate level easier, especially in relation to the activities of sub-units within a decentralised structure.

The significance of cost factors in organisational restructuring were seen to be important when it was established that the benefits of divisionalisation required to be linked to adequate volumes of business in order to ensure economies of scale and scope. Cost factors were further examined by considering the effect of a range of internal features within building societies on the statistical probability that they might engage in organisational restructuring. Here it was found that the higher the relative price of labour, profit growth, absolute administrative costs and asset size, the greater the probability that a building society would engage in organisational restructuring. This was provided that these factors were not outweighed by the negative impact of growth in employee numbers, the ratio of management expenses to branch numbers, and staff costs. It was recognised that probability models are just that and ultimately any form of organisational restructuring is a matter of strategic choice.

The difficulty of changing traditional values within the sector was alluded to. For instance, translated to the level of objectives, this chapter attempted to show how the shift from social to more commercial objectives can create new challenges for building societies, particularly in balancing the interests of a more complex constituency of members and customers. Yet the degree to which cultural change has occurred is clearly seen in the way most societies have embraced a more performance orientated culture. Clearly the intent is that payment, promotion and recruitment systems are more clearly linked to the creation of performance based organisations.

A correlation analysis was undertaken of salary levels of chief executives *vis a vis* the asset size and profit performance of societies. Positive correlations were found to exist in both cases, although in terms of profit performance the relationship was often extremely weak and even at times slightly negative. The age profile of chief executives was also examined and the wastage rate projected through retirements did not appear unduly high. If, however, it is accepted that the potential for transfers of engagements may be a function of the age of the chief executive, a different picture emerges concerning the potential wastage rate amongst chief executives in the local society segment. Nevertheless, in overall terms, the case was made that there was stability within the age profile given that the majority of chief executives were under 55 years of age, and this ensured that long term business plans could be directed by the current strategic leaders within the sector.

10. The Factors of Influence in the Relocation Decision

Introduction

In this chapter the relocation policies pursued by building societies over recent years are examined. In terms of the discussion relocation is viewed to be the situation where the financial institution relocates its business operations in part or in full from one geographic area to another. The relocation decision itself is invariably driven either by the desire to reduce operational costs or as part of a restructuring programme, as the financial institution, for example, expands its product range.

The most recent sustained period of relocation activity was during the late 1980s. Unlike earlier periods of major relocations, as in the late 1960s and early 1970s, this most recent period was led by the private sector with only limited government involvement. As would be expected the majority of these relocations were out of central London. Diplock *et al.* (1991) argued that a combination of commercial trends combined to create the necessary pressure for firms to move out of the capital. These included a steady rise in office costs, a reduction in the availability of office space plus a fall off in the volume of suitably trained labour. These pressures were particularly acute within the then growing financial services industry. Clearly, banks, insurance companies, credit card companies as well as building societies were all searching for the perfect office location outside London where the financial institution could not only avail of relatively lower property costs but could also tap into a more abundant and better qualified labour supply.

The recession has, however, now firmly taken hold in the UK with the financial services sector one of the hardest hit. Building societies along with other financial institutions are at present going through a period of retrenchment. In consequence a shortage of skilled labour is no longer an acute problem. The recession has also taken its toll on the property market. Central London is now characterised by property oversupply and falling rents. Indeed Diplock *et al.* (1991) indicated that Central London based firms, willing to consider relocation, are finding rents in areas such as Dockland much lower than in many of the provincial alternatives in the South-East and South-West of England. The authors further suggested that at present only some 10 percent of London based companies are "very seriously considering relocation". This then of course raises the question why analyse the relocation activity of building societies? The primary reason for pursuing the analysis is that much of the relocation undertaken by building societies has been driven by operational restructuring programmes, as societies have expanded their product portfolio and in addition rationalised administration and support activities at head-office level. Indeed given that unlike most other financial groupings, the vast majority of building societies' head-offices and operational functions are not London based, (see chapter 3), cost push factors are likely to be much less important than restructuring in their relocation decision.

In this chapter two broad angles of the relocation process of building societies are examined. The first concerns an analysis of those societies which have in recent years been involved in relocation in an attempt to discover which functions of their operations have been relocated, why they chose to relocate and what were the crucial factors in their choice of geographic destination. The second considers the building society industry as a whole and with the aid of a limited dependent model attempts to identify the characteristics of those societies most likely to be involved in the relocation process.

Before examining the survey results for those societies which have engaged in relocation consider first a breakdown of the front and back-office operations of building societies. Consideration of these operations should enable a picture to be formed of the areas most open to relocation.

Operational Structure

Taking as a start point that of the financial services offered by building societies an attempt is made to present the spectrum of front and back office operations associated with each financial service. The breakdown is presented in Table 10:I. A total of five broad groups of financial services are identified although it is recognised that some societies do not offer services in all of these areas.

Table 10:I
Front and Back Office Operations

Nature of Financial Service	Provision of Front Office Service by:	Provision of Back Office Service through:
Deposit and Payment Services	Counter staff Lobby terminals ATM's Telephone banking Home banking	Processing systems Credit Card Accounting Cheque card fraud monitoring Ordering cheque books Balance enquiries Calculating charges and interest Accounting records and pass book entries
Consumer Loans	Branch lending offices Telephone banking Agency arrangements	Loan and mortgage processing Credit scoring and control procedures Loan and mortgage servicing Customer databases
Primary Provision of Financial Market Services	Client liaison officers Institutional sales teams Telephone, telex, fax and other communications	Market intelligence systems Dealing systems Settlement systems
Investment Management Services	Institutional and business liaison officers Management teams	Processing and registration of securities' transactions Monitoring market developments
Insurance Services	In-house sales forces Independent agents Tied agents	Valuing asset portfolios Processing of policy proposals, policies and claims Actuarial activities Claims assessments

For the most part, and this applies to all financial institutions not just building societies, back-office functions have formed the bulk of the relocation traffic. Traditionally such back-offices have taken the form of remote paper factories for non-time-critical labour and space intensive activities. In the case of building societies back-office work which falls into this category would encompass loan and mortgage processing, accounting records and passbook entries, credit and cheque card processing, customer databases and fraud monitoring. It is through information technology that organisations have been able to shelve this processing end of the business from the strategic core and relocate it to new tailor-made high technology premises.

Front-office facilities in contrast are much less likely to move. These functions are invariably located where they can best interface with the institution's customer base and as a consequence relocation for the most part is not an option. Only in limited areas such as telephone banking could a relocation policy be successfully pursued.

Not explicitly detailed in Table 10:I are head-office functions. In the main most of what would be considered traditional head-office functions have been subsumed in Table 10:I within the back-office subcategory. There are of course a number of notable omissions, not least the personnel, training and treasury functions. Head-office functions, in that there is limited advantage in being located in close proximity to the customer base, are also prime candidates for relocation. Indeed if the debate is broadened to include other financial groupings it is clear that head-office functions are as likely to be decentralised as back-office facilities. Sun-Alliance, the insurance giant, was one of the first decentralisers, when it moved its entire head-office to Bristol in the 1970s. Lloyds Bank in the late 1980s constructed a 105,000 sq. ft. building in Bristol to house its head-office personnel, finance, treasury and UK retail banking divisions. By the middle of 1990, 700 people had already been relocated by Lloyds to Bristol with the expectation of a further transfer of 700 jobs in the near future.

Survey Results

The information upon which this analysis of specific relocations by building societies is based was obtained from two surveys carried out by the authors in 1991. The first survey which covered all UK building societies was extremely general in form and the information obtained on relocation related solely to whether the intermediary had been involved in the process over the period 1987 to 1991, (the main purpose of this survey was to obtain information on the organisational structure of building societies, see chapter 9). A total of 72 societies responded in a usable form to this survey and of that number 26 had been involved in relocation. A more detailed, relocation specific, questionnaire was forwarded to these societies of which 18 replied in a usable format.

From the analysis of the survey material it transpired that essentially relocation consisted of the transfer of back-office work. This back-office work was moved both out of the branches and out of head-office with a significant proportion of this work moved to purpose built developments. The back-office work on the move was data and information processing, mortgage processing and printing.

One example of a society which has actively pursued a policy of transferring administrative functions away from its branch network is that of the Halifax. At present the Halifax is in the process of converting its branches to an open-plan format. To obtain maximum return from this open-plan approach they are researching the benefits of combining this with the transfer of administrative functions from the branches to separate service centres. In the case of the Halifax the development of administration centres is called the "Conurbation Scheme" whereby one major administration centre forms the hub for a nunber of satellite branches. Early in 1991, they established their first remote service centre in Manchester which took over the administrative tasks of a small group of branches in the City of London.

> "there is no technical reason why a branch and its administration should not now be at opposite ends of the country." (Halifax, Annual Report, 1991)

The Abbey National, (not included in the survey), has also pursued such a policy. They have moved administrative work out of the branches into a network of 49 mortgage and 23 cheque centres. Abbey National's mortgage centre based in Birmingham, for example, processes mortgage paperwork for 13 branches.

An example of a society transferring administrative functions from head-office is that of the Woolwich, although they achieved this objective in a somewhat circuitous manner. By the mid-eighties the Woolwich had outgrown its head-office and as a consequence various corporate functions were spread around satellite offices in London. In order to bring together all key corporate control functions on one site a new corporate headquarters was built in Bexleyheath, Kent and became functional in 1989. The old head-office then became one of the Woolwich's administration centres.

The Nationwide, at the start of 1992, opened administrative centres in both Swindon and Northampton[1]. Administrative functions in Swindon had previously been scattered in office buildings throughout the town. The Nationwide has total computer interchangeability between Swindon and Northampton and argue that this is

> "a vital part of our disaster recovery plan...." (Nationwide, Annual Report, 1992)

As societies' sophistication has increased so also has their reliance on information technology. A number of societies as a consequence have found it necessary to construct purpose built computer centres. Information technology is therefore a further back-office function which has been moved by a number of societies from head-office. The Bristol and West established a new computer centre at Harry Stoke, Bristol in 1990. This facility enabled the Bristol and West to centralise information technology operations which had previously been divided between two sites. Abbey National in October 1991 opened a new computer centre in Milton Keynes. New up-to-date computer equipment now enables them to process 8,500 financial transactions per minute instead of 5,000.

A number of societies have also transferred specific head-office functions, although for the most part these transfers were to the branches. The most often cited function involved in transfer was that of training. In a few cases there has also been a total movement of head-office functions, although invariably within the same locality. Recent examples include transfers by the Cheltenham and Gloucester, The Heart of England, the Stroud and Swindon and the Yorkshire.

A breakdown of the various reasons which lie behind the decision to relocate plus the percentage of societies which attach importance to the respective reasons is provided in Table 10:II.

Table 10:II
Relative Importance of the Various Reasons Given for Relocation

Reasons	% weights
Financial:-	
Property cost saving	6.9
Labour cost saving	0.0
Operational/Organisational:-	
Consolidation	13.8
Provision for expansion	41.4
Locational efficiency	20.7
Shortage of office space	17.2
Labour:-	
Availability	0.0
Welfare	0.0
Total	100.0

These figures indicate that organisational/operational factors are the most frequently cited reasons for relocation. Within this category "provision for expansion" which refers to the securing of space to accommodate current developments is by far the most important factor with a weighted score of 41.4

percent. In the main the importance of this factor stems from organisational restructuring by societies. In chapter 9 it was demonstrated that building societies traditionally have possessed a simple, unitary organisational structure comprised of a head-office containing a mortgage department responsible for the administration of lending, a savings department responsible for deposit taking and a personnel department. The remaining staff were located in the branch network which in turn was supported by a small number of regional offices providing a personnel function. As societies have diversified it has proved necessary to devise appropriate organisational structures to complement their market diversification strategies. In chapter 9 it was demonstrated that the new structures to emerge were quasi-divisional in form, that is structures which are locally administered but centrally driven. Estate agency operations, new financial services etc. were all established as separate divisions with the strategic and administrative functions for these divisions either within the head-office or at centralised units usually within easy travelling distance of head-office. It is therefore this organisational restructuring programme which accounts for the importance of the subcategory "provision for expansion" in Table 10:II. In addition the expectation also is that organisational restructuring is the overriding explanatory reason for the importance of the other subcategories within "operational/organisational" in Table 10:II.

Financial factors and specifically property cost saving have also a role, albeit minor, to play in the relocation decision. It was found that this was particularly true for those societies with a London base. These societies have attempted to reduce administrative costs by decentralising parts of their central administration from the capital. The demise of cost factors as a reason for relocation can be clearly seen if the results in Table 10:II are compared with those obtained by Jones Lang Wotton (1990). This consulting and research group considered decentralisation from Central London over the period 1983 to 1989. Their analysis considered all types of firms and they found that property and labour cost factors accounted for approximately 45 percent of the total number of relocations over that period. The comparable figure in this relocation study of building societies is a mere 6.9 percent.

Operational/organisational and financial cost saving are also the salient factors in the establishment by a number of societies of administrative centres to undertake back-office work. The Nationwide, as mentioned earlier, has developed administrative centres at Northampton and Swindon; the Alliance and Leicester has administrative offices in Hove while the Bradford and Bingley has a centre at Horsham. These administrative centres are essentially remote paper factories for non-time-critical labour and space intensive activities.

The decision about where to locate is based upon a more diverse set of factors than is the decision about whether or not to relocate. The relevant factors and their proportionate weights are all detailed in Table 10:III.

Table 10:III
Relative Importance of the Various Reasons Given for the Choice of Relocation Destination

Reasons	% weights
Proximity to head office	13.9
Proximity to London	8.3
Supply of labour	2.8
Supply of office space	19.4
Financial incentives from local authorities	2.8
Property prices	5.6
Labour costs	0.0
Infrastructure	8.3
Business consolidation	38.9
Total	100.0

Many of the factors identified in Table 10:III are interrelated. A case in point is that of proximity to head-office, proximity to London and good infrastructure. The reason for the interrelationship is that an intermediary's relocation plan is likely to include a transport and communications analysis to gauge the ease of access to the main financial markets and if back-office work is involved the ease of access between the relocation site and head-office. In the relocation decision consolidation of business, allocated a weight of 38.9 percent, was by far the most crucial determinant. Business consolidation refers to the degree of physical integration of the building societies operations and the need, having established in the past in an area, to relocate additional functions in order to consolidate operations. The Woolwich's new head-office in Bexleyheath, Kent is, for example, on land adjacent to its main administration and computer centre.

Salient Characteristics of Societies Involved in Relocation

Having identified the functions of societies most likely to be involved in the relocation process and the reasons why societies relocate and why they chose specific areas rather than others, the discussion now proceeds to an analysis of the characteristics of societies most likely to be involved in relocation.

In line with Hendry's approach to econometrics (see, for example, Hendry and Richard (1983)), an econometric methodology which has been labelled the general to simple procedure was adopted. In this procedure the investigator's initial start position is with a very general hypothesis which should be acceptable to all and which is then narrowed down by the identification of simplifications that are acceptable on the data. Given the limited applied information on the statistical relevance or otherwise of specific variables the adoption of such a procedure is viewed as particularly pertinent.

As a start position the analysis initially focused upon a range of potential categories of influence upon the probability of a building society being involved in relocation. Eight categories of influence giving rise to a total of 21 variables were specified as possibly revealing indicators of the characteristics of societies most likely to be involved in relocation. These are detailed in Table 10:IV.

Table 10:IV
Data Matrix

(a)	**Scale**	
	(i)	asset volume, £'000s
	(ii)	employee numbers
	(iii)	branch numbers
	(iv)	staff costs
	(v)	administrative costs
(b)	**Efficiency**	
	(vi)	management expenses/total assets
	(vii)	management expenses/employee numbers
	(viii)	management expenses/branch numbers
(c)	**Labour Costs**	
	(ix)	staff costs/employee numbers
(d)	**Market Share**	
	(x)	total assets of building society/total assets of the market
(e)	**Profit**	
	(xi)	profits before tax/total assets
	(xii)	profits after tax/total assets
	(xiii)	reserves/total assets
(f)	**Growth**	
	(xiv)	growth in employee numbers, 1987 to 1990
	(xv)	growth in total assets, 1987 to 1990
	(xvi)	growth in profits, 1987 to 1990
(g)	**Branch Structure**	
	(xvii)	national society
	(xviii)	regional society
	(xix)	local society
(h)	**Organisational Structure**	
	(xx)	unitary form structure
	(xxi)	quasi-divisional structure

Two aspects with regard to the information documented in Table 10:IV should be noted. First, the values of the variables (i) through to (xiii) were computed as the mean values over the period 1987 to 1990. In this instance, as the survey itself was carried out in 1991, it was felt that it would be inappropriate to utilise 1991 values. Second, dummy variables were utilised to distinguish between national, regional and local building societies and also to distinguish between societies which had shifted their organisational form from unitary in nature to quasi-divisional, this information was in turn obtained from the survey on organisational structure referred to in chapter 9.

The dependent variable was constructed as a dichotomous binary choice variable which assumes a value of one if over the period under scrutiny the society has been involved in relocation. As indicated earlier the information set upon which this classification is based was obtained from questionnaire returns. The model utilised for estimation purposes was the probit model. The rationale for the use of this model coupled with its salient features are all detailed in Appendix 10:I.

Estimation and Results

A probit model incorporating each of the explanatory variables documented in Table 10:IV was postulated. A simplification search in line with the Hendry methodology was then carried out. Essentially this relates to the elimination of variables which add little to the explanatory power of the model and then re-estimating the specification with the procedure repeated until almost in iterative fashion a statistically significant simplification of the general specification is converged upon.

In Table 10:V a summary of those estimated coefficients which proved to be significant in the building society relocation decision is presented. The t-statistics associated with each of the estimated coefficients are also detailed. In addition the transformed probit coefficients which give a measure of the marginal effect of each independent variable on the probability $Y_i = 1$ are also reported in Table 10:V. These transformed probit coefficients are computed at the sample mean of the respective explanatory variables. Finally at the bottom of Table 10:V the pseudo R^2 which gives a measure of the goodness of fit of the estimation equation, the number of positive observations and the percentage of correct predictions are all detailed.

Table 10:V
Probability Assessment of Relocation by Building Societies

Variable	Probit Coefficient	t-statistic	Probability Impact
Constant	-4.03	3.295*	-1.11
Organisational Structure	1.006	2.52*	0.277
Staff costs/ employee nos.	0.27	2.861*	0.074
Growth in employee nos.	4.373	2.66*	1.205
Growth in profits	0.819	1.74**	0.226
Administrative costs/branch nos.	-0.005	1.962**	-0.001

*significant at 5% level
**significant at 10% level
$R^2 = 0.35$
% of correct predictions = 72.6

Overall the variance explained by the model is high as indicated by the pseudo R^2 value of 0.356[2]. The model itself appears to be good from a predictive perspective in that over 72 percent of the cases are correctly predicted. From Table 10:V it can be seen that those variables with a positive influence are the dummy variable which represents those societies which have shifted their organisational structure to a quasi-divisional form, staff costs/employee numbers, growth in employee numbers and growth in profits. The implication therefore is that organisational change, high employee and profit growth plus high staff costs relative to employee numbers all increase the probability that the society will undertake relocation in some form.

Only one variable negatively impacts upon the likelihood of relocation. It is administrative costs relative to branch numbers. Consequently the greater are administrative costs relative to branch numbers the lower the probability that the building society will engage in relocation. It should be noted, however, that with a probability impact of -0.001 this variable has only an extremely limited role to play in the identification of societies likely to engage in relocation.

These results for the most part are intuitively appealing and appear to reflect what is now occurring within the sector. Consider first the positive factors. As earlier documented organisational restructuring has been forced upon the societies as they have diversified their product portfolio. This diversification has resulted, in a number of cases, in the establishment of decentralised divisions which have in turn captured from head-office a range of strategic and administrative functions. The positive role of staff costs relative to employee numbers can be viewed in terms of societies, particularly those with a London base, attempting to reduce administrative costs by spatially decentralising parts of their central administration from a high cost urban location. An overview of the relative probability impact weights in Table 10:V identifies employee growth as the most crucial positive influence upon relocation. Employee growth, with the exception of a dip in 1989 with the removal of the Abbey National from the statistics, has risen steadily within the industry over the last decade, (see chapter 3). Relocation to larger purpose built centres for functions such as mortgage and cheque administration and data processing has proved to be the only alternative for societies which have experienced rapid employment growth. Finally, as would be expected, profit growth is a further positive determinant in that without such growth, funds would not be available to implement relocation decisions.

The one negative variable is that of administrative costs relative to branch numbers. Although the explanatory power of this variable is limited a rationale for its relevance may be obtained from the earlier finding that a number of societies are transferring a selection of administrative functions from head-office to their branches. To the extent that some societies have high administrative costs at head-office it may be the case that these societies are less prone to divest head-office functions to their branches.

Summary

In this chapter the discussion has focused upon relocation by building societies. In the background analysis of general relocation trends in the UK a key element to emerge was that while the economic downturn has led to the relocation plans of many financial groupings being placed on hold this, for the most part, has not occurred in the case of building societies. A part explanation for this is that relocation by building societies has tended to be driven by operational restructuring programmes in the face of product diversification as opposed to cost push pressure.

In the main body of the discussion two different though complementary tacts were pursued. The first centred upon survey material. On the basis of the survey work an attempt was made to identify which functions building societies relocate; why they relocate; and why they opt for certain locational areas rather than others. The dominant answers in response to these questions were: back office facilities were most frequently relocated; provision for expansion was the prime relocation cause; and consolidation of business was the main determinant in the choice of relocation site. The second angle pursued by the discussion was the identification of the characteristics of those societies most likely to be involved in relocation. In this instance, a range of variables proved significant with the dominant factor, on the basis of its probability impact, that of growth in employee numbers. Such growth was viewed as creating internal and space constraints within the society thus, in a sense, forcing the society down the relocation road.

Notes

[1]The Northampton office opened was on the same site as an existing administrative office - the former head-office of the Anglia building society.

[2]The pseudo R^2 was obtained by first calculating in-sample estimated probabilities which are equivalent to predicted values of the dummy variable and then computing R^2 as $R^2 = 1 - [\Sigma (\hat{Y}_i - Y_i)^2/\Sigma(Y_i - Y)^2]$.

Given that the predicted values are continuous in the 0 1 interval while the actual values of Y_i are either 0 or 1 even very good fits would not give R^2 values that close to 1. In addition cross section analyses in themselves tend not to generate high R^2 values.

Appendix 10:I

Econometric Methodology

Given the dichotomous nature of the dependent variable it would be improper to utilise ordinary least squares as special problems arise when the dependent variable is binary in format.

Consider the linear probability model

$$Y_i = X_i'\beta + u_i; \; i=1............n \tag{1}$$

where $Y_i = 1$ if the society has been involved in relocation

$Y_i = 0$ if the society has not been involved in relocation

$X_i'\beta$ represents those characteristics of building society i that makes it more or less likely to engage in relocation.

Problems with this model refer to the fact that the disturbance distribution does not have constant variance therefore the disturbances are heteroskedastic. Although OLS applied to transformed data eliminates this problem the model still suffers from the fact that it is theoretically possible for $X'\beta$ to take values outside the range 0 to 1 and this conflicts with the interpretation of $X'\beta$ as the probability that $Y_i = 1$.

An alternative approach and the one utilised in this study is the probit model in which there is an underlying response variable Y^*_i defined by the regression relationship.

$$Y^*_i = \beta' X_i + u_i \tag{2}$$

Y^*_i in turn determines the outcome observed for the zero-one dummy Y_i.

$$\begin{aligned} Y_i &= 1, \quad \text{if } Y^*_i > 0 \\ Y_i &= 0, \quad \text{otherwise} \end{aligned} \tag{3}$$

Since Y^*_i is not constrained to equal 0 or 1 there is no reason u_i cannot be associated with a continuous distribution and we can specify that u_i is normally distributed with zero mean and constant variance.

From (2) and (3)

$$\begin{aligned} Prob(Y_i = 1) &= Prob(u_i > \beta' X_i) \\ &= 1 - F\ (-\beta' X_i) \end{aligned} \tag{4}$$

Where F is the cumulative distribution function for u. If u_i is standard normal then F( ) is the standard normal cumulative density function and we have the probit model.

The probit model also permits the calculation of the marginal effect of each independent variable on the probability $Y_i = 1$.
Following Maddala (1983) if X_{ik} is the K_{th} element of the vector of explanatory variables, X_i and β_k is the kth element of β then the marginal impact is given as

$$\frac{\partial}{\partial X_{ik}}(x_i'\beta) = (x_i'\beta)\,\beta_k \qquad (5)$$

11. European Legislative Framework

Introduction

To date the analysis of building societies has essentially been couched within the strictures of the UK domestic market. In this chapter, and indeed chapter 12 which follows, an effort is made to broaden the focus of the discussion. More particularly the opportunities and threats offered by the wider European market are examined. In this chapter attention concentrates upon the European legislative framework. This legislative framework has two dimensions, broad based legislation and more sector/industry specific legislation.

Broad based legislation, while impacting upon building societies, has implications for all industrial and service industries. The most important of these broad based measures are those which relate to the regulation of capital movements; the harmonisation of taxation; the control of mergers and takeovers; and the promotion of monetary union. In contrast the sector/industry specific legislation considered is that which is directly aimed at credit institutions. The implications of the Second Banking Directive for building societies is considered, as are the directives on own funds of credit institutions and solvency ratios for credit institutions. In a more summarised manner directives on annual accounts, deposit guarantee schemes, reorganisation and winding up of credit institutions, money laundering, payment cards, and supervision on a consolidated basis are all examined.

The importance of this analysis of legislation rests with the fact that it dictates the activities which building societies can undertake in the wider markets of Europe and indeed the conditions which building societies must satisfy and the safeguards which they must have in place before being permitted to trade in these markets. Emphasis in the discussion is placed upon spelling out the ramifications for building societies of recent developments in the European Community. Notable examples include the European Commission's draft statute at the end of 1991 for a European mutual society and of course the setbacks which occurred during 1992 to the goal of monetary union.

General and Specific Legislative Measures

In broad terms the Treaty of Rome is about the achievement of a single integrated market to enable the free movement between member states, unimpeded by customs duties and quantitative restrictions, of goods, services, labour and capital. With respect to the financial services sector the measures utilised by the EC in the attainment of an integrated market can be divided into two groups. The first group encompasses a selection of general measures. While these general measures are of relevance to the financial services industry, and indeed each of the financial groups which make up that industry, they are also of importance to each and every other industrial and service sector.

The second group encompasses measures of a more market specific nature, that is, measures which are targeted at individual markets within the financial services sector. In the examination of these measures particular attention is paid to those which have ramifications for building societies.

Consider first the more pertinent general measures. As emphasised, they have importance not only for the financial services industry but for all sectors of the economy. Four areas stand out in terms of their particular importance, they are: the free movement of capital between member states; the creation of a monetary union in Europe; equalisation of tax treatment; and the control of mergers and takeovers.

Freedom of capital movements

Essentially capital movements mean the movement of money. It should be noted that the liberalisation of capital movements is a much wider concept than simply the abolition of exchange controls, in that it also permits access to and investment in local markets such as stock markets. Two directives passed in the 1960s liberalised movements of personal capital, commercial credit and direct investments. In 1986, Directive 86/566C was passed which liberalised capital movements in connection with long-term commercial credit and transactions in securities not listed on a stock exchange. The directive also abolished exchange controls on the admission of company securities of one member state to the capital market of another. In July 1988, Directive 88/361 was adopted. This directive liberalised all remaining EC capital movements. It was adopted by 8 out of the 12 member states in the middle of 1990. The adoption period for Greece, Ireland, Portugal and Spain was extended until the end of 1992 with Greece and Portugal having the opportunity for a further period of extension, if required. The practical effect of this directive is that it allows both individuals and enterprises complete capital freedom. This includes freedom to, for example, open current and deposit accounts, enter into financial loans and credits and invest in short-term financial instruments.

Monetary union

The first serious attempt to establish a monetary union in the European Community was set out in the Werner Report, issued on October 8, 1970. It outlined a programme for the establishment of a complete monetary union among member states by 1980. In this union there would be a single currency and a common European central bank, organised along the lines of the Federal Reserve System in the US. The union was to have responsibility for the conduct of domestic monetary policy and for the Community's foreign exchange policy, using in the process the pooled reserves of all member countries.

As a first step towards this ideal of monetary union the snake in the tunnel was proposed. Primarily this arrangement was an appendix to the Smithsonian Agreement. The snake in the tunnel, applying only to EC nations, operated on the principal that whenever the strongest EC currency's percentage premium over its parity plus the weakest currency's discount over its parity reached a 2.25 percent limit then intervention takes place with the weakest currency bought with the strongest. The scheme was a disaster, the UK having lost one third of its reserves trying to stabilise sterling withdrew from the system within the first few weeks of its operation, other countries gradually followed the UK lead.

Attempts to achieve monetary union remained largely in abeyance until 1977, at that stage there was growing dissatisfaction with the way in which exchange markets were functioning - uncertainties associated with exchange rate instability were having an adverse effect on employment, trade and investment. Thus the European Monetary System, EMS was established on March 13, 1979. Its objective was to stabilise exchange rates between the currencies of member states and to contribute to the strengthening of international monetary relations. The exchange rate mechanism, ERM, is at the heart of the EMS. Essentially the ERM is a system of bilateral exchange rates organised to maintain exchange rates within narrow bands. Most members adhere to a +/- 2.25 percent band of fluctuation for their currencies. The UK when it belatedly joined the ERM on October 8, 1990 availed of the option to follow the wider band of +/- 6 percent.

Until the start of the currency crisis in the middle of September 1992 the ERM functioned well and appeared to constitute a zone of relative monetary stability. The success of the ERM was aided by a convergence across member countries in both fiscal and monetary conditions which resulted in more closely linked inflation and interest rates and reduced pressure on exchange rates.

Encouraged by this apparent economic and monetary convergence the Delors Report was published in 1989. This Report documented a three stage approach in the achievement of monetary convergence. The first stage involved each of the EC currencies joining the +/- 2.25 percent fluctuation band, the abolition of capital controls and enhanced policy co-ordination. This stage officially got underway on July 1, 1990. The second stage was where the ERM parity bands were to be narrowed and an EC central bank was to be established. The third and final stage was to occur with the EC central bank assuming control over monetary policy in member states and with the establishment of a single currency throughout EC countries.

While the emergence of a single currency would result, through the elimination of both exchange transaction costs and exchange rate fluctuations, in the expansion of intra-country trade it would also be likely to impact adversely upon the foreign exchange business generated by financial institutions, including building societies. Although 1997 is reputed to be the provisional target date for the introduction of a single currency the recent deterioration in economic conditions; divergent economic performance between EC states; and continued speculative currency runs appears to have placed the objective of monetary union very much in abeyance. Both Italy and the UK have now temporarily withdrawn from the ERM and with enlargement negotiations to open during 1994 with Austria, Sweden, Finland and Norway, monetary union again appears a somewhat unlikely objective. Indeed it could be argued that there are currently many parallels to be drawn with the final days in 1973 of the snake in the tunnel.

Any assessment of whether the withdrawal from the ERM by the UK will have positive or negative ramifications for building societies can at best only be speculative. The weight of opinion does, nevertheless, tend to suggest that the net effect may be positive. Lower market interest rates as a consequence of no longer having to support sterling at an overvalued rate within the ERM may help to stimulate the housing market as well as easing the problem of mortgage arrears. In addition the break in the formal link between sterling and the D-mark suggests that the UK is no longer subject to the same degree of anti-inflationary pressure. This may eventually result in a more rapid growth in prices in the UK, including house prices, with house price growth helping to alleviate the negative equity problems faced by many in the south of England.

Tax harmonisation

The EC through directives has brought pressure to bear on the process of tax equalisation. Directive 88/361 put forward a series of tax harmonisation measures. To date only limited progress has been made in achieving agreement on the respective measures and there are still substantial differences in tax treatment between member states. VAT rates on financial services products differ across Europe. There are also differences in the tax treatment of capital gains and differences with respect to the withholding of tax on company dividends and interest.

Perhaps the most obviously serious problem relates to the differential VAT rates which provide the opportunity for individual EC countries to create an unfair advantage for their own financial services sectors (see, Fleming and Nellis, 1991). Nevertheless the expectation must be that once capital controls across all member states are removed fiscal harmonisation will follow to eliminate the potential for unfair advantage.

Mergers and acquisitions

As institutions within the wider European market endeavour to avail of the opportunity to attain economies of scale and perhaps also economies of scope an increased emphasis on mergers and acquisitions is likely to result. This in turn may have adverse consequences for the degree and level of competition within EC markets. Measures have been put forward and indeed adopted to enable the Commission to exercise control over mergers and acquisitions. These controls have been in place since 1990. The controls cover sizeable mergers or takeovers with an EC-wide dimension. In the financial sector, size thresholds based on asset holdings are the primary test of EC jurisdiction in the determination of whether a merger is compatible with the maintenance of competition. In situations where the market share in the EC is in excess of 25 percent the merger or acquisition is usually viewed as being undesirable within the framework of competition.

Up to the present the financial services industry has not produced any institution with a prominent position through Europe as a whole. The market shares of, for example, the two largest banks, Credit Agricole of France and the Deutsche Bank of Germany are both marginally in excess of 2 percent. The market share of individual financial institutions in Europe is expected to demonstrate upward trends in future years. Barchard (1992) suggests that a wave of mergers is likely to sweep through the banking and insurances sectors of several European countries with the onset of the single market. Indeed a significant number of mergers have already occurred in Spain, the Netherlands, Austria, Italy and Germany. One reason behind such mergers is that the new larger scale financial institutions are better placed to protect their home market share. An equally important reason is that the additional capital strength enables the institutions to venture into markets outside their home country.

Second Banking Co-ordination Directive

The next stage in the discussion is that of an examination of those measures which have been directed explicitly at the financial services industry. Given the volume and diversity of measures attention primarily focuses upon those measures with relevance for building societies.

In their programme for the liberalisation of financial services the European Commission has adopted a three stage approach. The first stage is that of the establishment of key prudential standards. The second stage is to provide for home country control of these standards while the third stage is to achieve mutual recognition and application of standards so that control in one country is accepted as adequate in another with the right of establishment in any country within the EC.

The most important single market measure affecting credit institutions is the Second Banking Co-ordination Directive of 1989. All other credit institution measures can be viewed as supportive to this Directive. Its implementation date is January 1, 1993. Details of the Second Banking Directive and other directives which impact upon credit institutions may be found in a number of publications including Credit Institutions Community Measures Adopted or Proposed, Commission of the European Communities, (1990), BSA (1990), European File (1992), Euro Service (1992a) and Euro Service (1992b). The Directive introduces the concept of a single banking licence through which institutions licensed in one Community country can trade in any other member country without further authorisation. A wide range of banking services are open to provision including deposit taking and lending, money transmission, share service and portfolio management and advice. The key feature of the Directive is that of home country authorisation and supervision although the Directive does detail minimum capital requirements and also places disclosure obligations and limitations on equity holding in non-financial companies.

The Directive also sets out the Community's approach to banking arrangements with non-EC countries. Article 7 of the Directive proposed handling the licensing of institutions from non-member countries in the context of reciprocity. The supposed intention is to ensure that the level playing field concept in Europe is not exploited unfairly by non-member countries. Consequently under reciprocity, a licence would only be granted to a third country's credit institutions if European institutions could operate on the same basis in that third country.

The specific implications for building societies of the Second Banking Directive must be viewed within the framework of the 1986 Building Societies Act and subsequent amendments. Section 14 of the Act details the statutory requirements for overseas operations. While the Act and statutory instruments passed in 1987 and 1988 permitted societies to operate directly in certain British overseas territories, namely the Channel Islands, the Isle of Man and Gibraltar they could only until recently conduct business in Europe through a subsidiary or an associated company subject to having commercial assets of at least £100m.

In 1988 societies were permitted to establish European lending companies which are defined as

> "A company with the object of carrying on in member states other than the United Kingdom business which consists wholly or mainly in lending money on the security of land and do not (where that is not the whole business) include lending on land in the United Kingdom."

Essentially this implies that in other European markets societies are limited to their core business, that is lending on the security of land, (class 1 and class 2 assets). The suggestion has nevertheless been made, Council of Mortgage Lenders (1990), that depending on how broadly the BSC interprets the business of "wholly or mainly" lending money on the security of land societies, through their European lending companies, may have the authority to exercise powers and provide services beyond those permitted to them in the UK. While the BSC is unlikely to interpret "wholly or mainly" in this manner it still remains a moot point. No society has as yet tested the extent of these powers. Indeed only the Woolwich has European operations and to date they have not strayed from the provision of mortgage products.

As the 1986 Act plus subsequent orders stood societies within the context of the Second Banking Directive were at a considerable disadvantage relative to other institutions. More specifically the Second Banking Directive extends the single banking licence only in respect of activities which can be carried out in the home country and under the 1986 Act subsidiaries established by societies to operate in Europe could neither lend nor take deposits in the UK. Heightened awareness of this problem, brought on by the imminent approach of the implementation date for the provisions of the Second Banking Directive, led the BSC to review the means by which societies can conduct business outside the UK. As a result of the review an order under Section 14 of the 1986 Act was placed which permitted societies to lend direct on the security of land in other European countries and in line with the treaty between the European community and the European Free Trade Area, EFTA countries, to also lend direct in EFTA countries. That is societies now had the choice of operating directly in EC markets and indeed in the markets of EFTA countries through branch outlets. This order took effect on July 1, 1992[1]. The BSC through orders which came into effect on June 1, 1992 also extended to Europe the range of other powers available to societies within the UK. These new orders are summarised in BSA (1992). Essentially societies are able to undertake syndicated lending, participate in joint ventures, invest in insurance companies and carry out financial services business in any of the European Community or EFTA states.

Before proceeding to examine other single market measures which impact upon credit unions it is perhaps important to dwell briefly on the implication for building societies of Articles 4, 10 and 12 of the Second Banking Directive.

Article 4 states that:

"The competent authorities shall not grant authorisation in cases where initial capital is less than ECU 5 million."

This requirement is not hard and fast in that an additional clause states that the authorities, subject to certain provisos can grant authorisation if they so wish as long as the initial capital is not less than ECU 1 million. This capital requirement applies to the authorisation of new institutions. Given that ECU 1 million translates to approximately £800,000, (1ECU = £1.246, November 1992), a measure of the problem for the establishment of a new society can be taken from the fact that 2 local societies, end 1991, had general reserves of less than £800,000.

Article 10 requires that the capital of credit institutions must not fall below the initial capital required when they were authorised. Member states do not have to apply this requirement to existing credit institutions but in this instance capital must not decline below the highest level reached after the date of notification of the Directive if this is less than the capital prescribed in Article 4. This means that for societies below the sterling equivalent of ECU 1 million on January 1, 1992, probably only the Ecology building society and the Londonderry Provident, capital must never be permitted to fall until it exceeds the sterling equivalent of ECU 1 million.

Article 12 provides that a credit institution cannot hold a shareholding of more than 15 percent of its own funds in an undertaking which is neither a credit institution nor a financial institution. This limitation is not applicable to insurance companies.

Own-Funds

Directive 89/299 of 17 April, 1989 defines own funds for the purpose of authorising financial institutions and is an essential complement to the Second Banking Directive. In the analysis of the capital strength of building societies, documented in chapter 4, particular attention was paid to the manner in which own funds are calculated. To briefly reiterate, own funds are calculated as the sum of Tier 1 plus Tier 2 capital less intangible fixed assets. Tier 1 capital is essentially reserves plus permanent interest bearing shares, PIBS. Tier 2 capital encompasses revaluation reserves plus subordinated debt. Two limitations are imposed, the first is that subordinated debt can be included up to only 50 percent of Tier 1 capital minus intangible assets, the second is that the total of Tier 2 capital may not exceed Tier 1 capital.

Solvency ratios

The Directive on solvency ratios establishes a minimum solvency ratio of 8 percent. The ratio is calculated between own capital of the financial institution and its assets weighted by the degree of risk they exhibit. The weights range from 100 percent for class 2 and class 3 assets to 0 percent for cash in hand. As indicated in chapter 4 the BSC, come the end of the first quarter of 1993, will have established a minimum threshold solvency ratio for each society which in actual fact will be in excess of the 8 percent ratio. The degree to which the ratio exceeds 8 percent is dependent upon the nature and inherent risks of the society's business. Factors such as the quality of management in the society plus the geographical spread of its business are likely to be of particular importance in the determination of the minimum threshold solvency ratio.

Quasi-solvency ratios are reported in the Data Appendix. These ratios were calculated as simply Tier 1 capital alone divided by the sum of risk weighted assets. It is clear from the calculated values that most societies on Tier 1 capital alone are likely to have little difficulty in meeting the European Commission's 8 percent minimum solvency ratio and indeed the computed values are such that societies are also well placed to meet the higher threshold requirements of the BSC.

Other measures of importance to credit institutions

In addition to these principal directives a number of secondary directives, proposed directives, recommendations and communications relevant to credit institutions operating in the single European market have been published by the European Commission.

Directive 86/635 on the annual accounts of credit institutions, adopted in 1986, and which came into force at national level in 1991 standardises the form of annual accounts for building societies and other financial institutions.

Directive 87/102 on consumer credit sets minimum standards for consumer credit laws throughout the European Community. It came into force *via* national legislation in 1990.

A Recommendation concerning the introduction of deposit guarantee schemes was adopted in 1986. This Recommendation related to ensuring that all member states had such schemes in place and that they met certain minimum criteria. In June 1992 a proposal for a Directive to establish common rules for deposit guarantee schemes across member countries was set out. This proposal requires European Community members to have deposit guarantee schemes that provide a minimum level of protection, (approximately £10,000). Member countries could if wished introduce a co-insurance element of up to 10 percent. Schemes would work on the basis of home country funding.

A Proposed Directive on re-organisation and winding up of credit institutions addresses the problem of dealing with credit institutions in financial difficulty. Under its terms responsibility rests with the authorities in the home country of the institution. Disqualification in one community country could under the Directive extend to the EC as a whole.

In December 1986 a Recommendation on large exposures was adopted. This Recommendation attempted to define and harmonise the treatment of large exposures. A draft Directive similar to the Recommendation was published in 1990. The draft Directive is intended to take effect from the start of 1993. There are two principal aspects of note with regard to the Directive. First a credit institution may not incur an exposure to a customer which exceeds 40 percent of own funds. This suggests that the Ecology building society with a capital base, end 1991 of £296,000 would not be able to make a loan in excess of £118,400. Secondly large exposures, defined as greater than 15 percent of own funds are limited in total to 800 percent of own funds. The Ecology building society would therefore be subject to a limitation on the number of loans in excess of £44,400 which it could provide. If each loan was on the 15 percent margin then no more than a total of 53 such loans could be provided. It should in addition be noted that it is argued in (BSA,1992) that the BSC is likely to impose a total limit on the aggregate of all large exposures at considerably less than the 800 percent own funds permitted by the Directive.

A Directive on money laundering was introduced in 1991. This Directive required credit institutions handling large cash flows to report transactions which they suspected to be associated with criminal activity.

The 1988 Recommendation on payments cards was converted to a draft Directive in 1990. The Directive essentially endeavours to establish clear rules on liability in the case of error or defect and to generally secure more information for cardholders.

In April 1992 the Directive on the supervision of credit institutions on a consolidated basis was formally adopted. The key elements of this Directive are that it requires the supervisors of a credit institution which is part of a larger financial group (whether as the parent or a subsidiary), to calculate and apply the prudential ratios and limits on the basis of the consolidated situation of the whole group. The Directive also requires supervisors of credit institutions to co-operate and exchange information with each other. Finally the Directive indicates that there should be a clear allocation of responsibility for carrying out consolidated supervision of a multi-national group. For example where a parent holding company is in one member country but most of the banking activity is carried out in another member country the relevant supervisors are expected to come to an agreement as to which of them is best placed to carry out consolidated supervision.

European Mutual Societies

In the BSA (1991) annual report it was suggested that the potential emergence of European mutual societies was a particularly significant development. At the end of 1991 the European Community produced a draft statute for a European mutual society. The rationale behind the statute is to provide mutuals

> "with adequate legal instruments capable of facilitating the development of their transnational business."

In other words to take advantage of the single market without having to convert to plc status. This piece of European Community legislation in effect could potentially be utilised to by-pass the constraints of the Building Societies 1986 Act. Building societies under this proposed legislation could convert to European mutual status and in so doing step outside the constraints of the 1986 Act. This still leaves the question of the appropriate regulator for the European mutual. Is it a case of establishing a completely new regulator or perhaps the European mutual opts for authorisation as a credit institution under the 1987 Banking Act? The BSA, among others, initially appeared to welcome the prospect for the creation of a European mutual

> "Developments in the European Community during 1991 had the potential to affect significantly the regulatory regime governing societies' operations in the UK. Perhaps the most important matter to emerge was the possibility of the creation of a European Mutual Society." (BSA, Annual Report 1991).

This initial enthusiasm has over recent months tended to abate, not least because the UK Government appears somewhat sceptical as to the merits of the proposal. The Government's position is that it is not clear that the relevant national bodies are experiencing difficulties in operating in more than one European Community member state. In part this concern relates to the much publicised concept of subsidiarity. Procedures to apply the principle of subsidiarity, under which the European Community acts only when member states cannot achieve the goal as well themselves, was one of the key decisions to stem from the Edinburgh European Community summit of December 1992. The introduction of measures to enable a mutual organisation to be formed under European law, outside the laws of individual states, appears to clash directly with the principle of subsidiarity. On this count it seems improbable that much progress will be made in the formation of European mutuals in the foreseeable future.

European Legislation and its Impact on Competition in the UK Mortgage Market

To date the discussion has focused upon the European legislative framework under which societies' fields of operation are shaped. Emphasis centred upon the market opportunities available to societies and the restrictions which still remain on the activities of societies. Omitted from the analysis was the fact that, for example, the single banking licence also opens up the traditional markets of building societies to competition from outside. Whether this can be perceived as a problem for societies is questionable in that the UK financial markets are already one of the most open group of markets in the world. As indicated in chapter 3 centralised mortgage lenders, which include among their number a significant number of foreign based institutions, already have a presence in the UK, although during the property downturn their market share has tended to contract.

Mostly it is the mortgage arm of foreign banks which have entered the UK market. Although specialist mortgage lenders such as Danish housing finance institutions, French home loan companies and Irish building societies are also present. The Irish building societies are among the more recent entrants. In establishing in the UK they have opted to by-pass the BSC and instead have applied direct to the Bank of England to be authorised under the 1987 Banking Act to accept deposits. This in part relates to the fact that the Building Societies Act of 1989 in Ireland, which was very much akin to the 1986 Act in the UK, chose not to vest supervisory responsibility in a body, such as the BSC in the UK, but instead delegated regulatory authority to the Central Bank of Ireland.

Given the relative openness of the UK financial markets the expectation must be that freedom of access, as a result of the dismantling of trans border restrictions, is unlikely to further increase competition levels in the UK mortgage market.

Summary

Consideration of European legislation and its impact upon building societies was pursued from two angles in this chapter. Initially a broad focus was adopted with areas such as tax harmonisation, merger and acquisition policy, freedom of capital movement and monetary union all considered. The importance of these areas rests not with the fact that they are specifically targeted at building societies but rather in that it is these areas where most is happening to shape market strictures, market opportunities and competition levels in Europe.

Most problematic was the discussion of monetary union not least as a consequence of the currency problems of September 1992 which saw both the UK and Italy withdraw from the exchange rate mechanism. It was argued that currency volatility coupled with economic divergence and recent commitments to an enlarged European Community has in all probability placed monetary union on long term hold. When viewed from the perspective of building societies such an outcome may, at least in the short to medium term, have a number of positive ramifications. The resultant lower interest rate structure may help stimulate the housing market and ease the problem of mortgage arrears. Furthermore if the break in the formalised link between the D-mark and sterling leads to moderate UK inflation, including house price inflation, the negative equity problem faced by many homeowners in the south of England may become a thing of the past.

In the examination of legislation more specific to building societies the obvious area of emphasis was that of the Second Banking Co-ordination Directive which provides for a single banking licence through which institutions licensed in one Community country can trade in another member country without further authorisation. Until recently, restrictions under the 1986 Act resulted in the concept of a single banking licence being essentially a nonsense from the perspective of building societies. More specifically the Second Banking Directive extends the single banking licence only in respect of activities which can be carried out in the home country and under the 1986 Act societies could only operate in Europe through subsidiaries which could neither lend nor take deposits in the UK. In June and July 1992 orders were passed which enabled societies to lend direct in other European countries and also extended to Europe the range of other powers available to societies within the UK.

A wide range of additional regulations specific to credit institutions over and above the Second Banking Directive were also considered. Regulation on own funds, solvency ratios, format of accounts, deposit guarantee schemes, large exposures, money laundering and supervision on a consolidated basis were all examined. For the most part these additional legislative measures were adopted or are in the process of being adopted to ensure the smooth function of the single banking licence.

One aspect of proposed legislation which received detailed scrutiny was that pertaining to the concept of a European mutual society. European mutuals may be viewed as taking the concept of the single banking licence a stage further in that the mutual organisation is formed under European law and outside the laws of individual states. While the idea was initially met by many within the building society movement with some anticipation, interest has now tended to wane. The recent enhanced importance ascribed to subsidiarity has essentially put paid to any ideas of establishing an organisation under European law and outside the laws of individual states. The principle of subsidiarity rests with the fact that the European Community should only act when member states cannot achieve the goal as well themselves.

Having established the legislative platform the task in the next chapter turns to an examination of the degree to which societies have availed of the opportunities open to them under legislation. More specifically, in chapter 12, the extent to date of diversification into Europe by building societies; the problems they have faced in this geographic diversification; and the vehicles they have employed to undertake this expansion are all explored.

Notes

[1]Subsequently the Swiss vote against the treaty agreement between the EC and EFTA has led the UK government to withdraw the order enabling societies to operate in EFTA countries.

12. Market Opportunities in Europe

Introduction

Diversification options for societies are not confined solely to the domestic market, building societies also have the opportunity to geographically expand their coverage to markets outside the UK. The single European market has provided societies with a potential customer base well in excess of 300m as opposed to a mere 60m when their operations were constrained to the UK.

On the basis of this customer potential one might therefore have expected to have seen societies enter, *en masse*, into the mortgage markets of Europe. Such a situation has not as yet materialised. In part this is a consequence of the fact that societies have been heavily involved in diversification within national boundaries and have not felt able, at this stage, to add the extra burden of geographic diversification. Another part of the problem for societies rests with the fact that there are significant differences in the house finance markets of Europe, in terms of market participants, mortgage products, the housing mix, government involvement and indeed cultural characteristics. These differences necessarily imply that to successfully diversify on a geographic basis a society must tailor both its operational structure and products to the specific requirements of the market in question.

In this chapter the objective is not to be prescriptive, not least because what holds in one country in Europe is unlikely to hold for others, but rather to identify both the opportunities and problems which are likely to arise in geographic diversification. The discussion begins with an examination of mortgage price differentials and differences in the level of home-ownership across Europe. In essence such analysis is an attempt to identify countries where building societies would have a relative price advantage and in addition where scope for mortgage expansion exists. A country specific analysis is then pursued. Four countries, France, Italy, Germany and Spain are considered. This part of the discussion highlights the major differences between the respective house finance markets and identifies the problems faced by societies involved in expansion. The Woolwich Building Society then becomes the focus of the discussion in that, amongst societies, only the Woolwich has to date diversified into Europe. To supplement the discussion the European diversification strategy of the Abbey National is also considered. The discussion is then completed with an overview of the various mechanisms through which societies could expand into Europe. Start-ups, acquisitions and alliances are considered with the advantages and disadvantages of each documented.

Product Price Differentials

The Cecchini Report (1988) was the first to attempt to quantify how much European companies were losing as a result of border controls. The Report was based on a survey of 11,000 business executives, conducted by 15 companies of consultants, economists and commission personnel. The Report estimated that effective implementation of the single market would result in a saving to European industry of approximately £130bn. This equated to some 5 percent of the Community's gross domestic product. While the actual estimate of the volume of saving has been subject to both dispute and criticism, nevertheless there is a consensus that the completion of the single market will result in some level of saving to European industry.

As part of the Cecchini Report the benefits likely to accrue from the establishment of a single market in financial services were examined. In the area of financial services the primary focus of the research was the estimation of the gains to consumers in the form of a fall in the price of financial products as a consequence of enhanced competition levels. The study covered 8 of the 12 community countries, with the financial products examined those of banking, insurance and security type products. The price of the respective financial products was calculated in terms of the cost of providing the financial product, that is price was computed as the margin in excess of wholesale money market rates. The impact of the completion of the single market was then gauged in terms of the likely squeeze on margins.

The Cecchini Report anticipated "substantial economic gains" from the integration of financial markets because of the integral role that financial services play in all aspects of business in each of the Community countries. The Report calculated that the integration of banking and credit, insurance, brokerage and securities would save the Community somewhere in the order of

£16bn. This cost saving would of course neither be spread equally across countries nor across product lines.

Product pricing in, for example, the Netherlands and the UK was considered to be already highly cost competitive and in consequence would experience only limited downward drift. Price falls in the Netherlands were expected to range between 1 percent and 9 percent while the drop in prices in the UK was calculated to be somewhere in the order of 2 to 12 percent. At the other extreme were those countries viewed as uncompetitive with respect to the pricing of financial products. Notable examples in this instance were Italy and worst of all Spain. In the case of Spain price reductions were expected to lie between 16 and 26 percent.

From this summary of anticipated price falls, on completion of the internal market, it is evident that consumers in the UK will benefit to a lesser degree than their counterparts particularly in Southern Europe. UK producers of financial services in contrast would appear to be well placed to exploit the relative uncompetitive pricing of financial products in other European countries. On the basis of the Cecchini Report the impression obtained is that UK financial services firms should be targeting consumers in countries such as Spain and Italy.

Earlier it was suggested that on individual product lines there was a non-uniformity in price differentials between countries. While margins on some financial products were broadly similar in Community countries, on other products there was wide variability. It is with those products where price variability is most extreme that the benefits to consumers and opportunities to producers are likely to most accrue with the completion of the internal market. In order to quantify the difference in the degree of cost mark-up between product lines, comparative "prices" of a selection of banking and insurance services as documented in the Cecchini Report, are reproduced in Table 12:IA. In Table 12:IB a description of each of the financial services under examination is provided.

As argued in the Cecchini Report care should be taken in any analysis of the "prices" detailed in Table 12:IA. This is due to the fact that the prices of financial services change frequently and the data therefore represents only a "snap-shot" at a given point in time. In addition the reported "prices" in some instances do not give a true assessment of product cost as in many cases there is cross-subsidisation between different financial services.

Table 12:IA
Comparative "Prices" of Purchases of a Range of Personal Financial Services, (ECUs)

Personal Financial Services	Countries							
	B	D	ES	F	I	L	NL	UK
Banking Services:								
Consumer Credit	12	46	27	40	43	14	26	43
Credit Cards	94	84	66	37	99	46	75	61
Mortgages	480	575	800	653	350	499	343	290
Travellers Cheques	7	5	7	8	7	5	7	5
Current Accounts	0	117	2	10	240	8	0	112
Insurance Services:								
Term Insurance	380	225	294	285	392	355	195	150
House Insurance	118	144	135	195	253	220	164	266
Motor Insurance	494	436	758	413	942	671	354	316

It is nevertheless clear that across product lines there is considerable disparity in the spread of "prices". Travellers cheques, home insurance and credit cards are product lines which do not appear to display excessive price variability. At the other end of the spectrum are current accounts, consumer credit and motor insurance. All these product lines demonstrate substantive price variability. From the perspective of UK financial firms what is also particularly noteworthy is that in the case of 4 out of the 8 personal financial services products, the UK is the lowest cost producer. These financial products are term insurance, motor insurance, travellers cheques and mortgages. The fact that mortgages are one of the product areas in which UK financial firms are lowest cost producers can also be said to augur well, at least at face value, for the expansion plans of UK building societies into the markets of Europe.

Table 12:IB
Description of Personal Financial Services

Personal Financial Services	Description of Service
Banking Services:	
Consumer Credit	Annual cost of consumer loan of 500 ECUs. Excess interest rate over wholesale rates.
Credit Cards	Annual cost assuming 500 ECUs debit. Excess interest rate over wholesale rates.
Mortgages	Annual cost of home loan of 25,000 ECUs. Excess interest rate over wholesale rates.
Travellers Cheques	Cost of purchasing 100 ECU's worth of Travellers Cheques.
Current Accounts	Annual cost assuming 200 cheques, 20 standing orders, 50 withdrawals and 20 credits.
Insurance Services:	
Term Insurance	Average annual cost of loan insurance
Home Insurance	Annual cost of fire and theft cover for house valued at 70,000 ECUs.
Motor Insurance	Annual cost of comprehensive insurance, 1.6 litre car, driver 10 years experience, maximum no claims bonus.

Comparison of Housing Tenure Statistics

While a price competitive product is a necessary condition for expansion into a new market it cannot be assumed to be a sufficient condition. A further condition which requires to be satisfied is that there is market potential for the sale of that product. With regard to opportunities for the sale of mortgages one method of assessment of market potential is through an examination of housing tenure statistics. More specifically there are markets in Europe where home ownership is not at anywhere near UK levels. It is in these markets that one would assume there are opportunities for selling mortgages.

In Table 12:II information is provided on the status of occupation of national housing stocks. Figures are provided in percentage form for the proportion of owner occupied housing and for the proportion of rented accommodation. For certain countries these figures do not necessarily sum to 100 due to other more limited housing forms. Presented also in Table 12:II is a breakdown of the rented sector into that of private rented accommodation and social rented accommodation. The latter comprises homes that are let at cheaper rents than market rents by subsidised rental organisations.

Table 12:II
Status of Occupation of National Housing Stocks

Countries	Owner Occupied	Rented Sector	Private Rented	Social Rented
Belgium	62.0	36.0	30.0	6.0
Denmark	55.5	43.3	22.1	21.2
Spain	76.0	18.0	16.6	1.4
France	54.2	36.8	19.7	17.1
Greece	70.0	26.5	26.5	-
Ireland	81.0	19.0	8.4	10.6
Italy	67.0	30.7	23.1	7.6
Luxembourg	68.0	32.0	31.0	1.0
Netherlands	45.0	52.0	15.7	36.3
Portugal	58.0	36.0	24.7	11.3
Germany	40.0	60.0	43.0	17.0
United Kingdom	67.6	32.4	7.0	25.4

From cursory observation of Table 12:II it is evident that substantive differences exist between countries in the level of owner-occupation. Countries such as Germany, the Netherlands and France have relatively low levels of owner-occupation while in contrast Ireland, Spain and Greece have high levels of home-ownership, all of which are in excess of 70 percent. At first glance the conclusion which might be drawn is that the markets of Germany, the Netherlands and France offer the most scope for selling mortgages and consequently should figure in the country diversification plans of UK building societies. France in particular looks a good option when the relative cost of French mortgages are compared with that of UK mortgages, (Table 12:IA).

The case for expansion into these markets is further strengthened when it is considered that over the last number of years there has been an increasing tendency for both national governments and indeed private investors to engage in a policy of disinvestment from the rented sector. It is argued in Social Europe Supplement 3/92 published by the European Commission that this change in direction by national governments

> "is due to a tightening of budgets and a reduction in State investment expenditure in favour of transfer expenditure. This is all part of a larger project to reorganise State finances, reduce budget deficits and, above all, ease taxation."

The change in policy by national governments has manifested itself in the form of cuts in the building of subsidised homes for rent coupled with the sale of subsidised housing to their occupants. In addition to these cutbacks in the provision of housing in the public sector European governments, almost to the exclusion of none, are actively promoting policies to encourage increases in the level of owner occupation. One example is that of Germany where the government has a target of 50 percent for home-ownership, this compares with a current level of ownership of 40 percent. In Spain the government has placed considerable importance on housing finance and has attempted to encourage more liberal means of housing finance. Birch (1989) argued that in France, despite heavy state intervention, successive governments have attached importance to housing construction and at keeping the volume of homes built in excess of 300,000 per annum. This is almost double the number built in the UK. Considerable opportunities therefore exist for societies to exploit these expanding private sector housing markets. This point was further reinforced by Birch (1989) when he stated

> "... some member states of Europe are under political and economic pressure to maintain housing construction programmes but find themselves increasingly unable to fund such programmes. There is no doubt that this situation creates opportunities for mortgage lenders not necessarily indigenous to these individual markets."

The problems faced by national governments in creating an adequate supply of housing and the opportunities open to societies for business in these markets are both further increased by trends in the private rented sector. Disinvestment by private investors in the rented sector is a trend which has become increasingly common to a large majority of member states over recent years. It is suggested that the trend is due to overly constricting rent legislation, as is the case in Italy, Greece and Denmark, although in countries which have initiated a process of freeing the rented market, such as the UK, Spain, the Netherlands and Portugal, disinvestment still continues.

> "Despite uneven results, these measures have not proved to be sufficient to counteract the trend towards disinvestment on the part of private investors. This raises the wider problem of the overall distribution of savings, of the shift of property investment flows from property to securities, stocks and shares." (Social Europe

Supplement, 3/1992, European Commission).

While the promotion of home-ownership plus scope for home-ownership development can again be classed as necessary conditions for the attraction of UK building societies into the markets of other European member countries, these may still not prove to be sufficient conditions. Across Europe considerable diversity still exists in terms of market competition levels; the mix in the provision of public and private sector finance for housing; tax incentives for housing investment; the form of the mortgage advance; plus of course cultural differences. Some or all of these factors may still bar building societies from the profitable entry into the housing markets of Europe. In order to obtain a flavour of the extent of this diversity it is necessary to consider a brief overview of structure and market conditions in four of the main housing markets in Europe - those of Spain, Italy, France and West Germany. Much of this information is based on Reid (1992), Steinherr (1992) and CML(1990).

Housing Finance in France

It has already been indicated that home-ownership levels in France are low and the cost of mortgage finance relatively expensive (see Table 12:IA and Table 12:II). In addition the expense of the housing transaction in France is further exacerbated by other cost elements in the house purchase. Reid (1992) emphasised this point when she stated

> "With fees and other costs in the order of 10-15% of the purchase price, it is hardly surprising that French consumers do not move house more than once or twice in their lifetime."

In terms of the market providers of mortgage loans commercial banks dominate. The largest commercial bank, Credit Agricole, has approximately 20 percent of the housing finance market. Other commercial banks which are viewed as major players in the mortgage market include Banque Nationale de Paris, Credit Lyonnais and Societe Generale. Together they account for a further 35 percent of the market. Savings banks are also prominent in this market with their aggregate market share around 20 percent. The French government is itself a further key participant. Through its agent, Credit Foncier, the government assists in the purchase of homes through the provision of subsidised mortgages. Credit Foncier's share of the mortgage loan market stands at around 10 percent, a share which has been subject to decline in recent years as a consequence of the decrease in the volume of subsidised mortgages provided. Finance companies and life assurance companies are the other players in the French house finance market.

Although finance companies' share of the mortgage loan market is a mere

5 percent it is perhaps worth briefly concentrating upon them because Abbey National, as part of its European expansion plans, purchased the French finance company, Ficofrance. Finance companies generally offer mortgage products at uncompetitive rates as a result of their reliance upon wholesale funds which in France are more expensive than retail deposits. No interest can be paid in France on cheque and short-term time deposits. Due to this cost disadvantage finance companies have tended to provide loans to purchasers for whom other sources of funds are not available, such as loans for second homes.

A typical French mortgage tends to be a packaged loan which consists of several different loan components, including a government subsidised loan, a house-savings related loan plus other approved loan forms. In terms of the discussion to date the house-savings component has not as yet been considered. Only financial institutions which are registered for this purpose by the French government can provide such schemes. The purchaser enters into the savings scheme, usually with one of the commercial banks or saving banks, and after a period of contractual saving they can obtain the housing loan at a preferential rate. The loan amount provided is 2.5 times the amount saved and its term to maturity cannot exceed 15 years.

Most mortgages provided in France are of the capital repayment type where the borrower pays equal instalments, comprising an interest component and a capital component. There are very few endowment or pension scheme mortgages. This rests, in part with the fact that tax relief on mortgage payments are only available for the first five years of the mortgage but perhaps of more importance is that, as indicated, mortgage loans in France rarely exceed 15 years. The relevance of this latter point relates to the fact that the short time scale over which mortgages extend results in investment based products such as endowment mortgages being decidedly more expensive than repayment mortgages. It should not be thought, however, that mortgage innovation is totally lacking in France. There has been some limited innovation. The most notable example is that of the introduction of mortgages with indexed rates. The mortgage interest rate in this instance is variable and is linked to one of the main interest indicators such as the interbank rate.

Finally, in France the sale of mortgages is primarily conducted through the branch network system of the commercial banks, savings banks and finance companies. In France insurance brokers and estate agents tend to be organised on an individual basis, rather than in the form of chains, as is the case in the UK, consequently intermediary third-party sale of mortgages is not very developed.

Housing Finance in Germany

Home-ownership in Germany is the lowest of all 12 members of the European Community while mortgages are the third most costly. Only mortgages in Spain and France are more expensive. Part of the reason for the low level of home-ownership rests with cultural characteristics. Most Germans do not purchase their first home until they are somewhere between the ages of 35 and 40. Until that stage they stay in rented accommodation. The preference in Germany is to save until the purchaser can afford a high quality home and then having chosen a home to remain in it for good.

In contrast to the situation in the UK where home loan finance is invariably provided by a single finance institution, the loan package in Germany is very often made up by a group of financial institutions. In the provision of home finance the financial grouping with dominant market position is that of the savings banks, (Sparkasse). There are approximately 600 savings banks in Germany and they control around 30 percent of the house finance market. While savings banks are permitted to accept deposits from anywhere in Germany they are only able to make loans within their own particular state. Savings banks are controlled by the local authority of that state which in turn guarantees their operations.

Bausparkassen, which deal exclusively with the provision of house finance, are the next most important financial group in the German home finance market. Their market share is of the order of 20 percent. There are 30 Bausparkassen in Germany, two-thirds of which are privately owned. For the most part the private owners are the insurance companies and commercial banks, and it is through the branch networks of these institutions that Bausparkassen provide home loans.

Mortgage banks, as their title suggests, are another financial grouping which operates in the German house finance market. There are almost 40 mortgage banks and their combined market share is 17 percent. Most are private organisations with the majority subsidiaries of other financial institutions, particularly the commercial banks. Mortgage banks are unable, through law, to take retail deposits, rather they generate funds by issuing mortgage and municipal bonds.

Credit co-operatives are also providers of house finance. They are community based institutions and number almost 3,500. They offer a wide range of banking services, with their aggregate share of the mortgage market standing at approximately 17 percent.

The final group of major players in the home loans market is the commercial banks. These institutions have country wide representation with branch outlets in most towns. They provide an exhaustive range of financial services, with their share of the house finance market around 10 percent. Although this market share may appear relatively small, especially when compared with the retail banks in the UK, it must be remembered that most commercial banks have as subsidiaries Bausparkassen and/or mortgage banks, both of which are specialist providers of home loans.

A typical home loan in Germany would comprise a Bausparkassen loan, a mortgage bank or savings bank mortgage and a bridging loan. The customer in all probability deals only with one institution, either a commercial or savings bank, which assembles the loan package on behalf of the customer. From the customer's perspective the most important component of the package is the loan from the Bausparkassen in that the only government incentive for house purchase is administered through the Bausparkassen. This incentive takes the form of a lump sum, payable once the loan is granted by the Bausparkassen. The loan is itself only made available once the borrower has fulfilled a period of contractual saving with the Bausparkassen. The period of contractual saving is usually in the order of 8 to 10 years at which stage the borrower receives a loan which can be no more than the total volume of funds saved over the period.

Product innovation is relatively weak in Germany. Most mortgages are provided at a fixed rate of interest although savings banks, mortgage banks and commercial banks do also offer variable rate mortgages. In terms of mortgage distribution channels the most frequently used medium is that of the branch networks of the commercial and savings banks. As in France very limited selling is conducted through third parties.

Housing Finance in Italy

The level of owner-occupation in Italy is high. At 67 percent it stands at a par with that in the UK. The cost of mortgages is also comparatively low, with lower cost mortgages only to be found in the UK. Most Italians do not purchase their first home until they are in their thirties. Until this stage the preference is to remain in the family home. This strong sense of family is further demonstrated in that some 70 percent of home financing is provided by domestic savings a good proportion of which is a family contribution to the purchase of the new home.

The large share of house finance provided through domestic own funds therefore limits the scope of financial institutions in the generation of mortgage business. The key financial group in this reduced market is the specialist mortgage credit institution. Most of these intermediaries, of which there are over 20, either operate as subsidiaries or separate divisions of the commercial and savings banks. The limited direct involvement of commercial banks in the mortgage market is due to legal demarcations which have been drawn between institutions empowered to offer short-term products, namely the commercial banks, and institutions permitted to provide medium and long-term products, principally specialist credit institutions. This is not to say that commercial and savings banks are not also directly involved in the provision of home finance, they are on two counts. First in recent years the strict demarcation lines between providers of short-term finance and providers of medium to long-term finance have been relaxed somewhat. Savings banks in particular have been offered the opportunity to hold a proportion of their assets in the form of medium and long-term loans. Secondly banks make house purchase loans to individuals in the form of either overdrafts or personal loans. On maturity the facility is then automatically rolled over creating a funding instrument with the characteristics of a long-term loan.

Most mortgage loans in Italy are initially made to home builders and developers, on the completion of the property development, the loans are subdivided and assumed by the home purchasers. Loans provided for the construction of new property are available up to 75 percent of the property value, the repayment period is usually between 10 and 35 years. Where loans are made on existing residential property, 50 percent of the property value can be advanced with the repayment period somewhere between 10 and 35 years. In the case where the house purchaser is a first time buyer the government may also become involved in the process, either through the provision of a loan subsidy or as a loan guarantor.

Both fixed and variable rate mortgages are available in Italy. Mortgage product development has, however, been somewhat sluggish. Those product innovations which have occurred include the introduction of monthly repayment mortgages, previously interest and principal were paid semi-annually; variable rate mortgages linked to the ECU; and insured loans which are somewhat akin to endowment mortgages.

Although, as earlier indicated, mortgages are supplied by specialist mortgage credit institutions they are distributed to customers primarily through the branch networks of the commercial and savings banks. Other distribution channels are utilised, most notably through banks entering into co-operative agreements with other financial institutions to use their sales forces, they nevertheless perform a relatively minor role.

Housing Finance in Spain

Spain has both a high level of owner-occupation, 76 percent, and a mortgage price structure which by international standards is uncompetitive. From Table 12:IA it transpires that out of the 8 countries under scrutiny the most expensive mortgages are to be found in Spain.

The main providers of house finance are the private banks, the savings banks and the mortgage credit companies. There are in excess of 130 private banks and they provide an extensive range of corporate and personal financial services including house finance. The savings banks which are non-profit organisations concentrate upon personal financial services with particularly strong emphasis upon mortgage lending. There are approximately 70 savings banks operating in Spain. Mortgage credit companies are a relatively new form of financial institution in Spain. They owe their existence to regulatory changes in the mortgage market in 1981. The purpose of these institutions is the granting of mortgage loans and guarantees for private housing and commercial property development. Unlike the private banks and the savings banks the majority of mortgage credit institutions' funds are not generated from the retail deposit market but rather through the issue of mortgage bonds. Mortgage credit institutions are also authorised to collect long-term deposits.

As in Italy most mortgage loans in Spain are initially made to housing developers with the loan on the completion of the development broken down and assumed by the individual house purchasers. Again mortgage product development is not as advanced in Spain as in the UK. Most mortgages are capital and interest repayment loans of an average maturity period of 15 years. The interest rate levied on the loan is usually fixed relative to some reference interest rate and is revised when variations in this rate occur. Government participation in the private sector mortgage market also takes place through the provision of both subsidised mortgages and tax allowances on mortgage interest.

The bulk of mortgages are distributed through the branch networks of the private banks and savings banks. Mortgage credit companies also, in the main distribute mortgages through their own branch network.

UK Building Societies in Europe

As is clear from this discussion of the house finance markets of Spain, Italy, Germany and France, there are fundamental differences not only between the UK market and these markets but also between each of the individual markets themselves. No consistent characteristics appear to emerge across markets, with the exception of course that in each country there is a strong demand for mortgage finance. There are differences in: cultural characteristics; the mix of institutions which provide home loans; the degree of government involvement; the level and nature of fiscal incentives; the criteria which must be satisfied before a loan is provided; and finally the form and sophistication of the mortgage products on offer. Therefore, even if as earlier identified there are countries with both low levels of owner occupation, and hence much scope for mortgage provision, and a mortgage cost structure markedly more expensive than that in the UK other barriers to entry are likely to exist which may negate a UK building society from entry into that market. A measure of the difficulty perceived by societies in establishment outside the UK may be taken from the fact that only one society, the Woolwich, has to date established operations in other European countries.

There are of course additional factors, domestic in origin, which have also reduced the attractiveness of Europe as a market destination for societies. These difficulties were documented in chapter 11 and centred upon the manner in which societies, under the provisions of the 1986 Act, were permitted to establish in Europe. Building societies could only provide services in Europe through subsidiaries and were restricted in their product provision solely to their core business, that is lending on the security of land. In addition subsidiaries established by societies to operate in Europe could neither lend nor take deposits in the UK. This latter point when taken in conjunction with the Second Banking Directive further compounded the problem faced by societies, as the Directive only extended the single banking licence in respect of activities which could be carried out in the home country.

As indicated in chapter 11, orders which became effective in June and July 1992 have removed many of these domestic obstacles to the establishment of societies in Europe. Societies now have the option to lend direct in other European countries plus any powers available to them in the UK are also now extended to Europe.

An additional hurdle faced by societies, again essentially domestic in nature, is that societies have only very recently entered the arena of product and market diversification. Indeed the majority of societies, in the domestic setting, have availed only of a limited number of the diversification options open to them under the 1986 Act. Expertise and resource constraints obviously necessitate that diversification is a gradual process which is implemented in a series of stages over a number of years. This being the case and given the relatively fruitful areas for diversification in the domestic market it is perhaps of no surprise that societies, with the notable exception of the Woolwich have not as yet entered the markets of Europe as providers of financial services. This then of course raises the questions: why has the Woolwich found it necessary to expand into Europe, how have they overcome the apparent problem of the major differences in the home finance markets of Europe, and in which countries and in which form has the Woolwich pursued geographic diversification?

Reid (1992) argued that the rationale for expansion by the Woolwich outside the domestic market stems from two forces, "domestic push and external pull." Reid outlined the characteristics of these two forces as follows

> "Features of domestic push are the maturity of the UK mortgage market and the additional pressure arising from new entrants to this domestic market. In such circumstances, there is a strong strategic argument for trying to expand and balance the Society's principal product portfolio over more than one geographical market-place. External pull is there in the shape of perceived opportunities waiting to be tapped in some of the other EC nations."

These then are the reasons for expansion by the Woolwich into Europe, but what of the apparent divergences between the various house markets in Europe. Recognition of this point was the start position for research carried out by the Woolwich into the house finance markets of Europe. Initially an in-house research team conducted desk research to explore the characteristics of house finance in other European countries, this was followed by local research including interviews with players in other countries. The research was then tied together by a firm of management consultants which identified for the Woolwich both product areas and countries which offered the greatest potential for gain. A total of five countries were identified. Given that resources are not unlimited and that there are obvious risks involved in a geographic diversification strategy the Woolwich opted for staged diversification, that is one country at a time.

To date the Woolwich has established in two European countries - Italy and France. Woolwich (Europe) Ltd., a wholly owned subsidiary of the society was launched in February 1990 to act as a holding company for other subsidiaries to be established in Europe. In October 1990 Woolwich SpA was launched as a wholesale funded mortgage lender based in Milan and servicing the Italian market, particularly Northern Italy, which research by the Woolwich had identified as an area of significant potential.

The next target country for the Woolwich was France. In this instance the method of establishment was different than that employed in the case of Italy. Entry into the French market was achieved through the purchase of an existing mortgage lending company, although not its mortgage book. Banque Woolwich was launched in July 1991, its headquarters are on the outskirts of Paris and it has a 19-strong branch network spread throughout France.

To date this is the extent of the Woolwich's operations in Europe and as yet there is limited information on the success or otherwise of these operations, although in their 1991 annual report and accounts they do indicate with regard to the subsidiary in Italy that

> "During its first full year of operation it has strengthened its distributional base and its reputation for fast, friendly and reliable service is growing."

It is obviously not possible to draw parallels with other building societies' experience of Europe, at this juncture it is therefore perhaps useful to consider the manner in which the Abbey National has expanded within the context of housing finance in Europe.

In Spain, at the start of 1988, the Abbey National established Abbeycor Nacional. Organised in form as a mortgage credit company, Abbeycor Nacional is a joint venture with Winterthur, a Swiss insurance group and Grupo Cor, a Spanish financial intermediary with experience of the Spanish mortgage market. Abbeycor sells mortgage products through branch offices which have already been established in most major cities in Spain and also through Winterthur's branch network in other cities and towns where Abbeycor has not as yet a presence. Subsequently in 1989, the Abbey National set up Cornerstone Espana to provide an estate agency service to customers of Abbeycor.

In 1989 Abbey National in conjunction with Diners Club which has a minor equity stake established the mortgage company, Abbey National Mutui in Italy. The intention in this instance is to market mortgages through the Italian distribution channels of Diner's Club as well as Winterthur's distribution network in Italy.

Abbey National continued its steady expansion into European markets in 1990. In January of that year it purchased Ficofrance, a French mortgage finance company. Ficofrance has an asset base of some Ffr 5.0bn and operates through 12 branches spread across France. The objective in this purchase by the Abbey National is to provide a house finance service to both French and UK buyers of French property. In their 1990 annual report and accounts, Abbey National indicated that

"The company has performed well and the outlook is good,"

Subsequently however, the performance of Ficofrance and indeed the Abbey National's operations in Spain has been less than pleasing and has necessitated that the Abbey National restructure its business in both countries. For the end year 1992 the Abbey National's European operations incurred a total loss of £50m a quite substantial jump from the £1m loss made in 1991.

From this limited sample there appears to be a degree of commonality in terms of the markets chosen for diversification. Abbey National like the Woolwich has targeted the house finance markets of France and Italy although in addition it has also ventured into the Spanish market. No doubt a range of factors were important in the choice of these countries. Perhaps of importance in the case of France and Spain was the high cost of mortgage finance, see Table 12:IA, while in the case of Italy the fact that its markets are one of the most open set of markets in Europe could be viewed as important. One, however, obtains the overriding impression that the determining factor in the choice of these countries is that in these markets, UK institutions are most likely to capture expatriate customers, that is, Britons abroad requiring house finance.

Methods of Expansion into Europe

It is clear even from the previous analysis of only two institutions that varied mechanisms can be utilised in the entry into foreign markets. Opting for the correct entry method, which fits in with the requirements of the home institution and also accommodates the idiosyncrasies of the foreign market, could arguably be considered as important a decision as the choice of the correct country for diversification. What then are the choices which face building societies? New start-ups, acquisitions and alliances are invariably viewed as the three primary mechanisms through which new markets can be accessed. There are of course a number of variants within each category which further increases the options open to institutions which desire to expand. For example, alliances encompass joint ventures, mergers and co-operation agreements. Institutions therefore appear to have many approaches to choose from. In reality, however, the organisational form of the home-based institution coupled with the constraints within which it operates is likely to rule out certain approaches. Furthermore given differences in market characteristics it is improbable that one method of expansion will be the first best option in all circumstances. Rather, the optimal approach is likely to vary between markets. In the light of these various points consider now the different approaches to market expansion and their relevance or otherwise for building societies, if and when they do decide to venture into the house finance markets of other European Community countries.

The start-up approach, as the name suggests, involves the establishment of a totally new business venture. The adoption of such an approach has much greater chances of success if the parent institution can, in some way, utilise its own infrastructure in the initial establishment of the start-up. A good case in point is the establishment by a number of banks of their own insurance companies, the TSB, Deutsche Bank and Credit Agricole are all examples of banks which have established insurance companies as start-up ventures. Perhaps the most successful of which is Predica Agricole. In under three years it grew to become the second largest life company in France. Nicholson (1992) suggested that

> "Their success is partly due to their large branch network - 6000 life assurance agents sell Predica products through Credit Agricole's network of ninety regional banks ...."

For building societies with neither an infrastructure in Europe nor a localised knowledge of market characteristics and conditions the start-up approach appears subject to above average risk. In addition the approach is likely to be expensive, not only in terms of the establishment costs of a network of outlets but also in terms of marketing campaigns which would be necessary in overcoming the inherent bias of customers in favour of domestic institutions. This is not to say that the start-up approach is in all instances wrong. Where the target of the society is that of a geographically contained *niche* market, such as the expatriate customer base which tends to be found only in certain countries and mainly within specific areas in these countries, a localised start-up arrangement with limited distribution channels may indeed be an effective mechanism in the capture of market share.

The acquisition route is another way in which an institution may forge entry into a new market. As with the start-up arrangement initial establishment costs can be high. Acquisition, as a means of entry into a market, has, however, much to commend it such as an already established product portfolio, customer base, distribution network and expertise of the local market. In addition when compared with the start-up approach the lead in time in the establishment of the business is much reduced, while in comparison to an alliance the parent institution has total control over the direction of the new business enterprise.

Both the Abbey National and the Woolwich in the establishment of operations in France have employed the acquisition approach. As indicated the pluses from such a strategy rest with the home institution being able to immediately distribute its products and learn from existing customers and staff how the market functions. There are, however, drawbacks. Cost of course, but perhaps of more importance is the potentially less than favourable long-term prospects for the purchased institution. The point of note is that building societies with their limited resources are in a position to purchase only small to medium sized enterprises, and as has been argued in this text *vis a vis* building societies in the UK but which equally applies to all financial groupings in most other countries, small to medium sized players are being squeezed from the market place.

The problem of the scale of the new enterprise can be alleviated to some degree, and this applies to both new start-ups and acquisitions, through entry into the arrangement in conjunction with another institution, that is a joint venture. Although total control of the new institution is lost, the additional resource base provided through the joint venture can be utilised to establish a larger scale more solidly based intermediary. Abbey National's approach to Europe is a case in point, where in both the start-up in Spain and acquisition in France they entered into joint ventures with other intermediaries. For example in the case of Abbeycor Nacional in Spain the Abbey National's stake is 67 percent, Winterthur the insurance group has 5 percent and the house finance specialist Grupo Cor 28 percent. This arrangement provides the Abbey National not only with additional resources, but also expertise and distribution channels if required.

In certain countries the structure of the house finance market would in itself make it inappropriate to establish a stand alone house finance operation. One example is that of the German house finance market. As earlier indicated the loan package in Germany is usually a combination of several loans from a number of institutions. The package is, however, invariably assembled by the customer's own commercial bank which probably has as subsidiaries those intermediaries which provide the various components of the loan package. A building society which establishes in Germany and fails to link into such an umbrella organisation would undoubtedly capture very little market share.

Cross-border alliances have increased dramatically in the past few years. Gugler (1992) details three factors which he views as influential in the growth of alliances. The first is that of technological advances which involve changes in the traditional competitive advantages of firms in an industry and in consequence leads firms to share risks and to find new ways to have rapid access to markets. Secondly the convergence of technologies. An example of technology convergence in operation relates to the alliance between the Royal Bank of Scotland and Spain's Banco Santander. The electronic banking system which these two banks operate allows each to treat the branches of its partner as if they were its own. The system covers basic transactions such as cash withdrawals and setting up standing orders although more sophisticated services such as cash-management accounts are to be introduced. Credit Commercial de France and Portugal's Banco de Comercio e Industria are also expected to join with the result that the Royal Bank of Scotland, a medium sized UK bank, will have branch outlets in Spain, France and Portugal. The third factor stressed by Gugler *op. cit.*, as important in the growth of alliances, is that of market globalisation which he argues creates a need for more flexible structures and new forms of organisations in order to allow firms to compete successfully outside their home market.

Alliances have been most common within the banking and insurance sector although the Skipton building society has also been involved in an alliance with the French bank, Societe Generale. The results from these alliances while in many cases positive, as with the Royal Bank of Scotland and Banco Santander and also with the formidable alliance between the Dresdner Bank and Banque Nationale de Paris, can in addition have their downside. The alliance between Germany's Commerzbank and France's Credit Lyonnais is one example of an alliance turned sour (see Alexander, 1991). The problems which arise usually centre upon issues such as which institution should retreat where operations overlap; which should take the lead in new ventures; the splitting of profits where ventures are shared; and particularly problematic is when the alliance becomes viewed as a means through which one institution achieves a toehold in the other's territory.

Accepting the above noted problems, an alliance for a UK society is likely to work best with foreign based intermediaries wishing to branch out into the provision of mortgage products. An alliance between a UK building society and for example a foreign based insurance company might take the form of the society distributing mortgages through the distribution outlets of the insurance company with a reciprocal arrangement whereby the insurance company markets its product through the branch network of the society. Indeed it would appear that the mortgage product expertise of UK building societies would fit neatly, as a third strand, into many of the current trans-border alliances between banks and insurance companies.

Summary

Under the broad theme of expansion by UK societies into the house finance markets of Europe a number of issues have been examined in this chapter. Initially a very simplistic approach was adopted to country diversification. Countries with low levels of house-ownership and expensively priced mortgage products were identified with the suggestion that it was in these countries where above average opportunities for mortgage business expansion by societies exist. At that juncture a country specific analysis was pursued, the objective in this instance was to demonstrate that price and demand were only two of many factors which should be considered in the identification of the appropriate markets for expansion. The form of the mortgage advance; the structure and mix of the suppliers of house finance; fiscal incentives for house purchase; and also cultural differences were all viewed as factors of equal importance to price and demand.

At one level a measure of the extent of the difficulties which confront societies can be taken from the fact that only the Woolwich has to date established a European presence. Furthermore the impression gained from the countries and indeed the specific areas within these countries targeted by the Woolwich, and also for that matter the Abbey National, in their expansion activities is that the objective is not country wide penetration but rather, the establishment of a *niche* market. In both cases the *niche* market was that of the expatriate customer requiring house finance.

The next step in the discussion was an examination of the various mechanisms through which societies could expand into Europe. Start-ups, acquisitions and alliances were the three main mechanisms considered although hybrid arrangements which spanned a mixture of approaches were also scrutinised. Each of the mechanisms had both advantages and disadvantages. It was not, however, possible to rank the various approaches in terms of a first best to least best method of entry. Differences in the structure of mortgage markets between countries implied that the first best option in one market did not necessarily hold good for other markets.

In this chapter more questions have been raised than answered and more problems identified than solved. This in part relates to the fact that an answer correct or problem solved for one market may in all probability be wrong for another. Such uncertainty is in turn further compounded by the changing structure not only of the respective house finance markets in Europe but also in the organisational structure of the institutions which provide finance in these markets. The latter point refers to the building of financial conglomerates both domestically and across national borders. In such circumstances knowledge of the correct questions to ask and the problems which are required to be solved, prior to the establishment of a building society in Europe, must surely be viewed as a solid advance.

13. Prospectus for Future Development

Introduction

This chapter considers not only the key issues that arise from the analysis so far undertaken in order to offer a commentary on the possible implications for the future development of the building society sector, but also the broader strategic options that currently confront the sector in respect of the development paths that might be taken. The early part of the chapter therefore concentrates on restating the insights gained from the internal analysis of the sector provided in previous chapters, whilst the latter part concludes with a more wide ranging discussion of the future potential for both evolutionary and radical change within the sector.

Currently, as a consequence of the changes induced by greater competition and deregulation, it is possible to detect an ongoing debate within the sector about the fundamental nature and purpose of building societies. The future evolution of the sector could take a number of different routes. The legal reform of the constitution and powers of building societies occupies the immediate agenda. Such legal reforms, if and when they occur, are likely to entail a less radical departure from traditional building society values than say the conversion option. Whether further legal reform forestalls the more radical transformation of the status of building societies is therefore a key question.

As distinctions between the building society and banking sectors diminish, modifying or adapting the role of the regulator is appropriate. Potentially, further legal reform within the sector might necessitate a change of regulator, with the possibility of the Bank of England taking responsibility for building societies as well as the banks. This is an issue also explored in this chapter.

As a starting point though, it is perhaps useful to draw together some of the main points arising from the appraisal of the internal features of building societies described in the previous chapters.

Reduction in Society Numbers

Most commentators accept that an increased concentration within the sector is almost certain. Whilst the actual pattern that this takes will be subject to a number of factors, it can be predicted that the number of societies will decline rapidly in the next decade. Should the harsh economic conditions of the early 1990s continue, then it can be anticipated that there may be other societies that have to be "rescued" in the same way as those in the south of England which have recently found themselves in difficulties. In explaining recent concentration in the sector, it was suggested that improving the geographic coverage of their branch network, motivated some national societies to participate in seeking transfer of engagements from smaller societies. Whether this source of concentration has been exhausted is doubtful, and it is likely to continue to be a factor of influence on future concentration.

Another obvious impetus to the process of concentration within the sector is the motivation to improve asset size. Society size is an important determinant of cost efficiency which, in turn, is a crucial factor in the maintenance of building society profitability. Therefore, the ultimate economic rationale for the process of increased concentration lies in the realisation of the benefits of economies of scale. It was demonstrated that cost efficiency gains are obtainable in the building society sector from economies of scale. Evidence was found of significant augmented economies of scale for national societies, and it was also indicated that, in terms of cost per unit of output, local societies could benefit from amalgamations. On these grounds, the momentum within the sector for concentration should continue unabated.

Predicting whether it is small to medium sized regional societies, or local societies which will contract most rapidly is a point of debate. Both are probably equally under threat from the larger institutions, and events in the building society sector look certain to mirror the concentration that previously occurred within the banking sector. Although the pace of transfer of engagements has slowed somewhat in recent months, and regardless of the eventual improvement in economic conditions, the logic of concentration within the sector seems fixed and the only uncertainty is in terms of the timespan involved in significantly reducing society numbers.

Experience of Product Diversification

Empirically documenting the extent and variation of product diversification within the sector has been an important concern. It was found that diversification programmes were graduated throughout the different segments; the larger national societies offered the most extensive product portfolios, with the remainder of the national societies and the larger regional societies providing product lines complementary to their savings and mortgage business and thereafter diversifying into a subset of other available product areas. For the smaller regional and local societies, product diversification has entailed staying very close to their core business.

Recently, retrenchment from particular kinds of diversification has been significant. For instance, share dealing, estate agency, commercial property lending and property development are areas from which some societies have withdrawn. Most affected by retrenchment have been those national and regional societies which opted to provide a broad product range. Indeed it is those societies which have undertaken extensive diversification programmes that have to date fared less well in terms of relative profit performance. From an analysis of building society results, it appears that profit performance is inversely related to diversification. In addition, in the cost function study, it was found that for regional and local societies cost inefficiencies existed in the production of mortgage and non-mortgage products, and although there was no evidence of cost inefficiencies for national societies, neither was there evidence of cost efficiency. It is, however, important that the conclusion should not be drawn that diversification *per se* is as a consequence unwise, even if specific examples can be found of less than circumspect lines of diversification. Establishing new products does initially require heavy investment which can only be recouped at later stages in the product life cycle. The point can also be made that it is the more extensively diversified societies which may be better placed to take advantage of any future economic upturn. Despite the experience of particular societies, the establishment of more balanced product portfolios may outweigh the inherent risks associated with the diversification process itself, and in the longer term contribute overall to greater risk reduction. Given the importance of this issue, there is a need to examine more closely this question of the relationship between risk and diversification in the building society sector, and it would be useful to conduct further research, to explore more extensively, the relationship between risk and diversification for different society types.

Diversification options for societies are not confined solely to the domestic market, building societies also have the opportunity to geographically expand their coverage to markets outside the UK. The single European market has provided societies with a potential customer base well in excess of 300m as opposed to a mere 60m when their operations were constrained to the UK. On the basis of this customer potential one might therefore have expected large numbers of societies to enter into the mortgage markets of Europe. Such a situation has not as yet materialised. In part this is due to the fact that societies have been heavily involved in diversification on the home front and have not felt able, at this stage, to add the extra burden of geographic diversification. Another part of the problem for societies is that there are significant differences in the house finance markets of Europe, in terms of market participants, mortgage products, the housing mix, government involvement and general cultural characteristics. These differences necessarily imply that the product portfolios and means of operation of UK building societies are not directly transferable to other member countries of the EC. Although European diversification is obviously not an easy option for societies, there is, nevertheless, significant market potential. Certainly in *niche* market mortgages as targeted by the Woolwich and the Abbey National but also the extensive customer base available in Europe offers societies much scope for future business in insurance services, money transmission as well as in mortgages.

The Rise of the Marketing Function

Greater emphasis on a more professional approach to marketing within the sector was evident. The predicted adoption of differential strategies for competitive advantage made by earlier studies of the sector do not appear to have materialised. The majority of societies now and for the future seem committed to cost strategies. The growth ambitions of most societies appear to be modest, aiming at a steady increase in market share. In terms of aggressiveness, it is the regional societies that are most inclined to view winning market share from competitors as the preferred means of achieving growth.

Building societies enjoy very favourable cost to income ratios compared to the banks which makes them highly competitive in the marketplace. Significantly, evidence was found of a deterioration in the cost to income ratios, particularly in the case of national and local societies. Given the current efforts of the banks to improve their cost structure, this trend of poorer cost to income ratios may prove particularly problematic for building societies. Undoubtedly, the costs of diversification have adversely impacted upon the cost to income ratios of national societies. In the case of local societies a significant number have invested heavily in refurbishment programmes which helps to explain their rising costs. It was clear that cost leadership strategies for competitive advantage would dominate in the regional and local society sectors in the future. It is those societies though which achieve economies of scale and control of costs that will have a stronger platform to mount such a strategy. Those societies which fail to create these characteristics will be on less firm ground.

Despite the dominance of cost strategies, differentiation strategies for competitive advantage are still important within the sector, particularly for some national societies. That there are inherent difficulties in product differentiation, where products can be copied, needs to be stressed, as does the difficulty of standing out from the crowd in a situation where the same positive attributes are used as promotional material by all societies, albeit in different guises. The continued increase in the use of branding is perhaps a reflection of the investment needed to counter the challenges associated with achieving differentiation.

Over and above the strengthening of the marketing function, which was most pronounced in the national and regional segments, there appears to be recognition that customer service is the ultimate key to competitive advantage. To rely purely on the conventional marketing mix of product, price and promotion is not enough. Compared to the banks, building societies have enjoyed a favourable reputation for providing accessible and friendly service, which obviously they would wish to protect and extend. If quality of service can be seen as the ultimate differentiator between institutions in the 1990s, the rise of customer care training programmes throughout the sector is an indication that building societies allocate critical importance to this factor. Interestingly, the emphasis given in quality service programmes is very much about changing culture, and training staff to be more responsive to the needs of customers moves building societies well away from the predominantly sales culture of the past.

Focused Use of Information Technology

Information technology investment, although much smaller in monetary terms than that of the banks, is nevertheless significant within the building society sector when taken as a proportion of non-interest costs. Building societies are focusing their investment in information technology to strengthen areas of traditional competitive advantage. This explains why mortgage and branch systems have been targeted for upgrading or replacement throughout the sector. Equally high on the agenda is the intent to unlock the potential afforded by more recent developments in information technology to improving their effectiveness, particularly in terms of marketing activities. Increasingly, the central feature of many building society computer systems is the customer relational database rather than the account based systems of the past.

It is not an exaggeration to claim that the sector stands on the threshold of a systems revolution. Only by incorporating state-of-the-art developments such as open and architected systems will building societies keep abreast of developments within the banking sector. Already, building societies are sophisticated users of data network systems which afford the potential to enhance the role of branches through greater devolution of responsibility to branch level. LINK, the building societies ATM network, was established more cheaply than rival networks, and is leading progress towards better integration with American and European networks. For the future, it is clear that ATM networks will attempt to differentiate on the basis of the range of functions available from machines. Throughout the financial services sector, greater emphasis will be given to lobby machines as opposed to holes-in-the-wall in an effort to entice customers back into branches.

Since debit card operations are set to rise spectacularly in the 1990s, the growth of ATM networks looks certain to be, as a consequence, halted. Currently, national building societies are increasingly engaged in debit card networks and it is likely that many regional societies will also enter this arena. Developments such as telephone banking and document image processing are generally not well developed throughout the sector. There are notable exceptions to this, and those societies which have pioneered these type of applications are enthusiastic about the benefits. An obvious brake on the rise of document image processing concerns the legal problems with the status of scanned documents. Once resolved, the attractions of this technological development to paperbound organisations like building societies should be very strong. Telephone banking similarly holds good potential within the sector and should increase in the future.

One important hallmark of the sector is its self-reliance in the development of computer projects, where many national and regional societies have well developed in-house expertise. Smaller regional societies and local societies are more likely to use outside help and consortia arrangements have been developed to further computer developments. It is perhaps more than idle speculation to suggest that such arrangements could contribute, due to a resulting systems compatibility, in making mergers easier between member societies of such consortia.

The comparison of the future course of computer development within the banking and building society sectors will provide an interesting case study. The efficacy of the more focused, bespoke approach in the building society sector as opposed to the universalistic, large scale computer systems being introduced by the banks will attract detailed scrutiny. If building societies prove more successful in their information technology strategy the parallel to David and Goliath will be an appropriate analogy.

Complex Organisational Structure and a Performance Culture

Evidence was found that the organisational structure of building societies had undergone significant change to better fit the new business environment. In the case of national and regional societies, divisionalised type structures have replaced the more traditional functional, departmentalised structures of the past. The use of joint ventures, the growth in subsidiaries and the development of strategic alliances have contributed to an increase in organisational complexity.

Yet analysis revealed that building societies displayed only some of the features related to the ideal type of organisational structure favoured in other commercial sectors. Whilst there was clear evidence of support for the increased use of delegation, there was little evidence of any "flattening" of the management hierarchy. In addition, building societies appeared not to favour the move towards the "leaner" head-office found in other sectors. In fact the opposite is the case, with staff numbers at head-office having expanded since deregulation. Rising staff numbers, plus rising administrative costs, are issues that require closer scrutiny given the need to control costs in an already strongly competitive market.

The use of spatial relocation as a means of optimising back-office operations and providing additional space for operational restructuring programmes has been a particular feature for some societies in recent years. The establishment of regional administration centres by some of the larger societies has allowed some dispersal of previously head-office functions to take place. Analysis of the factors that influence the relocation decision revealed that cost factors were less important than the pressure created by the need to fulfil expansion plans triggered by the process of diversification. Increasing complexity has led to a universal increase in the use of formalised planning and resource allocation within the sector. The organisational dilemma of devolving greater responsibility downward yet improving corporate co-ordination of activities can perhaps be viewed as the major challenge facing organisational redesign programmes within the sector. It is important to stress, however, that changes in organisational structure are only one dimension of the transformation taking place within the sector. Of perhaps greater significance is the culture change required to accompany a more competitive environment. Undoubtedly, there has been a shift from social to commercial objectives and this has helped to create a more performance orientated culture within the sector. For the future, it can be expected that payment, promotion and recruitment systems will be increasingly linked to a performance based ethos. Cultural change can be brought about within the sector by the process of diffusion, and senior appointments drawn from executives with banking experience will no doubt aid this process. Clearly, the building society sector is in a state of flux. Given this context, continuity in the progression of long term business plans could be viewed as a means of ensuring a degree of stability in the process of change. Interestingly, analysis revealed that the age profile of the current chief executives within the sector offered the prospect of stability and did not display an especially high wastage rate through projected retirements. The age profile of chief executives could, however, have a different impact, particularly on the concentration issue, if it is accepted that the likelihood of transfers of engagements at the local society level is in fact a function of the age of the chief executive.

Financial Performance of the Sector

The capital strength of the building society sector is healthier than that of the retail banks, and building societies are well placed to take advantage of any economic upturn. Within the sector, the capital strength of local societies is particularly high, although there is evidence that the capital ratios of the smaller and larger societies have begun to converge. The profit performance of building societies is consistently better than that of the banks. The contribution of fee income to total income has risen rapidly in the case of national building societies, although, as a source of income, it is less developed than for the retail banks. In terms of net interest income, local societies operate on higher margins than either national or regional societies.

Determining why building societies with their more limited product portfolios have consistently outperformed the retail banks in recent times is relatively straightforward. Largely, the success of the building society sector can be attributed to much lower cost to income ratios and comparatively insignificant bad debt problems. Whether this superior performance *vis a vis* the banks can be sustained in the longer term is an important question. The indications are that the banks are vigorously tackling the issues that resulted in placing them in their current position. It is probable that building societies will find occupying a lead position more difficult in the future.

On the note of an even tougher future environment, it is perhaps appropriate at this stage to change the focus towards the options concerning the future direction of the sector.

An Agenda of Change: Values, Purpose and Structure

The hallmark of building societies, prior to the effects of competition and deregulation, was that their values and essential purpose could be easily defined. In other words, for most of their long history, building societies have had a very clear purpose, namely, accepting savings from the public and making loans to home buyers. Currently, answering the question "what are building societies in business for?" might not be so straightforward. As societies begin to stray from their core business identity as savings and mortgage institutions the focus on this question needs to be sharpened. Recent proposals for the legal reform of the powers and constitution of building societies reflect a gradualist approach to the change process within the sector, where broadly a building society identity is retained but adapted further to suit the changing circumstances created by an evolving competitive environment. Where will this reform lead to? Some might argue that the momentum created by the intended future reform of building societies could be viewed as pointing ultimately to an inevitable convergence with the banking sector. Similarly, exercising the option of conversion to plc status for those societies eligible to do so could lead to an even more radical change process, where it was deemed that new values and purpose, and a new structural form, offered a more appropriate way forward in the current business context. Here, building societies would be following the Abbey National route with a necessary, immediate transformation to bank status being the outcome.

Within the industry, the view is expressed that societies are unwilling to forego the status of "building society", but at the same time do not wish the legal restrictions surrounding their status to hinder future strategic flexibility in an evolving marketplace. At a more pragmatic level, if the various development options are assessed in terms of the balance of consequences involved, the conversion option would need to be treated with some caution, particularly if the benefits to be achieved by legal reforms fulfil the need for flexibility of action by building societies, yet maintains their unique identity intact. In other words, it appears that there is a preference for gradual change within the industry, and the preferred mechanism for achieving this is through future legal reform.

Foregoing Building Society Status - The Conversion Option

Without the prospect of further legal reform, the attraction of the conversion option might be irresistible. Since there is currently strong pressure within the sector for legal changes it can be argued that this will prevent building societies being "forced" to exercise the conversion option.

Crossing over to the banking sector, which is necessary in the conversion process, undoubtedly guarantees the potential for strategic flexibility which societies increasingly see as a fundamental requirement in a financial services market typified by a high rate of change, increasing complexity and intense competition. Yet, to date, the successful adaptation by building societies to the changing business environment has been gradual and evolutionary. This has also been the case with the Abbey National, despite its shift to plc status. The Abbey National is indistinguishable from the building society sector in terms of what it is currently doing in regard to its business policy. Any difference in the strategic flexibility of the Abbey National and the building society sector appears to have remained largely theoretical[1].

The conversion of the Abbey National also demonstrated that the process involved is both complicated and costly. Taking 15 months to complete, the Abbey National conversion is reputed to have cost in the order of £80m. Merely considering the case for conversion cost the National and Provincial nearly £8m. The burden placed on the management of a society in dealing with conversion could cause severe strain where the board is already heavily occupied in discharging its duty towards the efficient management of a society. If simultaneous conversions occurred the regulatory body could suffer a similar overload problem. In addition, a number of stock flotations as adjuncts to conversion occurring in close proximity to one another could cause particular problems.

The actual provisions for conversion under the 1986 Act are sufficiently ambiguous that the Abbey National had to seek the approval of the High Court for its conversion scheme. By adding inducements in excess of the statutory requirements, such as giving free shares to voting members, a precedent has been created that would be difficult not to follow in any future conversion.

Since the process involved contains difficulties and uncertainties, it is not difficult to explain why this issue appears to be treated with a great deal of circumspection by societies. Whilst undoubtedly offering greater freedom of action under plc status, plus access to new sources of capital, conversion also means relinquishing the safeguards against hostile takeover enjoyed by the building society sector. However, the possibility of future conversions within the sector cannot be ruled out.

The future shape of the sector could also be influenced by the takeover of a society by an existing company, perhaps a bank or an insurance company. As was pointed out earlier the law and procedure for this is quite involved and requires the approval of the BSC, and the investing and borrowing members of the society. Also, the Bank of England must be prepared to give authorisation under the Banking Act if the takeover institution is a bank, while the Department of Trade would issue authorisation for insurance companies. Obviously, societies would have to be agreeable to such takeovers, and although the procedures are complex, it is not again impossible that such mergers could occur in the future.

Legislative Reforms

It is suggested that the pressure to engage in the conversion process will be inversely related to the liberalisation of the regime governing building societies by reforms to the legislative framework. In the future it looks likely that there will be additional secondary legislation under the 1986 Act and amendments through primary legislation to the Act itself, leading to the prospect of a new Building Societies Act in the longer term. The final desired outcome is to create a legal framework in which societies would not be constrained by restrictions on their powers. The BSA has recently published definitive proposals about the possible detail of this future legal reform (BSA,1992).

In relation to their lending powers, it is suggested that secondary legislation should be used to secure the power to make unsecured loans to small businesses and others in the same way as unsecured loans can be made to individuals. This change would, for instance, allow societies to provide banking services to schools. The ability to participate in syndicated lending on a Class 2 basis, plus the right to make loans secured by floating charges only, are additional powers that would enhance mainstream building society business. A range of amendments through secondary legislation are also being called for in order to enhance the provision of services by societies. These include offering full foreign exchange services to non-individuals, extending the range of permissable executorship and trusteeship services, allowing societies to act as a merchant acquirer in credit and debit card systems, and to remove the current restriction on owning a general insurance company, thereby permitting societies to provide general insurance underwriting. This latter point is particularly important in that it would allow building societies to escape from the attempts by insurance companies to increase premiums in order to compensate for the estimated £1.38bn losses suffered by them on mortgage indemnity policies in 1991.

In terms of conducting their business, secondary legislation is envisaged to have a role in allowing societies greater freedom to invest in premises which may not be immediately used for the conduct of business. Similarly, societies could be permitted to invest in joint venture bodies without the requirement to underwrite these bodies. And significantly, there is also a perceived need to remove the restrictions and complications concerning the operation of subsidiaries.

Central to the calls for legal reform is the desire to see key features of the 1986 Act amended. High on the agenda are revisions to permitted wholesale funding levels and asset class levels. The former might increase from 40 percent to 60 percent whilst the latter would see an improvement in the permitted ceilings for non Class 1 assets. The position regarding hedging, direct syndicated lending, and undertaking business through subsidiaries are all targeted as requiring reform through amendment to the primary legislation. It needs to be stressed, however, that this is regarded as purely an interim solution, with the best interests of the sector being served in the future by a completely new Building Societies Act which takes a permissive rather than a restrictive stance towards building society business operations. *De facto*, building societies would enjoy legal parity with other financial institutions, with justification for any residual restrictions that might exist expressed purely in terms of safeguarding mutuality. As an added precaution to the theoretically wider diversification opportunities that would exist under such a fundamental reform, the BSA has indicated its desire to see societies adopt a new memorandum of powers approved by its members as a required precursor to any implementation by societies of future permissive statutory powers envisaged under a completely new Act.

Regulatory Convergence?

The creation of a less restrictive legislative framework, where the powers permitted to building societies match more closely those of the banks, obviously has implications for the future supervisory regime. It is difficult not to concede that ultimately there might be a single regulator for banks and building societies and that logically this would be the Bank of England. It is interesting to note that in Ireland, building societies are already regulated by the Central Bank. The change of supervisory regime could happen abruptly, or alternatively extend over a lengthy period where dual supervision existed during the process of transition. The BSA is on record as expressing the view that it does not regard the identity of the supervisor as being of any particular significance. There is a rider to this in that, whatever the supervisory regime, the BSA does suggest that sensitivity to the particular characteristics of building societies is a pre-requisite.

Collaboration between the trade associations of the banking and building societies sectors is developing continuously. For instance, they have produced a joint code of banking practice, a code of conduct on the advertising of deposits and guidance notes on money laundering. Given their common interests in issues such as European legislation, the BSA and the British Bankers Association work closely together to influence policy makers. That the trade associations are concerned to work in unison with one another is a further reflection of the increasing commonality between the sectors.

Reconciling Mutuality with Wider Powers

If legislative reform does create the conditions whereby building societies are free to undertake wider diversification from their core businesses, the primacy of mutuality might be in danger of being undermined. The current constitutional arrangements within building societies for instance, holds that it is customers who have savings and mortgage accounts that are the owning members of a society. In order to retain a realistic claim to the status of mutuality, it looks likely that societies might be required to take constitutional steps to safeguard a continued provision for the special position of members as the defining characteristic of a building society.

It has been suggested by the BSA that the test of building society identity might lie in the formulation of appropriate nature limits regarding membership. Thus, under the BSA's proposals, the test for an appropriate level of mutuality could be where at least 25 percent of a society's funds is in the form of shares from members, and where at least 50 percent of commercial assets are in the form of loans to members. By instigating such nature limits, there would be a constitutional guarantee that societies retain their basic identity as a retail institution. In addition to this, it is possible to envisage a further test for mutuality comprising of a formula relating minimum numbers of members to a given amount of assets, where a sliding scale is developed for membership requirements for societies of different size.

It is clear from the proposals concerning the constitutional reform of building societies, that at the level of the Building Societies Association, there is a preference to retain the concept of ownership by members, albeit in a modified form, as the distinctive feature of building society identity. Essentially, the suggested reforms are a pragmatic response to, what in theory, could be viewed as a difficult problem.

From a different perspective, it might be held that to the extent that societies are freed from legal restrictions on their powers that this in fact merits a fundamental change in their status, and it would be more appropriate for them to relinquish the status of "building society" and adopt the status of "mutual bank", regulated under the Banking Act.

In so far as it is the preference of the building society sector, as expressed by the BSA, to preserve the distinctiveness of mutual building societies, it can be anticipated that pressures to instigate a fundamental change in the status of societies to that of a mutual bank will be resisted. The future prospectus for building societies is one where *de facto* societies will increasingly be seen as banks with a mutual constitution. Whilst the name "building society" may be retained, the complexion of societies in the future is likely to be very different, comprising of a multiple constituency where the challenge for management lies in reconciling a plurality of interests. Achieving a balance between the interests of members and other elements of a diverse constituency will undoubtedly be a major challenge, and for institutions that were once typified by a unified view of what they are, it would appear that this is about to be replaced by a more ambiguous reality as the price to be paid for the freedom to exercise greater strategic flexibility.

Summary

This chapter has attempted to provide an appreciation of the key internal features of building societies and how these might progress in the future. Although dealt with in discrete terms, it is the case that developments in marketing, information technology, organisational restructuring, product diversification and so on are not isolated from one another. The overall impression is that societies are adapting well to the challenges that face them, and that by any objective measure they are successful institutions. In order to maintain their position, societies are currently taking a long term view of what requires to be done *via* legal reform to equip them with a new degree of self-determination and flexibility considered essential for their future well being.

The preferred development path for the sector as a whole is a gradual approach to change. Even so, this has instigated a need to re-examine the constitutional basis of mutuality and the proposed derivation of new membership formulae or nature limits to guarantee that the distinctive identity of building societies can endure. Although called building societies, institutions in the future are likely to have the attributes of a bank. Reconciling the different interests of a more diverse constituency will be the feature that distinguishes the depth of change from their origins as savings and loan institutions. Critics might claim that in the institutions of the future the building society component may in fact be purely a residual element, maintained purely for pragmatic reasons, and that the freedom to diversify spells in the long term the seeds of destruction for building societies as we have known them.

Notes

[1]It should be noted that the Abbey National's treasury section is involved in the provision of a number of services which building societies are not permitted to provide.

Data Appendix

(prepared in conjunction with L. Barton and S. Bradley)[1]

Data from Society Accounts

Total Assets, £m
Branch Numbers
Total Share, Deposit and Loan Liabilities
Bad Debt, £m
Management Expenses, £m
Labour Costs, £m
Net Interest, £m
Other Income, £m
Profits Before Tax, £m
General Reserve, £m
Employee Numbers

Computed Ratios

Management Expenses/Total Income, %
Other Income/Total Income, %
Wholesale Funds/Share, Deposit and Loan Liabilities, %
Class 1 Assets/Total Commercial Assets, %
Class 2 Assets/Total Commercial Assets, %
Class 3 Assets/Total Commercial Assets, %
Liquid Assets/Total Assets, %

Tier 1 Capital/Risk Weighted Assets, %
Gross Capital/Share, Deposit and Loan Liabilities, %
Profits Before Tax/Mean Total Assets, %
Profits Before Tax/Mean Reserves, %

Cost Function Estimates

Augmented Economies of Scale
Product Specific Economies of Scale w.r.t. Mortgage Products
Product Specific Economies of Scale w.r.t. Non-Mortgage Products
Cost Complementarity

[1]Liam Barton and Suzanne Bradley are research assistants in the Department of Accounting and Finance, Queens University Belfast.

	Total Assets £m		Branch Numbers	
	1991	1990	1991	1990
NATIONAL SOCIETIES				
Halifax	58710.2	54145.9	726	744
Nationwide	34119.0	31124.9	757	895
A & L	20479.8	18401.8	411	407
Woolwich	20164.8	18195.2	531	546
Leeds Permanent	16210.8	14648.7	422	482
C & G	14789.3	11570.9	210	180
Bradford & Bingley	11910.3	9047.6	280	250
National & Provincial	10707.6	9257.1	315	321
Britannia	8523.8	7422.8	245	248
Bristol & West	7140.8	5646.6	186	171
REGIONAL SOCIETIES				
Northern Rock	4418.8	3420.4	119	125
Yorkshire	4184.8	3586.1	134	141
Birmingham Midshires	3745.2	3652.2	120	135
Skipton	2717.3	2223.5	60	57
Portman	2594.0	2444.4	100	129
Coventry	2369.9	2022.2	66	65
Chelsea	2277.4	2089.5	57	55
Leeds & Holbeck	2236.5	1827.8	78	75
Derbyshire	1350.6	1182.2	59	60
Norwich & Peterborough	1276.9	1157.9	63	65
North of England	1224.3	1008.4	45	52
WBBS	1110.2	1022.6	66	80
Cheshire	1101.1	905.6	59	56
Principality	1030.9	908.7	49	50
Heart of England	1015.4	920.9	50	51
Newcastle	971.5	852.1	55	54
Staffordshire	848.0	740.8	55	54
Nottingham	652.8	539.1	46	49
Dunfermline	644.1	547.9	37	37
Lambeth	517.0	481.0	13	13
Stroud & Swindon	493.6	481.9	26	25
Cumberland	482.8	410.3	31	27
Scarborough	371.0	348.7	14	17
National Counties	339.9	305.8	0	0
Furness	304.0	275.7	17	17
Leek Utd	284.0	243.7	16	16
Cambridge	266.1	232.9	12	9
Progressive	256.3	210.4	10	10
Hinckley & Rugby	226.7	219.6	18	18
Darlington	225.0	201.8	11	9
Marsden	218.4	194.2	15	14
Kent Reliance	217.0	207.8	12	12
Newbury	203.6	189.1	11	10

LOCAL SOCIETIES	Total Assets £m 1991	1990	Branch Numbers 1991	1990
Saffron Walden	188.5	173.9	11	9
Market Harborough	181.6	168.5	7	6
Melton Mowbray	168.9	151.6	4	3
Universal	157.4	140.8	13	13
Barnsley	155.1	140.5	8	4
Ipswich	151.6	140.9	7	8
Hanley	151.2	133.9	5	3
Greenwich	139.5	133.9	6	6
Monmouthshire	125.4	108.5	8	7
Haywards Heath	124.9	115.0	6	6
Mercantile	115.9	107.8	11	10
Teachers	110.4	104.8	0	0
Vernon	99.6	90.4	6	5
St.Pancras	95.1	91.5	5	5
Scottish	91.8	85.2	5	5
Mansfield	90.6	82.4	4	3
City & Metropolitan	84.7	82.2	4	4
Loughborough	78.6	70.1	3	3
Surrey	78.3	73.8	5	5
Tipton & Coseley	73.5	64.1	4	4
Manchester	71.2	61.5	0	0
Dudley	65.7	59.5	6	5
Chesham	59.9	51.3	3	2
Holmesdale	54.1	50.9	0	1
Earl Shilton	49.2	44.8	2	2
Chorley & District	48.5	43.2	2	0
Bath Investment	47.4	42.8	6	5
Tynemouth	44.7	40.4	0	0
Penrith	42.3	39.0	1	1
Buckinghamshire	40.4	38.5	1	0
Stafford Railways	37.4	35.8	0	0
Harpenden	37.0	35.7	2	2
Nottingham Imperial	32.3	28.7	2	2
West Cumbria	31.6	29.6	4	4
Beverly	31.2	26.7	0	0
Shepshed	28.5	25.1	0	0
Swansea	23.9	22.3	0	0
Catholic	20.2	18.4	0	0
Gainsborough	20.1	17.1	0	0
Ilkeston	15.9	14.6	2	2
Bexhill	15.7	14.9	1	1
Clay Cross	14.4	13.3	0	0
Standard	13.8	13.2	1	0
Century	9.3	8.7	0	0
Ecology	8.1	6.2	0	0
Londonderry Provident	5.0	4.1	0	0

	Total Share, Deposit and Loan Liabilities £m		Bad Debt £m	
	1991	1990	1991	1990
NATIONAL SOCIETIES				
Halifax	54828.1	50621.8	229.20	106.90
Nationwide	31808.0	28913.4	235.90	94.80
A & L	18743.2	16486.8	215.10	62.70
Woolwich	18922.2	17045.8	72.40	23.00
Leeds Permanent	14985.0	13634.6	44.30	19.90
C & G	13953.8	10866.9	71.70	17.20
Bradford & Bingley	11077.0	8429.3	30.45	8.40
National & Provincial	10055.9	8571.3	52.10	44.60
Britannia	8015.2	6876.6	33.67	7.33
Bristol & West	6610.9	5235.9	15.56	4.40
REGIONAL SOCIETIES				
Northern Rock	3065.1	2441.3	6.00	0.84
Yorkshire	3882.2	3323.3	15.35	9.03
Birmingham Midshires	3486.2	3366.9	21.40	8.20
Skipton	2557.9	2067.0	24.19	3.33
Portman	2393.1	2240.4	23.84	3.10
Coventry	2229.0	1882.7	9.88	3.86
Chelsea	2135.9	1911.9	16.70	3.20
Leeds & Holbeck	2099.2	1706.7	5.48	0.27
Derbyshire	993.1	888.4	0.76	0.06
Norwich & Peterborough	1179.2	1065.5	5.82	3.14
North of England	1135.4	940.8	0.43	0.45
WBBS	1003.0	919.1	12.60	4.48
Cheshire	1023.0	836.3	1.95	0.41
Principality	953.5	828.3	1.45	0.07
Heart of England	950.0	854.3	8.50	2.16
Newcastle	905.7	791.7	1.85	0.22
Staffordshire	793.3	694.9	2.11	2.98
Nottingham	605.7	495.2	1.81	0.21
Dunfermline	603.0	510.8	0.18	0.06
Lambeth	463.1	429.2	2.33	2.44
Stroud & Swindon	452.1	448.2	5.12	1.26
Cumberland	445.5	376.0	0.53	0.06
Scarborough	343.4	324.4	3.39	2.11
National Counties	278.8	247.1	0.79	0.15
Furness	282.8	255.3	0.16	0.01
Leek Utd	263.8	225.3	0.54	0.07
Cambridge	244.2	213.3	0.23	0.31
Progressive	240.5	194.7	0.10	0.03
Hinckley & Rugby	205.9	198.5	1.08	0.32
Darlington	208.9	187.0	0.09	0.02
Marsden	201.2	178.1	0.22	0.00
Kent Reliance	202.2	193.2	1.85	0.98
Newbury	187.5	173.9	0.41	0.17

	Total Share, Deposit and Loan Liabilities £m		Bad Debt £m	
	1991	1990	1991	1990
LOCAL SOCIETIES				
Saffron Walden	174.9	160.0	1.98	0.68
Market Harborough	169.7	157.1	0.82	0.54
Melton Mowbray	158.1	141.7	0.54	0.21
Universal	147.6	129.9	0.10	0.02
Barnsley	140.8	125.7	0.10	0.00
Ipswich	142.3	131.7	0.54	0.75
Hanley	138.1	121.9	0.02	0.03
Greenwich	130.1	125.0	1.01	0.32
Monmouthshire	115.4	99.7	0.24	0.03
Haywards Heath	116.5	106.3	0.39	0.24
Mercantile	107.2	99.7	0.02	0.00
Teachers	98.9	92.8	1.49	0.54
Vernon	94.5	84.7	0.19	0.12
St.Pancras	88.8	85.1	0.68	0.51
Scottish	83.7	77.8	0.08	0.04
Mansfield	78.0	70.5	0.01	0.00
City & Metropolitan	77.1	74.3	0.13	0.07
Loughborough	72.1	65.1	0.23	0.01
Surrey	73.5	68.9	0.39	0.26
Tipton & Coseley	66.0	57.4	0.06	0.00
Manchester	66.9	56.2	0.22	0.03
Dudley	59.0	53.3	0.05	0.00
Chesham	53.5	45.6	0.02	0.00
Holmesdale	49.6	46.6	0.25	0.03
Earl Shilton	43.5	39.7	0.02	0.00
Chorley & District	43.9	38.8	0.00	0.00
Bath Investment	32.2	30.2	0.15	0.04
Tynemouth	42.4	38.0	0.09	0.01
Penrith	37.0	34.0	0.05	0.00
Buckinghamshire	36.9	35.4	0.08	0.02
Stafford Railways	33.9	32.5	0.05	0.01
Harpenden	33.8	32.6	0.23	0.09
Nottingham Imperial	30.3	26.9	0.05	0.01
West Cumbria	29.1	27.3	0.01	0.00
Beverly	29.2	25.0	0.03	0.00
Shepshed	25.9	22.8	0.02	0.10
Swansea	22.1	20.7	0.03	0.01
Catholic	18.7	17.0	0.03	0.00
Gainsborough	18.7	15.9	0.05	0.01
Ilkeston	14.7	13.5	0.01	0.02
Bexhill	14.5	13.5	0.07	0.00
Clay Cross	13.1	12.1	0.01	0.00
Standard	12.8	12.2	0.04	0.02
Century	7.5	6.9	0.02	0.47
Ecology	7.6	5.9	0.03	0.00
Londonderry Provident	4.5	3.6	0.02	0.00

	Management Expenses £m		Labour Costs £m	
	1991	1990	1991	1990
NATIONAL SOCIETIES				
Halifax	663.00	657.70	298.10	271.90
Nationwide	539.10	493.80	215.00	192.00
A & L	606.60	390.00	185.90	132.50
Woolwich	312.40	227.10	139.90	103.20
Leeds Permanent	178.10	164.60	80.80	75.50
C & G	89.30	61.60	44.80	30.30
Bradford & Bingley	123.20	93.70	50.56	38.90
National & Provincial	152.50	104.40	50.10	48.80
Britannia	91.70	80.20	40.45	35.79
Bristol & West	103.60	67.90	49.47	31.13
REGIONAL SOCIETIES				
Northern Rock	55.20	49.90	23.69	20.51
Yorkshire	48.40	42.10	24.87	20.69
Birmingham Midshires	57.70	60.10	30.00	27.40
Skipton	36.20	21.40	16.61	10.09
Portman	33.10	22.60	16.65	10.59
Coventry	23.70	20.00	10.55	8.42
Chelsea	24.70	22.20	10.10	9.30
Leeds & Holbeck	18.50	15.10	8.70	7.33
Derbyshire	19.00	16.40	7.85	6.66
Norwich & Peterborough	25.30	22.40	11.02	10.16
North of England	13.90	11.70	5.35	5.77
WBBS	17.50	14.80	8.48	7.47
Cheshire	11.10	9.40	6.35	5.20
Principality	16.50	11.90	6.15	5.38
Heart of England	15.40	14.00	6.50	5.79
Newcastle	15.20	11.80	5.87	5.09
Staffordshire	9.20	8.70	5.07	4.47
Nottingham	11.40	9.00	5.11	4.01
Dunfermline	7.90	6.90	3.67	3.28
Lambeth	5.70	5.60	2.70	2.33
Stroud & Swindon	5.50	4.50	2.74	2.29
Cumberland	6.70	5.70	3.40	2.74
Scarborough	5.00	5.30	3.07	2.40
National Counties	2.70	2.20	1.58	1.36
Furness	4.20	3.40	1.92	1.64
Leek Utd	3.70	3.30	1.85	1.62
Cambridge	2.80	2.50	1.27	1.03
Progressive	2.80	2.50	1.14	0.94
Hinckley & Rugby	3.30	3.00	1.55	1.30
Darlington	3.10	2.70	1.67	1.43
Marsden	3.80	3.50	2.03	1.81
Kent Reliance	2.80	2.70	1.43	1.34
Newbury	2.80	2.50	1.41	1.17

LOCAL SOCIETIES	Management Expenses £m 1991	Management Expenses £m 1990	Labour Costs £m 1991	Labour Costs £m 1990
Saffron Walden	2.30	2.40	1.11	1.18
Market Harborough	1.90	1.60	0.85	0.72
Melton Mowbray	1.60	1.30	0.60	0.52
Universal	2.50	2.15	1.21	1.03
Barnsley	3.10	2.60	1.48	1.16
Ipswich	2.67	2.08	1.12	1.00
Hanley	1.89	1.52	0.80	0.70
Greenwich	2.02	1.89	1.19	1.13
Monmouthshire	1.54	1.28	0.74	0.58
Haywards Heath	2.15	1.63	0.90	0.66
Mercantile	1.63	1.37	0.79	0.65
Teachers	1.47	1.49	1.01	0.97
Vernon	1.09	1.04	0.56	0.50
St.Pancras	1.30	1.22	0.61	0.58
Scottish	1.53	1.37	0.67	0.57
Mansfield	1.61	1.60	0.77	0.65
City & Metropolitan	1.07	0.99	0.58	0.58
Loughborough	0.94	0.79	0.35	0.29
Surrey	1.44	1.44	0.76	0.67
Tipton & Coseley	0.96	0.82	0.36	0.31
Manchester	1.37	1.22	0.50	0.42
Dudley	1.01	0.92	0.42	0.40
Chesham	0.87	0.68	0.37	0.31
Holmesdale	0.48	0.42	0.31	0.27
Earl Shilton	0.77	0.73	0.36	0.31
Chorley & District	0.49	0.41	0.26	0.21
Bath Investment	1.17	1.18	0.53	0.51
Tynemouth	0.56	0.50	0.18	0.18
Penrith	0.40	0.36	0.20	0.18
Buckinghamshire	0.44	0.38	0.20	0.17
Stafford Railways	0.55	0.49	0.21	0.19
Harpenden	0.64	0.56	0.30	0.28
Nottingham Imperial	0.46	0.39	0.20	0.18
West Cumbria	0.69	0.63	0.33	0.30
Beverly	0.44	0.39	0.20	0.16
Shepshed	0.43	0.38	0.13	0.14
Swansea	0.44	0.37	0.23	0.18
Catholic	0.39	0.31	0.21	0.14
Gainsborough	0.23	0.22	0.11	0.10
Ilkeston	0.42	0.34	0.18	0.13
Bexhill	0.33	0.27	0.14	0.13
Clay Cross	0.33	0.27	0.07	0.06
Standard	0.24	0.21	0.09	0.07
Century	0.21	0.22	0.05	0.07
Ecology	0.16	0.13	0.09	0.07
Londonderry Provident	0.08	0.06	0.05	0.04

	Net Interest £m		Other Income £m	
	1991	1990	1991	1990
NATIONAL SOCIETIES				
Halifax	1188.30	1035.40	331.70	321.90
Nationwide	721.30	678.40	255.60	194.90
A & L	537.00	418.60	384.20	232.70
Woolwich	389.40	344.20	131.80	78.90
Leeds Permanent	309.00	266.20	103.60	89.60
C & G	289.60	171.60	55.20	51.90
Bradford & Bingley	201.41	158.20	60.01	45.54
National and Provincial	212.50	177.40	66.50	49.30
Britannia	144.33	131.63	33.95	27.31
Bristol & West	117.38	93.45	69.16	39.44
REGIONAL SOCIETIES				
Northern Rock	83.45	70.74	32.30	22.28
Yorkshire	92.85	78.82	24.14	16.01
Birmingham Midshires	62.20	61.90	26.40	22.30
Skipton	44.01	39.91	28.21	16.96
Portman	60.51	34.15	8.59	5.23
Coventry	46.57	40.82	8.31	6.97
Chelsea	42.70	40.20	6.80	7.20
Leeds & Holbeck	28.18	30.69	9.17	6.28
Derbyshire	32.40	25.32	5.98	5.20
Norwich & Peterborough	27.75	26.57	10.11	7.45
North of England	24.71	21.88	5.01	4.54
WBBS	33.12	32.50	8.09	5.38
Cheshire	22.44	17.92	5.16	4.10
Principality	22.40	20.03	7.61	6.31
Heart of England	23.39	18.47	3.57	3.44
Newcastle	21.99	18.71	7.19	4.14
Staffordshire	16.82	17.13	3.11	2.90
Nottingham	17.81	13.22	3.31	2.36
Dunfermline	15.24	14.79	2.09	1.54
Lambeth	11.34	12.01	1.73	1.22
Stroud & Swindon	13.41	10.49	1.95	1.18
Cumberland	11.94	10.69	2.25	2.09
Scarborough	7.44	7.27	4.01	2.49
National Counties	10.34	10.14	1.24	0.98
Furness	6.32	6.13	0.92	0.67
Leek Utd	6.08	5.45	0.65	0.62
Cambridge	4.93	4.81	0.58	0.57
Progressive	5.31	4.94	0.51	0.44
Hinckley & Rugby	5.14	5.49	0.82	0.73
Darlington	4.66	3.91	0.79	0.58
Marsden	5.24	5.04	1.05	0.86
Kent Reliance	5.71	5.20	0.53	0.43
Newbury	4.45	3.80	0.49	0.54

LOCAL SOCIETIES	Net Interest £m 1991	Net Interest £m 1990	Other Income £m 1991	Other Income £m 1990
Saffron Walden	4.25	4.58	0.69	0.58
Market Harborough	3.92	3.50	0.31	0.27
Melton Mowbray	3.55	3.20	0.39	0.36
Universal	3.43	3.36	0.70	0.43
Barnsley	3.38	3.74	1.27	1.00
Ipswich	2.99	2.82	0.42	0.42
Hanley	3.12	3.23	0.40	0.42
Greenwich	3.57	3.14	0.27	0.25
Monmouthshire	2.87	2.26	0.22	0.28
Haywards Heath	2.48	2.35	0.36	0.29
Mercantile	2.46	2.04	0.46	0.39
Teachers	3.10	3.30	0.41	0.35
Vernon	1.90	1.86	0.21	0.20
St.Pancras	2.08	2.04	0.15	0.17
Scottish	2.60	2.51	0.27	0.18
Mansfield	2.67	2.80	0.25	0.28
City & Metropolitan	1.72	1.67	0.20	0.23
Loughborough	1.68	1.25	0.29	0.23
Surrey	1.90	1.66	0.22	0.13
Tipton & Coseley	2.03	1.70	0.23	0.19
Manchester	1.93	1.61	0.25	0.19
Dudley	1.57	1.40	0.19	0.17
Chesham	1.46	1.40	0.16	0.12
Holmesdale	1.05	1.02	0.12	0.11
Earl Shilton	1.36	1.31	0.09	0.12
Chorley & District	1.18	0.96	0.11	0.11
Bath Investment	1.33	1.24	0.31	0.44
Tynemouth	0.75	0.65	0.05	0.03
Penrith	0.91	1.10	0.09	0.10
Buckinghamshire	0.91	0.75	0.11	0.11
Stafford Railways	0.89	0.85	0.06	0.06
Harpenden	1.13	1.06	0.09	0.09
Nottingham Imperial	0.72	0.70	0.09	0.09
West Cumbria	0.87	0.76	0.12	0.09
Beverly	0.70	0.54	0.09	0.08
Shepshed	0.62	0.53	0.05	0.05
Swansea	0.63	0.58	0.06	0.05
Catholic	0.60	0.47	0.03	0.03
Gainsborough	0.46	0.42	0.04	0.03
Ilkeston	0.41	0.37	0.18	0.13
Bexhill	0.43	0.43	0.02	0.02
Clay Cross	0.32	0.33	0.05	0.03
Standard	0.29	0.28	0.05	0.04
Century	0.33	0.04	0.01	0.01
Ecology	0.28	0.22	0.02	0.01
Londonderry Provident	0.15	0.14	0.01	0.00

	Profits before Tax £m		General Reserves £m	
	1991	1990	1991	1990
NATIONAL SOCIETIES				
Halifax	628.00	592.70	2619.80	2202.40
Nationwide	201.90	284.70	1385.70	1243.10
A & L	99.50	198.60	802.80	723.00
Woolwich	136.40	173.00	919.30	843.60
Leeds Permanent	190.20	171.30	753.10	628.30
C & G	183.80	144.70	642.10	515.70
Bradford & Bingley	107.78	100.62	482.34	394.31
National & Provincial	100.40	59.80	514.30	449.80
Britannia	64.04	73.60	356.98	323.46
Bristol & West	67.39	60.56	226.39	186.39
REGIONAL SOCIETIES				
Northern Rock	54.56	42.29	202.86	166.41
Yorkshire	52.58	43.70	225.36	190.10
Birmingham Midshires	9.50	15.90	143.10	137.00
Skipton	11.47	32.08	98.11	88.70
Portman	10.47	13.68	135.53	128.43
Coventry	21.30	23.95	105.24	90.84
Chelsea	8.10	21.97	95.80	90.04
Leeds & Holbeck	12.31	20.35	88.57	80.37
Derbyshire	17.67	14.05	73.75	62.19
Norwich & Peterborough	6.71	8.50	49.98	45.81
North of England	15.43	14.23	62.05	51.81
WBBS	11.14	18.60	77.14	71.80
Cheshire	14.59	12.25	55.21	45.21
Principality	15.09	14.42	63.82	53.53
Heart of England	2.27	5.74	43.03	41.65
Newcastle	12.17	10.85	49.46	41.42
Staffordshire	8.59	8.31	39.44	33.80
Nottingham	7.95	6.40	39.93	34.95
Dunfermline	9.23	9.32	34.20	27.93
Lambeth	5.03	5.15	46.67	43.34
Stroud & Swindon	4.76	5.87	26.05	22.68
Cumberland	6.92	7.00	28.80	24.17
Scarborough	1.63	2.32	14.17	13.08
National Counties	8.09	8.78	56.66	51.29
Furness	2.85	3.35	14.58	12.61
Leek Utd	2.51	2.73	13.67	12.02
Cambridge	2.50	2.61	17.37	15.70
Progressive	2.90	2.86	11.97	10.03
Hinckley & Rugby	1.58	2.91	14.95	13.92
Darlington	2.25	1.73	13.24	11.74
Marsden	2.23	2.38	11.74	10.24
Kent Reliance	1.58	1.91	12.18	11.11
Newbury	1.70	1.62	11.72	10.58

	Profits before Tax £m		General Reserves £m	
	1991	1990	1991	1990
LOCAL SOCIETIES				
Saffron Walden	0.62	2.10	11.68	11.23
Market Harborough	1.49	1.67	9.49	8.48
Melton Mowbray	1.83	2.03	9.83	8.62
Universal	1.53	1.62	9.03	7.99
Barnsley	1.39	2.11	11.48	10.56
Ipswich	0.20	0.40	7.07	6.91
Hanley	1.61	2.10	9.31	8.24
Greenwich	0.81	1.17	7.07	6.50
Monmouthshire	1.31	1.23	7.19	6.31
Haywards Heath	0.10	0.03	6.21	6.16
Mercantile	1.26	1.07	6.97	6.11
Teachers	0.33	1.27	9.13	9.05
Vernon	0.83	0.90	4.61	4.04
St.Pancras	0.25	0.48	4.67	4.49
Scottish	1.26	1.29	6.60	5.75
Mansfield	1.31	1.48	10.87	10.02
City & Metropolitan	0.72	0.85	6.27	5.78
Loughborough	0.79	0.68	4.12	3.61
Surrey	0.28	0.09	4.01	3.83
Tipton & Coseley	1.24	1.06	5.75	4.91
Manchester	0.58	0.55	2.85	2.46
Dudley	0.69	0.65	5.22	4.73
Chesham	0.72	0.83	5.25	4.75
Holmesdale	0.44	0.69	3.62	3.31
Earl Shilton	0.66	0.70	4.25	3.77
Chorley & District	0.79	0.67	3.96	3.41
Bath Investment	0.33	0.46	2.73	2.50
Tynemouth	0.16	0.16	1.84	1.72
Penrith	0.54	0.84	4.39	4.00
Buckinghamshire	0.50	0.46	2.88	2.53
Stafford Railways	0.34	0.42	2.99	2.74
Harpenden	0.35	0.50	2.50	2.25
Nottingham Imperial	0.30	0.40	1.69	1.47
West Cumbria	0.29	0.23	1.97	1.76
Beverly	0.32	0.23	1.39	1.17
Shepshed	0.23	0.10	1.90	1.74
Swansea	0.23	0.25	1.34	1.17
Catholic	0.20	0.19	1.18	1.02
Gainsborough	0.18	0.22	1.05	0.92
Ilkeston	0.16	0.14	0.99	0.87
Bexhill	0.06	0.19	0.98	0.94
Clay Cross	0.04	0.09	1.01	0.97
Standard	0.06	0.10	0.82	0.80
Century	0.08	0.13	1.65	1.58
Ecology	0.12	0.11	0.30	0.21
Londonderry Provident	0.07	0.04	0.46	0.40

	Employee Numbers		Management Expenses/ Total Income %	
	1991	1990	1991	1990
NATIONAL SOCIETIES				
Halifax	20860	21023	43.61	48.46
Nationwide	13627	14385	55.18	56.54
A & L	11059	8431	65.85	59.88
Woolwich	8154	6149	59.94	53.68
Leeds Permanent	5090	5055	43.17	46.26
C & G	2452	1909	25.90	27.56
Bradford & Bingley	3200	2687	47.13	45.99
National & Provincial	3031	4821	54.66	46.05
Britannia	2631	2434	51.44	50.46
Bristol & West	2565	1986	55.54	51.09
REGIONAL SOCIETIES				
Northern Rock	1540	1491	47.69	53.64
Yorkshire	1677	1507	41.37	44.39
Birmingham Midshires	1948	2180	65.12	71.38
Skipton	599	599	50.12	37.63
Portman	1001	683	47.90	57.38
Coventry	758	687	43.19	41.85
Chelsea	621	619	49.90	46.84
Leeds & Holbeck	588	559	49.60	40.84
Derbyshire	600	566	49.51	53.73
Norwich & Peterborough	750	718	66.82	65.85
North of England	452	427	46.78	44.28
WBBS	571	592	42.47	39.07
Cheshire	410	382	40.22	42.68
Principality	454	425	54.99	45.18
Heart of England	398	411	57.13	63.89
Newcastle	404	381	52.10	51.63
Staffordshire	370	362	46.16	43.42
Nottingham	325	296	53.96	57.78
Dunfermline	262	244	45.60	42.27
Lambeth	128	116	43.61	42.31
Stroud & Swindon	187	166	55.67	63.19
Cumberland	255	236	47.20	44.59
Scarborough	196	171	43.67	54.31
National Counties	90	73	23.30	19.79
Furness	159	152	58.01	49.96
Leek Utd	133	131	54.94	54.35
Cambridge	110	92	50.80	46.45
Progressive	75	69	48.17	46.49
Hinckley & Rugby	102	99	53.00	50.38
Darlington	127	122	56.90	60.08
Marsden	143	133	60.40	59.31
Kent Reliance	97	99	44.86	47.93
Newbury	90	83	56.61	57.70

	Employee Numbers		Management Expenses/ Total Income %	
	1991	1990	1991	1990
LOCAL SOCIETIES				
Saffron Walden	77	79	46.61	46.50
Market Harborough	65	55	44.91	42.47
Melton Mowbray	42	40	40.68	36.47
Universal	88	85	60.63	56.65
Barnsley	118	105	66.81	54.82
Ipswich	71	71	78.14	64.32
Hanley	46	42	53.72	41.56
Greenwich	57	59	52.51	54.28
Monmouthshire	50	48	49.82	50.42
Haywards Heath	51	53	75.48	62.01
Mercantile	66	62	56.01	56.17
Teachers	57	62	41.80	40.82
Vernon	57	54	51.85	50.83
St.Pancras	37	36	58.33	54.98
Scottish	45	44	53.37	50.91
Mansfield	51	49	55.01	51.84
City & Metropolitan	27	27	55.72	51.73
Loughborough	31	29	48.00	53.59
Surrey	37	36	68.24	80.58
Tipton & Coseley	27	26	42.38	43.52
Manchester	30	29	63.21	67.51
Dudley	37	37	57.59	58.44
Chesham	22	21	53.85	44.75
Holmesdale	15	16	40.94	36.64
Earl Shilton	23	20	53.08	51.16
Chorley & District	21	18	38.06	38.04
Bath Investment	37	37	71.20	69.94
Tynemouth	20	21	69.15	74.62
Penrith	17	18	40.42	30.13
Buckinghamshire	12	12	43.26	43.90
Stafford Railways	11	11	58.21	53.30
Harpenden	19	19	52.94	48.62
Nottingham Imperial	16	14	57.05	49.31
West Cumbria	31	29	69.90	73.25
Beverly	15	14	55.45	63.54
Shepshed	12	12	63.52	65.18
Swansea	13	12	63.21	58.94
Catholic	7	7	62.48	62.31
Gainsborough	8	7	45.53	47.89
Ilkeston	18	16	71.43	68.00
Bexhill	11	11	71.87	58.92
Clay Cross	7	7	87.95	74.65
Standard	8	8	70.32	64.64
Century	8	8	67.50	55.54
Ecology	8	7	51.70	53.47
Londonderry Provident	5	5	47.85	41.70

	Other Income/ Total Income %		Wholesale Funds/ Share, Deposit and Loan Liabilities %	
	1991	1990	1991	1990
NATIONAL SOCIETIES				
Halifax	21.82	23.72	13.28	15.15
Nationwide	26.16	22.32	21.56	18.66
A & L	41.71	35.73	26.31	25.84
Woolwich	25.29	18.65	22.26	20.07
Leeds Permanent	25.11	25.18	19.94	19.11
C & G	16.01	23.22	23.86	22.58
Bradford & Bingley	22.95	22.35	24.62	25.76
National & Provincial	23.84	21.75	25.45	19.63
Britannia	19.04	17.18	19.31	20.57
Bristol & West	37.08	29.68	25.05	26.34
REGIONAL SOCIETIES				
Northern Rock	27.91	23.95	34.28	30.27
Yorkshire	20.64	16.89	22.94	18.72
Birmingham Midshires	29.80	26.48	22.07	20.84
Skipton	39.06	29.82	18.71	14.22
Portman	12.43	13.28	15.96	11.26
Coventry	15.14	14.58	17.13	10.97
Chelsea	13.74	15.19	17.54	18.41
Leeds & Holbeck	24.59	17.00	23.88	20.79
Derbyshire	15.58	17.05	26.76	22.90
Norwich & Peterborough	26.70	21.90	22.22	22.22
North of England	16.84	17.19	19.23	18.31
WBBS	19.62	14.21	6.22	7.12
Cheshire	18.69	18.62	20.95	17.64
Principality	25.35	23.97	16.00	18.59
Heart of England	13.23	15.69	24.58	23.77
Newcastle	24.63	18.12	15.52	13.13
Staffordshire	15.59	14.49	11.34	9.32
Nottingham	15.68	15.12	10.73	8.53
Dunfermline	12.06	9.41	9.64	7.62
Lambeth	13.21	9.25	13.10	14.00
Stroud & Swindon	19.77	16.56	14.21	18.31
Cumberland	15.87	16.38	10.81	5.94
Scarborough	35.02	25.50	21.22	9.21
National Counties	10.72	8.82	10.10	10.66
Furness	12.75	9.89	1.70	1.12
Leek Utd	9.71	10.23	4.86	1.07
Cambridge	10.52	10.63	0.40	0.67
Progressive	8.74	8.20	10.89	8.65
Hinckley & Rugby	13.09	12.34	7.07	8.84
Darlington	14.44	12.95	6.02	5.45
Marsden	16.72	14.61	6.65	0.00
Kent Reliance	8.52	7.67	1.35	2.43
Newbury	9.98	12.37	10.84	9.01

	Other Income/ Total Income %		Wholesale Funds/ Share, Deposit and Loan Liabilities %	
	1991	1990	1991	1990
LOCAL SOCIETIES				
Saffron Walden	13.98	11.22	3.57	4.98
Market Harborough	7.33	7.09	7.12	7.13
Melton Mowbray	9.87	10.15	3.42	2.99
Universal	16.97	11.40	5.37	4.71
Barnsley	27.26	21.17	3.91	0.15
Ipswich	12.37	12.91	2.53	2.30
Hanley	11.33	11.64	0.55	0.92
Greenwich	6.98	7.04	12.05	11.26
Monmouthshire	7.06	11.08	5.47	4.24
Haywards Heath	12.66	10.85	8.49	1.91
Mercantile	15.78	16.03	3.33	3.46
Teachers	11.67	9.62	0.00	0.00
Vernon	9.87	9.59	5.03	3.73
St.Pancras	6.58	7.78	7.11	5.96
Scottish	9.39	6.77	3.28	3.29
Mansfield	8.60	9.12	1.08	2.67
City & Metropolitan	10.21	12.27	14.41	7.01
Loughborough	14.61	15.84	9.20	5.40
Surrey	10.31	7.43	10.05	8.43
Tipton & Coseley	9.99	9.99	1.96	1.42
Manchester	11.41	10.80	9.30	10.31
Dudley	10.77	10.78	1.91	3.39
Chesham	9.82	7.97	0.16	0.16
Holmesdale	10.13	9.82	1.07	1.02
Earl Shilton	6.49	8.38	0.15	0.70
Chorley & District	8.36	10.32	1.17	0.05
Bath Investment	18.88	26.27	33.65	27.69
Tynemouth	6.84	3.85	11.63	6.03
Penrith	8.65	8.24	0.00	0.00
Buckinghamshire	10.89	12.63	1.13	1.15
Stafford Railways	6.45	6.62	1.40	1.44
Harpenden	7.08	7.81	1.89	1.66
Nottingham Imperial	10.64	11.22	15.33	15.80
West Cumbria	11.74	11.60	1.74	0.75
Beverly	11.85	12.32	12.77	9.99
Shepshed	8.04	8.61	0.26	0.28
Swansea	8.83	7.82	6.69	4.24
Catholic	4.43	5.77	4.08	3.79
Gainsborough	7.46	7.54	0.00	0.00
Ilkeston	30.38	25.42	3.78	1.36
Bexhill	4.07	4.78	0.92	2.06
Clay Cross	13.65	9.63	0.00	0.00
Standard	16.11	13.28	0.00	0.00
Century	2.56	1.79	2.52	1.60
Ecology	5.79	5.96	0.00	0.00
Londonderry Provident	6.80	2.71	6.03	5.96

	Class 1 Assets/Total Commercial Assets %		Class 2 Assets/Total Commercial Assets %	
	1991	1990	1991	1990
NATIONAL SOCIETIES				
Halifax	97.20	96.80	1.40	1.60
Nationwide	94.00	93.20	4.20	4.70
A & L	90.90	90.00	5.00	6.80
Woolwich	96.20	95.10	3.00	3.20
Leeds Permanent	98.20	98.30	0.30	0.40
C & G	95.20	95.32	4.10	4.03
Bradford & Bingley	93.60	97.17	3.00	2.33
National & Provincial	96.50	96.20	2.20	2.90
Britannia	93.30	94.20	5.40	5.10
Bristol & West	92.70	94.80	5.30	3.60
REGIONAL SOCIETIES				
Northern Rock	95.93	97.18	3.84	2.53
Yorkshire	93.96	94.40	4.90	5.00
Birmingham Midshires	97.40	96.90	2.30	2.80
Skipton	86.77	89.84	11.99	9.76
Portman	91.44	90.64	6.94	7.50
Coventry	98.56	98.13	1.31	1.73
Chelsea	96.74	96.70	2.67	2.50
Leeds & Holbeck	98.32	98.36	1.68	1.64
Derbyshire	99.43	99.39	0.53	0.56
Norwich & Peterborough	92.12	93.04	6.96	6.19
North of England	85.75	87.88	10.96	10.30
WBBS	97.84	96.78	2.15	3.21
Cheshire	96.54	97.18	3.46	2.78
Principality	97.02	98.73	1.14	1.06
Heart of England	92.61	92.00	7.33	7.90
Newcastle	93.99	95.10	5.46	4.35
Staffordshire	96.99	95.84	2.98	4.16
Nottingham	97.84	98.24	2.06	1.63
Dunfermline	95.79	96.80	4.03	3.10
Lambeth	98.96	98.27	1.02	1.70
Stroud & Swindon	85.26	86.23	14.74	13.64
Cumberland	93.75	95.00	6.14	4.90
Scarborough	90.41	90.60	9.47	9.10
National Counties	99.04	99.48	0.96	0.52
Furness	94.57	95.08	5.43	4.92
Leek Utd	98.47	97.65	1.53	2.35
Cambridge	94.90	96.10	5.10	3.90
Progressive	89.70	89.27	10.30	10.73
Hinckley & Rugby	93.90	93.30	5.97	6.56
Darlington	95.54	97.56	4.46	2.44
Marsden	90.52	91.42	9.45	8.58
Kent Reliance	88.20	88.70	11.80	11.30
Newbury	93.81	95.20	6.19	4.80

LOCAL SOCIETIES	Class 1 Assets/Total Commercial Assets % 1991	1990	Class 2 Assets/Total Commercial Assets % 1991	1990
Saffron Walden	87.25	88.00	12.12	11.30
Market Harborough	95.40	96.01	4.60	3.99
Melton Mowbray	97.89	97.86	2.11	2.14
Universal	97.44	98.07	2.56	1.93
Barnsley	94.76	95.00	5.24	5.00
Ipswich	94.93	93.55	5.07	6.45
Hanley	96.16	96.35	3.84	3.65
Greenwich	93.80	95.80	6.20	4.20
Monmouthshire	92.96	94.79	7.04	5.21
Haywards Heath	92.30	90.71	7.70	9.29
Mercantile	97.00	95.48	2.97	4.49
Teachers	97.78	97.32	2.22	2.68
Vernon	88.73	88.00	11.27	12.00
St.Pancras	94.21	94.74	5.79	5.26
Scottish	94.80	95.20	5.20	4.80
Mansfield	97.96	99.54	2.04	0.46
City & Metropolitan	88.78	91.47	11.22	8.53
Loughborough	92.01	92.80	7.99	7.20
Surrey	90.90	90.51	9.10	9.49
Tipton & Coseley	90.31	93.14	9.69	6.86
Manchester	84.05	86.99	15.95	13.01
Dudley	99.04	98.61	0.96	1.39
Chesham	93.27	94.35	6.73	5.65
Holmesdale	92.55	93.34	7.45	6.66
Earl Shilton	85.77	87.30	14.23	12.70
Chorley & District	94.00	97.80	6.00	2.20
Bath Investment	85.20	90.10	14.70	9.70
Tynemouth	92.33	93.10	7.67	6.90
Penrith	92.82	94.78	7.18	5.22
Buckinghamshire	86.85	88.90	12.75	11.00
Stafford Railways	92.77	94.91	7.23	5.09
Harpenden	90.53	91.89	9.47	8.03
Nottingham Imperial	92.90	92.94	7.10	7.06
West Cumbria	91.69	93.93	8.31	6.07
Beverly	89.55	90.82	10.35	9.17
Shepshed	88.80	91.10	11.20	8.90
Swansea	93.84	95.00	6.16	5.00
Catholic	97.47	97.85	2.53	2.15
Gainsborough	93.26	94.43	6.74	5.57
Ilkeston	98.57	99.12	1.20	0.62
Bexhill	95.56	95.69	4.44	4.31
Clay Cross	98.28	98.35	1.72	1.65
Standard	97.13	97.06	2.87	2.94
Century	88.86	93.65	11.14	6.35
Ecology	91.06	91.95	8.94	8.05
Londonderry Provident	94.03	95.97	5.97	4.03

	Class 3 Assets/ Total Commercial Assets %		Liquid Assets/ Total Assets %	
	1991	1990	1991	1990
NATIONAL SOCIETIES				
Halifax	1.40	1.60	15.52	15.30
Nationwide	1.80	2.10	16.10	16.49
A & L	4.10	3.20	24.19	23.06
Woolwich	0.80	1.70	16.71	16.37
Leeds Permanent	1.50	1.30	15.33	16.33
C & G	0.70	0.65	16.03	17.26
Bradford & Bingley	3.40	0.50	17.79	17.31
National & Provincial	1.30	0.90	13.50	14.44
Britannia	1.30	0.70	16.43	17.02
Bristol & West	2.00	1.60	17.03	16.89
REGIONAL SOCIETIES				
Northern Rock	0.23	0.29	14.86	15.55
Yorkshire	1.14	0.60	15.48	17.48
Birmingham Midshires	0.30	0.30	17.35	16.66
Skipton	1.24	0.40	18.12	16.92
Portman	1.62	1.86	21.73	21.20
Coventry	0.13	0.14	17.64	19.76
Chelsea	0.59	0.80	20.19	17.71
Leeds & Holbeck	0.00	0.00	16.31	15.60
Derbyshire	0.04	0.05	16.14	15.93
Norwich & Peterborough	0.92	0.77	18.49	18.01
North of England	3.29	1.82	18.58	19.31
WBBS	0.01	0.01	20.00	19.46
Cheshire	0.00	0.04	16.38	15.36
Principality	1.84	0.21	17.41	18.02
Heart of England	0.06	0.10	22.68	20.17
Newcastle	0.55	0.55	19.03	17.68
Staffordshire	0.03	0.00	14.95	15.15
Nottingham	0.10	0.13	16.95	18.78
Dunfermline	0.18	0.10	16.32	16.85
Lambeth	0.02	0.03	21.68	17.33
Stroud & Swindon	0.00	0.13	20.49	17.45
Cumberland	0.11	0.10	20.34	16.57
Scarborough	0.12	0.30	19.93	20.17
National Counties	0.00	0.00	15.56	18.04
Furness	0.00	0.00	22.04	20.46
Leek Utd	0.00	0.00	19.44	17.65
Cambridge	0.00	0.00	21.85	21.91
Progressive	0.00	0.00	18.09	16.37
Hinckley & Rugby	0.13	0.14	16.66	16.43
Darlington	0.00	0.00	19.25	18.39
Marsden	0.03	0.00	15.46	22.37
Kent Reliance	0.00	0.00	17.07	18.38
Newbury	0.00	0.00	20.25	19.30

	Class 3 Assets/ Total Commercial Assets %		Liquid Assets/ Total Assets %	
	1991	1990	1991	1990
LOCAL SOCIETIES				
Saffron Walden	0.63	0.70	20.26	16.91
Market Harborough	0.00	0.00	19.97	19.71
Melton Mowbray	0.00	0.00	19.22	19.40
Universal	0.00	0.00	15.73	18.72
Barnsley	0.00	0.00	16.24	19.54
Ipswich	0.00	0.00	19.03	18.74
Hanley	0.00	0.00	20.72	18.96
Greenwich	0.00	0.00	21.56	22.73
Monmouthshire	0.00	0.00	17.50	16.04
Haywards Heath	0.00	0.00	15.58	16.83
Mercantile	0.03	0.03	23.95	21.39
Teachers	0.00	0.00	20.06	20.22
Vernon	0.00	0.00	18.38	18.96
St.Pancras	0.00	0.00	17.32	18.50
Scottish	0.00	0.00	21.32	21.51
Mansfield	0.00	0.00	19.90	19.50
City & Metropolitan	0.00	0.00	18.42	23.35
Loughborough	0.00	0.00	16.96	18.11
Surrey	0.00	0.00	17.92	21.91
Tipton & Coseley	0.00	0.00	17.68	18.26
Manchester	0.00	0.00	16.98	15.30
Dudley	0.00	0.00	21.64	20.58
Chesham	0.00	0.00	20.60	18.44
Holmesdale	0.00	0.00	22.50	23.43
Earl Shilton	0.00	0.00	19.76	18.78
Chorley & District	0.00	0.00	18.89	21.82
Bath Investment	0.10	0.20	14.07	15.17
Tynemouth	0.00	0.00	19.33	17.38
Penrith	0.00	0.00	25.18	19.10
Buckinghamshire	0.40	0.10	20.00	23.27
Stafford Railways	0.00	0.00	21.84	21.16
Harpenden	0.00	0.08	20.63	20.94
Nottingham Imperial	0.00	0.00	17.11	17.74
West Cumbria	0.00	0.00	18.15	23.26
Beverly	0.10	0.01	18.54	17.85
Shepshed	0.00	0.00	27.20	20.05
Swansea	0.00	0.00	19.94	18.14
Catholic	0.00	0.00	21.36	17.89
Gainsborough	0.00	0.00	19.46	24.33
Ilkeston	0.23	0.26	17.63	18.03
Bexhill	0.00	0.00	16.17	19.21
Clay Cross	0.00	0.00	23.94	28.88
Standard	0.00	0.00	21.28	21.72
Century	0.00	0.00	21.48	22.62
Ecology	0.00	0.00	25.89	32.70
Londonderry Provident	0.00	0.00	29.11	28.74

	Tier 1 capital/ Risk Weighted Assets, %		Gross Capital/ Share, Deposit and Loan Liabilities %	
	1991	1990	1991	1990
NATIONAL SOCIETIES				
Halifax	9.89	8.64	5.60	5.04
Nationwide	8.38	8.24	6.02	6.29
A & L	8.34	8.23	6.19	6.40
Woolwich	9.80	9.72	5.75	5.32
Leeds Permanent	10.92	9.24	6.54	5.71
C & G	9.13	9.46	5.41	5.21
Bradford & Bingley	9.69	9.34	5.84	5.27
National & Provincial	10.03	10.13	5.71	5.95
Britannia	8.62	9.08	5.84	5.84
Bristol & West	8.68	6.84	5.50	4.71
REGIONAL SOCIETIES				
Northern Rock	9.58	10.31	8.59	8.49
Yorkshire	11.13	11.14	6.19	6.17
Birmingham Midshires	8.20	7.97	6.61	6.61
Skipton	7.17	7.97	4.81	5.02
Portman	10.89	10.86	6.94	7.10
Coventry	9.71	9.93	5.65	5.92
Chelsea	9.15	9.22	5.62	6.23
Leeds & Holbeck	8.53	9.45	5.14	5.07
Derbyshire	11.88	11.41	7.43	7.00
Norwich & Peterborough	8.04	8.08	6.57	5.97
North of England	10.02	10.40	5.46	5.51
WBBS	15.30	15.27	7.69	7.81
Cheshire	10.62	10.53	5.98	6.14
Principality	13.29	12.76	6.69	6.46
Heart of England	8.94	9.29	5.52	5.93
Newcastle	10.76	10.28	5.46	5.23
Staffordshire	9.79	9.51	5.41	5.37
Nottingham	13.19	14.20	6.59	7.06
Dunfermline	11.18	10.86	5.67	5.47
Lambeth	20.42	19.78	10.08	10.10
Stroud & Swindon	10.33	9.10	7.85	5.71
Cumberland	12.60	12.26	6.46	6.43
Scarborough	7.92	7.81	6.16	5.57
National Counties	35.72	37.22	20.32	20.76
Furness	10.39	9.84	5.15	4.94
Leek Utd	10.56	10.60	5.53	5.74
Cambridge	14.15	14.89	7.11	7.36
Progressive	9.44	9.48	5.60	5.92
Hinckley & Rugby	13.70	13.05	7.26	7.01
Darlington	12.60	12.57	6.34	6.28
Marsden	10.68	11.13	5.83	5.75
Kent Reliance	11.20	10.81	6.08	5.81
Newbury	12.23	11.94	6.25	6.08

	Tier 1 capital/ Risk Weighted Assets %		Gross Capital/ Share, Deposit and Loan Liabilities %	
LOCAL SOCIETIES	1991	1990	1991	1990
Saffron Walden	12.49	12.79	6.68	7.02
Market Harborough	11.31	10.94	5.59	5.40
Melton Mowbray	12.70	12.40	6.21	6.08
Universal	12.22	12.42	6.12	6.15
Barnsley	15.29	15.95	8.15	8.40
Ipswich	9.89	10.30	4.97	5.25
Hanley	13.47	13.39	6.74	6.76
Greenwich	10.92	10.70	5.43	5.20
Monmouthshire	11.90	12.17	6.23	6.33
Haywards Heath	10.02	10.74	6.21	6.75
Mercantile	13.53	12.35	6.50	6.12
Teachers	18.24	18.90	9.38	9.90
Vernon	9.30	8.97	4.92	4.81
St.Pancras	9.63	10.37	5.93	5.97
Scottish	16.57	14.65	7.89	7.39
Mansfield	26.40	27.01	14.24	14.54
City & Metropolitan	14.81	14.91	8.28	7.93
Loughborough	10.76	10.70	6.24	6.12
Surrey	10.46	10.84	5.91	6.04
Tipton & Coseley	15.93	16.09	9.05	8.93
Manchester	7.73	7.81	5.76	6.15
Dudley	17.68	17.69	8.84	8.88
Chesham	18.47	19.50	9.81	10.43
Holmesdale	14.40	14.21	7.30	7.10
Earl Shilton	17.14	16.92	9.77	9.50
Chorley & District	17.24	17.74	9.03	8.80
Bath Investment	10.68	11.33	11.23	11.26
Tynemouth	8.61	8.83	4.45	4.65
Penrith	22.95	22.08	11.88	11.78
Buckinghamshire	14.40	13.87	7.81	7.16
Stafford Railways	17.21	16.74	8.81	8.43
Harpenden	14.04	13.28	8.19	7.72
Nottingham Imperial	10.83	10.64	5.80	5.72
West Cumbria	12.68	12.77	6.77	6.44
Beverly	9.00	8.89	4.74	4.65
Shepshed	14.32	14.41	7.67	7.96
Swansea	11.90	11.19	6.70	6.33
Catholic	12.94	11.97	6.45	6.12
Gainsborough	10.94	11.92	5.59	5.76
Ilkeston	13.56	13.07	6.70	6.46
Bexhill	13.16	13.58	6.76	6.92
Clay Cross	15.77	17.34	7.69	8.06
Standard	13.24	13.48	6.61	6.76
Century	36.80	39.61	22.11	22.84
Ecology	7.86	7.79	3.88	3.56
Londonderry Provident	20.59	22.45	10.04	11.06

	Profits Before Tax/ Mean Total Assets %		Profits Before Tax/ Mean Reserves %	
	1991	1990	1991	1990
NATIONAL SOCIETIES				
Halifax	1.11	1.16	26.05	29.46
Nationwide	0.62	0.99	15.36	24.89
A & L	0.51	1.24	13.04	30.48
Woolwich	0.71	1.04	15.47	22.94
Leeds Permanent	1.23	1.24	27.54	29.96
C & G	1.39	1.54	31.75	34.14
Bradford & Bingley	1.03	1.24	24.59	27.87
National & Provincial	1.01	0.68	20.83	13.90
Britannia	0.80	1.07	18.82	24.04
Bristol & West	1.05	1.17	32.65	34.44
REGIONAL SOCIETIES				
Northern Rock	1.39	1.36	29.55	27.65
Yorkshire	1.35	1.31	25.31	24.81
Birmingham Midshires	0.26	0.47	6.78	11.97
Skipton	0.46	1.67	12.28	41.03
Portman	0.42	0.74	7.93	13.34
Coventry	0.97	1.31	21.72	28.81
Chelsea	0.37	1.12	8.72	26.63
Leeds & Holbeck	0.61	1.23	14.57	27.64
Derbyshire	1.39	1.26	25.99	24.41
Norwich & Peterborough	0.55	0.78	14.00	19.79
North of England	1.38	1.61	27.10	30.15
WBBS	1.04	1.96	14.96	28.43
Cheshire	1.45	1.53	29.07	29.73
Principality	1.56	1.72	25.71	29.51
Heart of England	0.23	0.68	5.35	14.42
Newcastle	1.34	1.37	26.79	28.62
Staffordshire	1.08	1.19	23.45	26.74
Nottingham	1.33	1.32	21.24	19.44
Dunfermline	1.55	1.82	29.72	37.45
Lambeth	1.01	1.13	11.18	12.37
Stroud & Swindon	0.98	1.43	19.55	30.12
Cumberland	1.55	1.84	26.12	31.99
Scarborough	0.45	0.74	11.99	18.96
National Counties	2.50	3.03	14.98	18.11
Furness	0.98	1.29	21.00	29.00
Leek Utd	0.95	1.20	19.55	24.51
Cambridge	1.00	1.18	15.10	17.73
Progressive	1.24	1.52	26.37	31.44
Hinckley & Rugby	0.71	1.43	10.95	22.43
Darlington	1.05	0.89	18.01	15.46
Marsden	1.08	1.29	20.25	25.12
Kent Reliance	0.74	0.96	13.57	18.13
Newbury	0.87	0.94	15.27	16.07

	Profits Before Tax/ Mean Total Assets %		Profits Before Tax/ Mean Reserves %	
	1991	1990	1991	1990
LOCAL SOCIETIES				
Saffron Walden	0.34	1.25	5.38	19.91
Market Harborough	0.85	1.05	16.59	21.00
Melton Mowbray	1.14	1.39	19.83	25.41
Universal	1.03	1.22	17.97	21.68
Barnsley	0.94	1.57	12.60	21.16
Ipswich	0.14	0.30	2.88	5.96
Hanley	1.13	1.64	18.31	27.81
Greenwich	0.59	0.89	11.92	19.04
Monmouthshire	1.12	1.21	19.36	20.78
Haywards Heath	0.09	0.03	1.68	0.55
Mercantile	1.13	1.06	19.32	18.56
Teachers	0.31	1.32	3.62	14.67
Vernon	0.87	1.07	19.13	23.89
St.Pancras	0.26	0.55	5.37	11.13
Scottish	1.42	1.59	20.38	24.07
Mansfield	1.52	1.91	12.57	15.46
City & Metropolitan	0.87	1.11	11.98	15.42
Loughborough	1.06	1.04	20.30	19.98
Surrey	0.37	0.13	7.21	2.46
Tipton & Coseley	1.81	1.78	23.32	23.26
Manchester	0.88	1.03	21.87	24.23
Dudley	1.11	1.18	13.90	14.46
Chesham	1.30	1.72	14.45	18.60
Holmesdale	0.84	1.43	12.71	22.51
Earl Shilton	1.41	1.66	16.50	19.83
Chorley & District	1.73	1.66	21.54	20.85
Bath Investment	0.72	1.19	12.42	19.65
Tynemouth	0.37	0.42	8.90	9.67
Penrith	1.34	2.26	12.96	22.53
Buckinghamshire	1.26	1.31	18.39	19.44
Stafford Railways	0.93	1.23	11.94	16.17
Harpenden	0.95	1.48	14.53	24.16
Nottingham Imperial	0.99	1.49	19.08	30.08
West Cumbria	0.95	0.82	15.67	13.78
Beverly	1.10	0.93	25.01	20.77
Shepshed	0.84	0.42	12.40	6.06
Swansea	0.97	1.23	17.91	22.80
Catholic	1.05	1.05	18.49	19.61
Gainsborough	0.94	1.39	17.84	26.74
Ilkeston	1.03	0.99	16.88	16.41
Bexhill	0.37	1.30	5.96	21.59
Clay Cross	0.29	0.73	4.04	9.85
Standard	0.47	0.75	7.88	12.39
Century	0.92	1.53	5.14	8.56
Ecology	1.61	2.04	45.48	64.58
Londonderry Provident	1.56	0.92	16.55	9.26

	Augmented Economies of Scale	Product Specific Economies of Scale: 1	2	Cost Complementarity
NATIONAL SOCIETIES				
Halifax	0.83	1.24	5.55	0.01
Nationwide	0.88	1.17	6.53	0.01
A & L	0.95	1.07	6.79	0.01
Woolwich	0.92	1.13	6.81	0.02
Leeds Permanent	0.92	1.15	6.91	0.05
C & G	0.98	1.06	5.86	0.02
Bradford & Bingley	0.96	1.07	6.80	0.04
National & Provincial	0.96	1.12	6.41	0.04
Britannia	0.98	1.06	6.95	0.03
Bristol & West	1.00	1.05	6.80	0.03
REGIONAL SOCIETIES				
Northern Rock	1.01	1.05	5.65	0.07
Yorkshire	1.00	1.05	7.29	0.05
Birmingham Midshires	1.00	1.08	7.37	0.14
Skipton	1.04	1.01	7.08	0.05
Portman	1.01	1.06	8.06	0.06
Coventry	1.01	1.07	7.57	0.32
Chelsea	1.02	1.04	7.56	0.21
Leeds & Holbeck	1.01	1.07	7.45	0.29
Derbyshire	1.00	1.10	6.74	1.12
Norwich & Peterborough	1.02	1.05	8.41	0.12
North of England	1.03	1.04	8.04	0.07
WBBS	1.00	1.11	8.16	0.35
Cheshire	1.02	1.08	7.61	0.25
Principality	1.00	1.09	8.83	0.98
Heart of England	1.02	1.06	8.85	0.15
Newcastle	1.02	1.06	8.31	0.18
Staffordshire	1.01	1.09	7.79	0.35
Nottingham	1.00	1.10	8.53	0.53
Dunfermline	1.01	1.07	8.13	0.32
Lambeth	1.01	1.08	8.34	2.36
Stroud & Swindon	1.02	1.06	8.78	0.16
Cumberland	1.01	1.07	8.80	0.29
Scarborough	1.02	1.07	8.39	0.29
National Counties	1.04	0.99	6.20	3.49
Furness	1.01	1.09	8.89	0.59
Leek Utd	1.00	1.11	8.90	1.78
Cambridge	1.01	1.07	8.58	0.75
Progressive	1.01	1.07	8.15	0.36
Hinckley & Rugby	1.00	1.12	7.86	0.65
Darlington	1.01	1.09	8.44	0.91
Marsden	1.00	1.09	8.81	0.42
Kent Reliance	1.01	1.09	8.31	0.40
Newbury	1.00	1.10	8.38	0.76

1 refers to mortage products
2 refers to non-mortage products

	Augmented Economies of Scale	Product Specific Economies of Scale 1	2	Cost Complementarity
LOCAL SOCIETIES				
Saffron Walden	1.00	1.09	8.86	0.44
Market Harborough	1.00	1.09	8.26	1.08
Melton Mowbray	1.00	1.09	8.09	2.51
Universal	0.99	1.13	8.57	1.64
Barnsley	1.00	1.08	8.16	1.10
Ipswich	0.99	1.10	8.79	1.14
Hanley	1.00	1.08	8.01	1.73
Greenwich	1.00	1.12	8.37	1.02
Monmouthshire	0.98	1.11	8.27	0.82
Haywards Heath	0.99	1.11	8.22	0.92
Mercantile	0.98	1.14	9.19	1.59
Teachers	1.00	1.07	7.52	1.34
Vernon	0.98	1.12	8.69	0.83
St.Pancras	0.98	1.14	8.96	1.71
Scottish	0.98	1.13	7.93	1.58
Mansfield	0.97	1.12	8.28	3.97
City & Metropolitan	0.98	1.14	7.92	1.02
Loughborough	0.98	1.12	7.97	1.33
Surrey	0.98	1.15	8.21	1.27
Tipton & Coseley	0.98	1.15	7.66	1.07
Manchester	0.98	1.08	7.56	1.12
Dudley	0.96	1.18	9.31	9.03
Chesham	0.96	1.14	8.16	2.01
Holmesdale	0.96	1.13	8.13	2.26
Earl Shilton	0.96	1.16	8.25	1.14
Chorley & District	0.96	1.11	7.61	1.04
Bath Investment	0.95	1.17	5.40	1.00
Tynemouth	0.96	1.12	7.91	2.78
Penrith	0.95	1.16	8.16	2.78
Buckinghamshire	0.96	1.14	7.42	1.12
Stafford Railways	0.95	1.15	7.62	1.52
Harpenden	0.95	1.19	8.03	1.29
Nottingham Imperial	0.94	1.19	7.94	1.92
West Cumbria	0.93	1.20	8.73	1.40
Beverly	0.94	1.15	7.96	1.61
Shepshed	0.94	1.17	8.50	1.16
Swansea	0.93	1.19	7.97	1.60
Catholic	0.92	1.21	8.00	1.14
Gainsborough	0.92	1.19	7.68	1.44
Ilkeston	0.91	1.27	7.89	1.73
Bexhill	0.92	1.26	6.76	1.22
Clay Cross	0.89	1.23	8.49	1.69
Standard	0.91	1.24	7.83	1.54
Century	0.87	1.25	5.75	1.92
Ecology	0.87	1.29	8.23	1.30
Londonderry Provident	0.85	1.35	6.48	1.27

1 refers to mortage products
2 refers to non-mortage products

References

Alexander, J., 1991, Europe: The sweet and sour - European cross-border romances continue to blow hot and cold, The Banker, 11th November.
Ansoff, I., 1965, Corporate strategy, McGraw-Hill, New York.
Aksoy, A., and Marshall, N., 1992, The changing corporate head office and its spatial implications, Regional Studies, Volume 26, 147-161.
Balmer, J.M., 1990, Towards a corporate identity, Journal of the Chartered Building Societies Institute, Vol. 44, Number 198, 12-13.
Bank of England Quarterly Bulletin, 1987, Building societies : A changing role, August, 400-403.
Bank of England Quarterly Bulletin, 1990, The development of the building societies sector in the 1980s, November, 503-510.
Barchard, D., 1991a, Financial Times, 15th April.
Barchard, D., 1991b, Survey of computers in finance: Holding on against banking goliath - building societies, Financial Times, 12th November.
Barchard, D., 1992, Conference on international banking: European merger wave predicted, Financial Times, 27th February.
Barnes, P. and Dodds, C., 1983, The structure and performance of the UK building society industry 1970-78, Journal of Business Finance and Accounting, 10, 37-56.
Baumol, W.J., Panzar, J.C. and Willig, R.D., 1982, Contestable markets and the theory of industry structure, (Harcourt Brace Jovanovich, New York).
Birch, P., 1989, Building societies and the European challenge, Banking World, June 1989, 26-29.

Black, G., 1990, ATM's move back into the lobby, Financial Times, 7th November.

Boleat, M., 1982, The building society industry, Allen and Unwin.

Boleat, M., 1987, The mortgage market, theory and practice of housing finance, Allen and Unwin.

Boleat, M., 1988, Building societies: the regulatory framework, Building Societies Association.

Boddy, M., 1980, The building societies, MacMillan.

Bradley, J., 1978, Changing the image, Bankers Magazine, Volume 232, Number 1613.

Brooks, N. A., 1989, Strategic issues for financial services marketing, International Journal of Bank Marketing, Volume 5, Number 2, 5-19.

Building Societies Association, 1990, Building societies and 1922, 2nd Ed., BSA, London.

Building Societies Association, 1992, Building societies the regulatory framework, BSA, London.

Building Societies Association, 1992, Building Society Powers and Constitution.

Building Societies Commission, Annual Report of the Building Societies Commission, 1989-90, HMSO, London.

Building Societies Commission, Annual report of the Building Societies Commission, 1990-91, HMSO, London.

Building Societies Commission, Annual report of the Building Societies Commission, 1991-92, HMSO, London.

Cane, A., 1989b, Survey of information technology in finance: No need for an albatross - the building societies' prospects, Financial Times, 9th November.

Cane, A., 1989a, Banking on information systems: building societies will spend heavily on software, Financial Times, 14th June.

Cecchini, P., 1988, Research on the cost of non-Europe in financial services, Commission of the European Communities.

Clark, J.A., 1988, Economies of scale and scope at depository financial institutions: a review of the literature, Economic Review, Federal Reserve Bank of Kansas City, September/October, 16-33.

Cleary, E.J., 1965, The building society movement, Elek.

Commission of the European Communities, 1990, Credit institutions: Community measured adopted or proposed, Office for Official Publications of the European Communities.

Commission of the European Communities, 1992, Social Europe, towards a Europe of solidarity: housing, Supplement 3/92.

Council of Mortgage Lenders, 1990, Housing finance in Europe, CML, London.

Coles, A., 1992, Building societies and the mortgage market in 1991/92, Building Societies Year Book, 1992-93, 106-114.

Cooper, J.C.B., 1980, Economies of scale in the UK building society industry, Investment Analyst, 55, 31-36.
de Moubray, G., 1989, Quality of service - the key to competitive advantage, The Journal of the Chartered Building Societies Institute, Volume 43, Number 194, 19-22.
Diplock, N., Knight, S. and Ellis, R., 1991, Relocation and inward investment: Short-term thinking, long-term disaster, Investors Chronicle, Vol. 96.
Drake, L., 1989, The building society industry in transition, MacMillan.
Druker, P.E., 1988, The coming of the new organisation, Harvard Business Review, Volume 88, 45-53.
Economist, 1990, If it looks like a bank: Building societies as banks, October.
Edgett, S. and Thwaites, D., 1990, The influence of environmental change on the marketing practice of building societies, European Journal of Marketing, Volume 24, Number 12, 35-47.
Ennew, C. T., Wright, D.M., and Watkins, T., 1989, Marketing strategies in a changing competitive environment: the financial services sector in the UK, in Moutinho, L., Brownlie, D., and Livingstone, J.,(Eds) Marketing Audit of the 80s, Marketing Education Group, Glasgow Business School, 943-969.
European File, 1992, Towards a single market in financial services, Commission of the European Communities, 3/1992.
Euro Service, 1992a, Abolishing tax payments at frontiers, Commission of the European Communities, No. 13, December.
Euro Service, 1992b, Financial services and the single market, Commission of the European Communities, No. 11, December.
Ferguson, C. and McKillop, D G., 1992, Internal performance features of UK building societies and their effect on organisational structure, Applied Financial Economics, Volume 2, Number 4, 199-204
Fleming, M. and Nellis, J., 1991, European economic and monetary union - implications for financial services - Part II, The Journal of the Chartered Building Societies Institute, Vol. 45, No. 208, pp 17-21.
Fleming, M. and Nellis, J., 1992, The future of centralised mortgage lenders in the UK mortgage market, The Journal of the Chartered Building Societies Institute, Vol.46, No.211, pp 17-20.
Ford, D., 1989, Develop your technology strategy, Long Range Planning, Vol.21, No.5, 85-95.
Frazer, D., 1990, Survey of building societies, Financial Times, 20th Feb.
Fuss, M. and Waverman, L., 1981, The regulation of telecommunications in Canada (Technical Report No. 7, Economic Council of Canada, Ottawa).
Gough, T.J., 1979, Building society mergers and the size efficiency relationship, Applied Economics, 11, 185-194.
Gough, T.J., 1982, The economics of building societies, Macmillan Press, Ltd.

Gugler, P., 1992, Building transnational alliances to create competitive advantage, Long Range Planning, Vol. 25, No. 1, 90-99.
Hanoch, G., 1975, The elasticity of scale and the shape of average costs, American Economic Review, 65, 492-497.
Hardwick, P., 1989, Economies of scale in building societies, Applied Economics, 21, 1291-1304.
Hardwick, P., 1990, Multi-product cost attributes: A study of UK building societies, Oxford Economic Papers, Vol 42, 446-461.
Hendry, D.F. and Richard, J.F., 1991, The econometric analysis of economic time series, International Statistical Review, 51, pp. 111-163.
Hooley, G. and Mann, S., 1988, The adoption of marketing by financial institutions in the UK, The Services Industry Journal, Volume 8, Number 4, 488-500.
Hutchinson, R. and McKillop, D., 1991, The financial services industry in Northern Ireland, Northern Ireland Economic Council, Report 91.
Iles, C., 1992, The Dilemma of the branch manager in financial institutions, Journal of the Chartered Building Societies Institute, Vol. 46, No. 210, pp 6-7.
Jenkins, P., 1992, Viewpoint: The profit formula for the 1990s, The Banker, 1st August.
Jones Lang Wootton, 1990, The decentralisation of offices from central London: An annual special survey, JLW Consulting and Research.
Judge, G.G., Griffiths, W.E., Carter Hill, R. and Tsoung-Chao Lee, 1980, The theory and practice of econometrics, (Wiley, New York).
Kallas, J., 1990, Survey of building societies: Acumen touched by conscience - housing initiatives, Financial Times, 20th Feb.
Kanter, R.M., 1989, The new managerial work, Harvard Business Review, Volume 89, 85-92.
Kaye, J., 1989, Building societies and financial services, Building Societies Association, London.
Kmenta, J., 1986, Elements of econometrics, MacMillan, New York.
Llewellyn, D., 1988, The challenge from the building societies, Banking World, July, 32-35.
Macey, R. and Wells, D., 1987, New legislation accelerates change in building society culture, Management Accounting, 34-35.
Maddala, G.S., 1983, Limited-dependent and qualitative variables in econometrics, Cambridge University Press.
Martin, P., 1990, Return of the invisible hand, Financial Times, May.
McKillop, D.G. and Hutchinson, R.W., 1990, Regional financial sectors of the British Isles, Avebury, Gower, Aldershot.
McKillop, D.G. and Glass, J.C., 1994, A cost model of building societies as producers of mortgages and other financial products, Journal of Business Finance and Accounting, forthcoming.
Merton Associaties, 1990, UK Building Societies: A prognosis for the 1990s,

London.
Mester, L.J., 1987, A multiproduct cost study of savings and loans, Journal of Finance, 42, 423-445.
Miles, R.H., 1982, Coffin nails and corporate strategies, Prentice-Hall.
Miles, R.E. and Snow, C.C., 1986, Organisations: New concepts for new forms, California Management Review, Volume 28, 62-73.
Morgan, N. A., 1989, Developing information strategies in the UK financial services sector, Marketing Intelligence and Planning, Volume 7, Number 7/8, 42-28.
Murray, K., 1992, Leading your own life, Building Societies Yearbook, 1992-93, 127-132.
Nicholson, G., 1992, Competition between banks and insurance companies - the challenge of bancassurance, in Steinherr, A., The new European financial market place, Longman.
Norkett, P., 1989, Building societies and their subsidiaries, Routledge.
Pawley, M., Winstone, D. and Bentley P., 1991, UK financial institutions and markets, MacMillan.
Peters, T. and Waterman, 1982, In search of excellence: lessons from America's best run companies. Harper Row.
Porter, M.E., 1980, Competitive strategy: Techniques for analysing industries and competitors, New York: Free Press.
Porter, M.E., 1985, Competitive advantage, New York Free Press.
Porter, M.E., 1990, The competitive advantage of nations, New York: Free Press.
Price Waterhouse, 1991, New building society legislation: Consultants Report, Building Societies Association.
Ramanujam, V., and Varadarajan, P., 1989, Research on corporate diversification : A synthesis, Strategic Management Journal, Vol. 10, 523-551.
Ray, S.C., 1982, A translog cost function analysis of US agriculture, American Journal of Agricultural Economics, 64, 490-498.
Reid, K., 1992, Opportunities and challenges for building societies in Europe, Journal of the Chartered Building Societies Institute, Vol. 45, No. 209, 2-7.
Rumelt, R., 1982, Diversification strategy and profitability, Strategic Management Journal, Vol. 3, 359-369.
Silverman, M., and Castaldi, R.M., 1992, Antecedents and propensity for diversification : A focus on small banks, Journal of Small Business Management, April, 42-52.
Snowball, A., 1992, Have building societies mistakenly entered the estate agency market? , The Chartered Building Societies Institute Journal, Vol. 45, No. 211, 2-5.
Speed, R., 1990, Building societies: New strategies for a competitve era, The Service Industry Journal, Vol. 10, No. 1, 110-123.
Steele, L., 1983, Managers' misconceptions about technology, Harvard

Business Review, November, 133-140.
Steinherr, A., 1992, The new European financial market place, Longman.
UBS Phillips and Drew, 1992a, Building societies research investing for the next millennium, June.
UBS Phillips and Drew, 1992b, Building societies research the major players, August.
Wales, T.J., 1977, On the flexibility of flexible functional forms: an empirical approach, Journal of Econometrics, 5, 183-193.
Wyllie, A., 1992, Lenders widen range of banking services, Building Societies Yearbook, 1992-1993, 133-135.

Subject Index

FSC
www.fsc.org
MIX
Papier | Fördert gute Waldnutzung
FSC® C083411

Kolibri 360 GmbH
Ferdinand-Jühlke-Straße 7
99095 Erfurt, Deutschland
produktsicherheit@kolibri360.de